Richard Bizier
Roch Nadeau

ULYSSES
TRAVEL PUBLICATIONS
Travel better... enjoy more

Editorial *Series Director:* Claude Morneau; *Project Supervisor:* Pascale Couture; *Editor:* Daniel Desjardins.

Research and Composition *Authors:* Richard Bizier, Roch Nadeau; *Contributors:* Paquerette Villeneuve, Gilles de Lalonde, Paul Haince, Jami Mitchell, Marie Rodrigue, John Tessier, Marie Tousignant.

Production *Design:* Patrick Farei (Atoll Direction); *Proofreading:* Jennifer McMorran; *Translation:* Tracy Kendrick, Danielle Gauthier, Emmy Pahmer, Sarah Kresh; *Cartography:* André Duchesne, Patrick Thivierge (Assistant); *Layout:* Sarah Kresh.

Illustrations *Cover Photo:* Tim Beiber (Image Bank); *Chapter Headings:* Jennifer McMorran; *Drawings:* Lorette Pierson.

Special Thanks to Researcher P. Villeneuve and her team, B. Giana and C. Decuir (New Orleans Metropolitan Convention and Visitor Bureau), J. Clevenger, J. Kirkpatrick, F.S. Rochefort. Thanks to SODEC and the Department of Canadian Heritage for their financial support.

Distributors

AUSTRALIA:
Little Hills Press
11/37-43 Alexander St.
Crows Nest NSW 2065
☎ (612) 437-6995
Fax: (612) 438-5762

BELGIUM AND
LUXEMBOURG:
Vander
Vrijwilligerlaan 321
B-1150 Brussel
☎ (02) 762 98 04
Fax: (02) 762 06 62

CANADA:
Ulysses Books & Maps
4176 Saint-Denis
Montréal, Québec
H2W 2M5
☎ (514) 843-9882,
ext.2232 or
1-800-748-9171
Fax: 514-843-9448
www.ulysse.ca

GERMANY AND AUSTRIA:
Brettschneider
Fernreisebedarf
Feldfirchner Strasse 2
D-85551 Heimstetten
München
☎ 89-99 02 03 30
Fax: 89-99 02 03 31

GREAT BRITAIN AND
IRELAND:
World Leisure Marketing
9 Downing Road
West Meadows, Derby
UK DE21 6HA
☎ 1 332 34 33 32
Fax: 1 332 34 04 64

ITALY:
Centro Cartografico del
Riccio
Via di Soffiano 164/A
50143 Firenze
☎ (055) 71 33 33
Fax: (055) 71 63 50

NETHERLANDS:
Nilsson & Lamm
Pampuslaan 212-214
1380 AD Weesp (NL)
☎ 0294-465044
Fax: 0294-415054

SCANDINAVIA:
Scanvik
Esplanaden 8B
1263 Copenhagen K
DK
☎ (45) 33.12.77.66
Fax: (45) 33.91.28.82

SPAIN:
Altaïr
Balmes 69
E-08007 Barcelona
☎ 454 29 66
Fax: 451 25 59

SWITZERLAND:
OLF
P.O. Box 1061
CH-1701 Fribourg
☎ (026) 467.51.11
Fax: (026) 467.54.66

U.S.A.:
The Globe Pequot Press
6 Business Park Road
P.O. Box 833
Old Saybrook, CT 06475
☎ 1-800-243-0495
Fax: 1-800-820-2329

New Orleans has inspired every artist, poet and writer who was either born here or who has passed through. From William Faulkner to Tennessee Williams (born Thomas Lanier), from the great Louis Armstrong to the prolific Anne Rice, the "Crescent City" has been lauded and criticized by many. New Orleans has always elicited as much passion in elites as it has disconcertment in conservatives.

Among the quotes which sing the praises of New Orleans, it is certainly the following one that best captures the soul of this unique city....

> "There seems to be a certain insidious chemical in the atmosphere which tends to destroy Puritanism."

> *Fabulous New Orleans*
> Lyle Saxon

TABLE OF CONTENTS

LIST OF MAPS

Help make Ulysses Travel Guides even better!

The information contained in this guide was correct at press time. However, mistakes can slip in, omissions are always possible, places can disappear, etc. The authors and publisher hereby disclaim any liability for loss or damage resulting from omissions or errors.

We value your comments, corrections and suggestions, as they allow us to keep each guide up to date. The best contributions will be rewarded with a free book from Ulysses Travel Publications. All you have to do is write us at the following address and indicate which title you would be interested in receiving (see the list at the end of guide).

Ulysses Travel Publications
4176 Rue Saint-Denis
Montréal, Québec
Canada H2W 2M5
www.ulysse.ca
e-mail: guiduly@ulysse.ca

Canadian Cataloguing in Publication Data

Bizier, Richard

    New Orleans

    (Ulysses travel guides)
    Translation of: Nouvelle-Orléans
    Includes index.

    ISBN 2-89464-074-9

1. New Orleans (La.) - Guidebooks.   I. Nadeau, Roch. II. Title. III. Series.

F379.N53B5913 1997   917.63'350463   C97-941449-0

TABLE OF SYMBOLS

🌴	Our favourites
☎	Telephone number
≕	Fax number
≡	Air conditioning
⊗	Ceiling fan
≈	Pool
ℜ	Restaurant
⊛	Whirlpool
ℝ	Refrigerator
K	Kitchenette
△	Sauna
⊘	Exercise room
tv	Colour television
pb	Private bathroom
sb	Shared bathroom
bkfst	Breakfast

ATTRACTION CLASSIFICATION

★	Interesting
★★	Worth a visit
★★★	Not to be missed

HOTEL CLASSIFICATION

Unless otherwise indicated, the prices in the guide
are for one room in the high season,
double occupancy, not including taxes.

RESTAURANT CLASSIFICATION

$	$10 or less
$$	$10 to $20
$$$	$20 to $30
$$$$	$30 or more

Unless otherwise indicated, the prices in the guide are for a
meal for one person, including taxes, but not drinks and tip.

All prices in this guide are in American dollars.

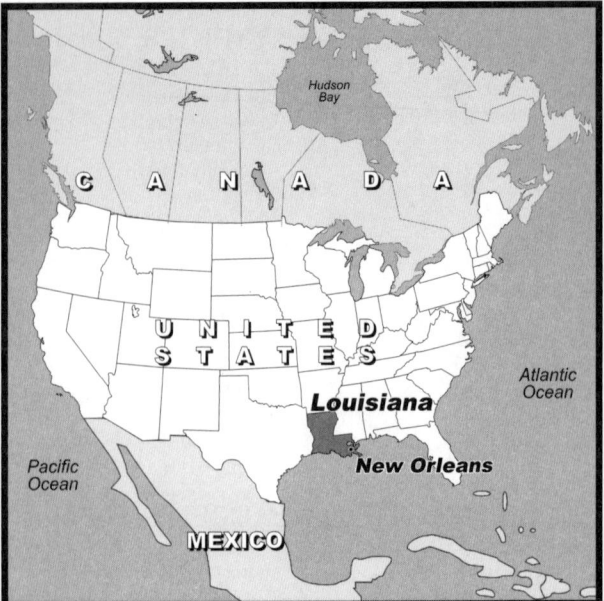

Hudson
Bay

C A N A D A

U N I T E D
S T A T E S

Atlantic
Ocean

Louisiana

Pacific
Ocean

New Orleans

MEXICO

*Where is
New Orleans ?*

Louisiana	New Orleans
Capital: Baton Rouge Population: 4,220,000 inhab. Currency: American dollar Area: 125,674 km²	Population: 497,000 inhab. Metropolitan region: 1,239,000 inhab.

Prime Meridian
0° longitude
(Greenwich Mean Time)

Louisiana

equator
(0° latitude)

© ULYSSES

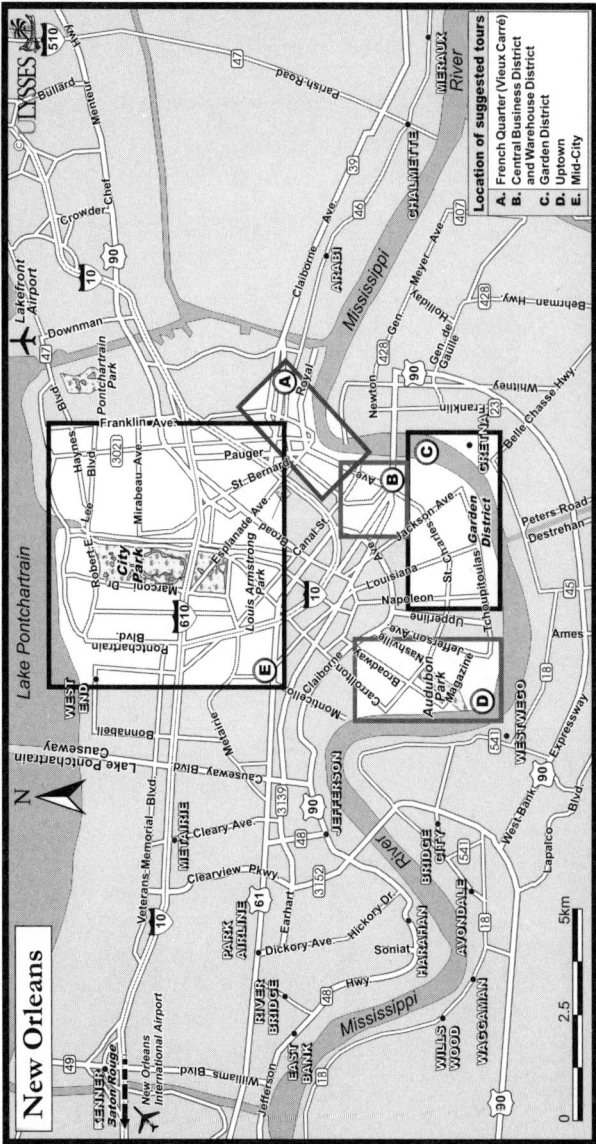

PORTRAIT

New Orleans seems to rise up out of the twists and turns of the Mississippi. The river and the proximity of the Gulf of Mexico both favoured the city's development. Indeed, as soon as it was founded, New Orleans became an important economic pivot between Europe and the fledgling European colonies in America. Today, its port ranks second in the United States in terms of tonnage handled.

Renowned for its gastronomy, music, festivals, architecture and history, New Orleans is like no other place on earth. All sorts of epithets can be used to describe it: magical, boisterous, debonair, flamboyant, even decadent. A 19th-century chronicler called it the most cosmopolitan of provincial cities and the most provincial of cosmopolitan cities. Ensconced on a curved stretch of land between the Mississippi and Lake Pontchartrain, it has a distinctive, almost insular location that has also earned it the nickname "Crescent City". Due to the city's complicated topography, standard points of reference are of little use here; fashionable Uptown is located to the west, commercial Downtown to the east. The city is bounded to the north and south by the shores of Lake Pontchartrain and the Mississippi, respectively.

New Orleans has succeeded in preserving its rich heritage. Its French Quarter, or Vieux Carré, is of impressive size and boasts a remarkable number of period houses. The architecture here reflects French and Creole, more than Spanish, influences. With its inner courts decked out with flowers, finely worked balconies, charming streets and public squares, New Orleans is truly enchanting. Around Jackson Square (the former Place d'Armes), dominated by the spires of St. Louis Cathedral, and throughout a maze of streets with names like Bienville, Toulouse, Bourbon, Dauphine, Conti, Ursulines, Levée, Dumaine, Chartres and Esplanade, the historic area reveals all sorts of unexpected charms. The French left an indelible stamp on New Orleans; during the Spanish occupation, the Creoles continued speaking French. And if French can still be heard here today, it is because Cajun country is right nearby; Cajun musicians and singers often perform in the local cafés.

Feverish New Orleans is without a doubt one of the most captivating urban centres in the United States. Even those visiting the marvelous Mississippi city for the first time fall madly in love with it. The richness of its architecture, the fabulous diversity of its cultural heritage (French, Creole, African-American and Spanish), its unique gastronomy and its proud inhabitants... everything here is harmonious, delightful, sensuous. Americans adore New Orleans more than any other city. Each day, thousands of tourists flood into the Vieux-Carré or French Quarter. They come from all over the country—New York, Boston, Los Angeles and Chicago—by bus, chartered flight or car. Just as others make a pilgrimage to Mecca, Americans go to New Orleans to get back to their roots in a place that has been instrumental in shaping their culture. And no one from anywhere else in the world will ever feel completely lost in New Orleans, with its myriad cultures; everyone has roots here.

The city, a cultural crossroads for three centuries, was fertile ground for the emergence of a new culture. New Orleans, the city of music, thrilled to the sounds of jazz greats like Louis Armstrong and Sidney Bechet, both of whom were born here. In the New Orleans of Tennessee Williams, you'll catch yourself looking for *A Streetcar Named Desire* (Desire being the English translation of Désirée, the first name of a Creole celebrity, Désirée Montreuil, after whom a local street was named). Playwright Tennessee Williams borrowed the name for his famous streetcar. New Orleans, a city even more beautiful than you'd think, a city that leaves no one indifferent.

A BRIEF HISTORY

Some anthropologists and archaeologists hypothesize that human beings have been living in the Mississippi Valley for several thousand years. Vestiges found at Poverty Point, in West Carroll Parish, confirm that permanent indigenous settlements were established in the lower Mississippi Valley between AD 700 and 1700. Three large native groups lived in the territory now known as Louisiana: the Tunicas, the Caddos and the Muskogees. It was these natives who met the first Europeans—the Spanish in the 16th century then the French in the 17th.

Spaniards Alonzo de Pineda (1519), Pánfilo de Narváez (1528) and Hernando de Soto (1541), the last of whom found the mouth of the Mississippi in April of the same year, deemed these swampy expanses too hostile to be colonized. It wasn't until a century later that the French started taking a genuine interest in this mysterious region.

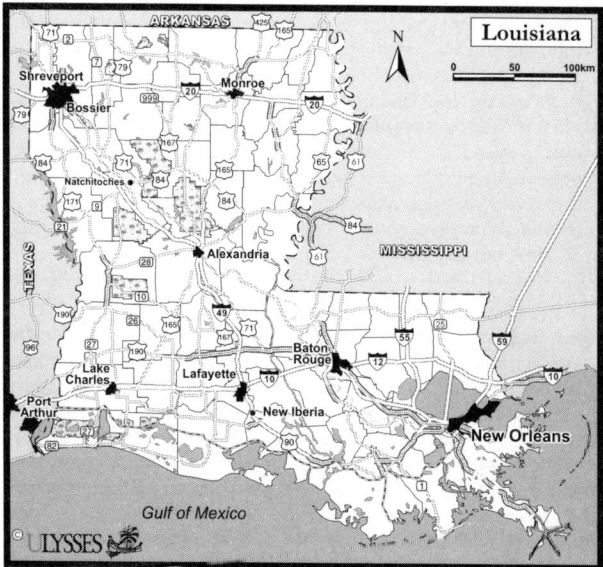

The history of Louisiana and New Orleans, founded in 1718 by Jean-Baptiste Le Moyne, Sieur de Bienville, is intertwined with that of New France. The region had been visited earlier by Louis Joliet and Père Marquette in 1673, followed by Cavelier de La Salle in 1682. That same year, La Salle took possession of the vast territory and named it Louisiane in honour of King Louis XIV. In 1699, through the efforts of Pierre Le Moyne, Sieur d'Iberville, the first colonists settled here.

The Le Moyne Brothers

No family in New France was more illustrious than the Le Moynes. Pierre Le Moyne, Sieur d'Iberville founded the colony of Louisiana (Louisiane) in 1698, while his brother, Jean-Baptiste Le Moyne, Sieur de Bienville, played an important role in the colony's development, serving three terms as its governor.

Bienville spent almost his entire life in the American wilderness. He first became governor at the tender age of 21, and was responsible for the construction of Forts Maurepas, Rosalie and St. Louis (on the shores of Mobile Bay) and for the establishment of numerous trading posts all along the Mississippi. It is to Bienville that we owe the founding of New Orleans (1718). He was a brilliant linguist who mastered several native dialects, a shrewd strategist and a valiant combatant. Historians are unanimous in acknowledging the unparalleled patience and tenacity he displayed while establishing the French colony in America. It was during his governorship, furthermore, that the first schools in New Orleans were built.

Jean-Baptiste Le Moyne, Sieur de Bienville, picked the site for New Orleans in 1718 for economic reasons. In order to control the maritime traffic in the lower Mississippi, it was necessary to build a city on the banks of the river, as close as possible to the Gulf of Mexico. This site, which Bienville chose over that of Baton Rouge, despite opposition from the King's engineers, made it possible to distribute products even when the mouth of the river was clogged up with alluvial sediments. Once unloaded in New Orleans, the goods needed only to be transported a short distance over land to Lake Pontchartrain.

There, they would be loaded onto boats that would carry them through the Passe-du-Sauvage to the Gulf of Mexico, which, 100 kilometres farther, gave access the world market. It wasn't until after New Orleans was founded in 1718 that the young French colony truly started to thrive. By 1726, just eight years later, the city had nearly 4,000 inhabitants (colonists, slaves, troops and natives) and was starting to look like a small port capital. Once the land was cleared, the settlers grew rice, tobacco, indigo, sugar cane, corn and cotton, which was exported to Europe and the other French colonies in North America.

In 1762, France ceded Louisiana to Spain, which returned it in 1800. On April 30, 1803, Napoleon sold the territory of Louisiana, which covered 2,600,000 square kilometres, to the United States for 80 million francs. New Orleans thus became American.

The Louisiana Purchase: "Buy Now, Pay Later!"

When Napoleon sold Louisiana to the Americans on April 30, 1803, President Thomas Jefferson had to borrow money in order to amass the colossal sum required, some 15 million dollars. If you can believe it, the American Treasury had only 10 million dollars at the time. The Emperor needed the money desperately to sustain his war efforts in Europe. By an irony of fate, the Americans borrowed the missing five million from Dutch and English banks. These two nations, both at war with Napoleon at the time, thus helped back their own enemy.

The Battle of New Orleans

The Battle of New Orleans, which took place in Chalmette in 1812, was a heroic victory of a kind unprecedented in American history, and in more ways than one. The Battle of New Orleans put an end to any designs the English might still have had on their former colonial possessions in the United States. It was also the first time that inhabitants from various parts of the fledgling nation joined together to fight a common enemy. Remarkably enough, Acadians from the bayous, francophile Germans from Côte-des-Allemands, slaves and freed slaves, Creoles, Kentuckians, Tennesseans and Jean Lafitte and his band of privateers from Barataria Bay all shared the same cause. This glorious battle claimed the lives of 2,000 English soldiers but just seven Americans. The great hero of the Battle of New Orleans was Andrew Jackson, who subsequently became President.

The Civil War

In the fledgling American republic, each state enjoyed a certain degree of autonomy, and was thus responsible for decisions such as whether or not to abolish slavery within its borders. However, when a new state or territory joined the Union, it was up to Congress to determine whether or not slavery would be permitted in that region. The Northern states opposed slavery, which was not necessary for their economic growth and which they considered inhumane. However, in those states south of the Ohio, as well as those west of the Mississippi, where more and more cotton plantations were springing up, slavery provided landowners with an inexpensive workforce. Before long, a confrontation started brewing between the slave states of the South and the abolitionist states of the North.

The South first started protesting when Missouri was admitted to the Union as a slave state in 1821, following the Missouri Compromise, while efforts were being made to abolish the "peculiar institution" in states west of the Mississippi and in the North. In 1844, after several other states were admitted, the level of discontent reached its peak, and a secessionist movement prepared to break up the Union in order to maintain slavery took shape. In the 1860 elections, Republican candidate Abraham Lincoln, an avowed abolitionist, became President, thus excluding the pro-slavery democrats from power. Perceiving this election as a veritable provocation, the Southern states started seceding in 1861. They joined together as the Confederate States of America, naming Richmond, Virginia their capital city and declaring Jefferson Davis President. This was the start of a long conflict between the North and the South. The Civil War as such lasted from the spring of 1861 to 1865.

The Southerners, who were better prepared, won many victories in the first two years of the war. They were outnumbered, however, by the Northerners, who occupied the entire territory west of the Mississippi, where they mobilized their troops; it was from there that the Union launched most of its attacks on the Confederates. Between Washington, the capital of the Union and Richmond, the capital of the Confederacy, the conflicts became bloodier and bloodier. The latter city was the scene of the decisive battle between the troops of Confederate General Robert E. Lee and those of Union General Ulysses Grant. The fighting lasted 10 days and resulted in Lee's surrender. This terrible war between the South and the North claimed 600,000 lives. Five days after it ended, on April 14, Northerners were thrown into a state of shock when Abraham Lincoln, who had just begun his second term as President, was assassinated by an enraged Southerner, actor John Wilkes Booth. The outcome of the Civil War meant that the United States would remain intact. By 1863, in the middle of the war, the North had abolished slavery in all states where it was still legal, and in 1865, immediately after the war, slavery was officially banned in all parts of the United States.

Two of the eight Confederate generals, Braxton Bragg and Pierre Gustave Toutant Beauregard, were from Louisiana. It was under the command of the latter, a Creole, that the first shots of the Civil War were fired at Fort Sumter, in South Carolina, on April 12, 1861. Both had distinguished themselves during the Mexican War.

Important Dates in the History of New Orleans

1541: After his expeditions to Peru, New Spain (Mexico) and the Antilles, Hernando de Soto explores the coast of Florida, then proceeds farther around the Gulf of Mexico, where he discovers the mouth of an immense river, which, more than a century later, will be named the "Mississippi".

1682: René Robert Cavelier, Sieur de La Salle, travels from New France to the mouth of the "great river", arriving at his destination on April 9. He claims this vast territory for France and names it "Louisiane" after his King, Louis XIV.

1699: Pierre Le Moyne, Sieur d'Iberville, establishes a colony at Fort Maurepas. That same year, he explores the area around modern-day Baton Rouge. On the way back, the natives show him a lake north of the future city of New Orleans, and he names it Pontchartrain after his benefactor.

1708: Louis Juchereau de Saint-Denis founds the town of Bayou Saint-Jean (Bayou St. John). Other colonists settle in the area, from Bayou Sauvage (Gentilly) to Metairie.

1709: The ship *La Vierge de Grâce* sets out from Havana with the first shipment of African slaves destined for New Orleans.

1716: Under the supervision of Jean-Baptiste Le Moyne, Sieur de Bienville, brother of Pierre Le Moyne, Sieur d'Iberville, Fort Rosalie welcomes its first inhabitants.

1718: Jean-Baptiste Le Moyne, Sieur de Bienville, founds La Nouvelle-Orléans (New Orleans), named after Philippe d'Orléans, the reigning king, on the banks of the Mississippi (then known as the Missisipy or the Fleuve Saint-Louis).

1720: The population of Louisiana reaches 6,000 inhabitants, 10% of whom are slaves. By the end of 1721, the population of New Orleans can be broken down as follows: 147 men, 65 women, 38 children, 28 servants, 73 slaves and 21 natives, for a total of 372 people.

1722: Following the destruction of the city by hurricane in 1721, Sieur de Bienville commissions Pierre Le Blond de La Tour to draw up new plans for the city of New Orleans. La Tour puts the finishing touches on the design for his famous "Carré" in April of the same year.

1727: The Ursulines arrive in New Orleans on August 6 and open a school for the native, French and black children in the young colony.

1728: France sends a first contingent of young women to be married off. The Ursulines take charge of these "*filles à la cassette*" (casketgirls), thus named because they got off the boat carrying the trousseaus they had been given.

1763: The Treaty of Paris confirms the retrocession of Louisiana to Spain, effected secretly the year before with the signing of the Treaty of Fountainbleau. The same year, the Jesuits are expelled, and all their assets, some 900,000 livres, including the land granted to them by Bienville, are confiscated.

1768: The Creoles of New Orleans contest the new Spanish rule and refuse to recognize the authority of Governor Don Antonio de Ulloa. Some 560 Creoles even sign a petition to protest the economic policies of the new administration, which devalue their currency and force them to trade only with Spain and its colonies. Furthermore, in defiance of the terms stipulated in the agreement reached by Charles III of Spain and Louis XV, the French troops refuse to join the Spanish militia.

1769: Determined to curb the rebellion gathering speed in its newly acquired colony and to restore order there, Spain resorts to force to deal with the defiant Creoles, sending an army of 2,056 soldiers with plenty of artillery. Under the command of Don Alejandro O'Reilly, an Irishman who fled to Spain to escape religious persecution in his own country, the soldiers enter New Orleans. After having the keys to the city symbolically handed over to him on the Place d'Armes (now Jackson Square), O'Reilly orders the arrest of the major opponents of the regime: five rebels are shot and a number of others are imprisoned. Thereafter, the Creoles to refer to him by the inglorious nickname "Bloody O'Reilly".

1785: According to a census taken by the Spanish authorities, the population of New Orleans stands at 4,980 inhabitants; that of Louisiana, which still includes the western part of Florida, at 32,000.

1794: On December 8, a fire destroys more than 200 homes and other buildings in New Orleans. That same year, printer Louis Duclot starts publishing *Le Moniteur de la Louisiane*, New Orleans's first newspaper.

1795: Don Luis de Penalver y Cárdenas is named the first Catholic bishop of New Orleans and St. Louis Cathedral becomes the episcopal see; until this point, Quebec City had held this position for all of New France.

1800: Napoleon and King Charles IV of Spain sign the Treaty of San Ildefonso. Louisiana is returned to France in exchange for the French emperor's guarantee that he will protect the kingdom of Italy.

1803: Napoleon sells Louisiana to the United States for the sum of 15 million dollars.

1804: The population of New Orleans is now 8,056 out of a total of 49,473 for Louisiana as a whole.

1809: Fleeing the island of Santo Domingo, where Dessalines had declared Haiti's independence on January 1, 1804, 6,000 refugees arrive in New Orleans after trying to settle in Cuba, where Spanish authorities deported them to protest Napoleon's invasion of Spain the same year.

1812: Having set out from Pittsburgh, the *New Orleans*, the first steamboat to sail the Mississippi, arrives at the port of New Orleans.

1815: In Chalmette, the combined forces of General Andrew Jackson and the buccaneers of pirate Jean Lafitte win a decisive victory over the British troops. The famous Battle of New Orleans puts an end to English colonial designs on American territory.

1837: The *Picayune* becomes the first English-language newspaper to be published in New Orleans. It is now the city's oldest daily.

1840: With 102,193 inhabitants, New Orleans is the fourth largest city in the United States, with the second largest port in the country.

1859: Inauguration of the Opéra Français de La Nouvelle-Orléans.

1865: The Civil War ends after four years of bitter fighting. President Abraham Lincoln is assassinated by a southern extremist. Many rich families from New Orleans and elsewhere in Louisiana were ruined by the war.

1878: An epidemic of yellow fever claims thousands of lives in Louisiana, including 3,800 in the city of New Orleans alone.

1900: The great jazz trumpeter, singer and conductor Louis Armstrong, is born in New Orleans.

1904: The Jesuits found Loyola College. Eight years later, the institution becomes Loyola University.

1915: The word "jazz", designating a kind of music played by African-Americans from New Orleans, appears in Chicago, where the style becomes very popular.

1953: Louisiana celebrates its 150th anniversary as part of the United States. New Orleans marks the occasion with splendid festivities and welcomes its guests of honour, including President Eisenhower and the French Ambassador to the United States, with great pomp.

1971: Death of jazz great Louis "Satchmo" Armstrong.

1977: For the first time in its history, New Orleans elects an African-American mayor, Ernest N. Morial.

1984: New Orleans inaugurates the Louisiana World Exposition. Though the event is not officially recognized by the Bureau of International Expositions, it nonetheless attracts 7,300,000 visitors.

1987: Pope John Paul II visits New Orleans on September 12.

GEOGRAPHY

Located on the southern edge of the United States, the city of New Orleans lies in the southeasternmost part of the state of Louisiana, which is bordered by the states of Texas to the west and Arkansas and Mississippi to the north. Mississippi also borders the eastern side of Louisiana, just a short distance from New Orleans.

Situated at latitude 30° north and longitude 90° west, on the east bank of the Mississippi, New Orleans lies nestled inside one of the many curves at the river's southern end. It was on this sharp bend that the city first developed, hence its nickname, the Crescent City. Lake Pontchartrain, an immense body of water covering over 1,500 square kilometres, washes the north edge of the city. West of the lake, after crossing the swampy parts of St. John the Baptist Parish south of Lake Maurepas, the Mississippi heads up to Baton Rouge, the capital of the state of Louisiana. On its southeast side, which is just a few kilometres from the state of Mississippi, Lake Pontchartrain empties into Lake Borgne, then Chandeleur Sound and finally the Gulf of Mexico. The Gulf itself is 110 kilometres from New Orleans by land and 145 kilometres by river.

New Orleans is situated at the same latitude as Shanghai, China, another major port city located on the other side of the world.

The Parishes

Another typical trait of Louisiana is the way it is divided up—not into counties, like other American states, but into parishes, the same way it was under the Catholic French Regime. Today, metropolitan New Orleans has three parishes: Orleans, Jefferson and St. Bernard.

Geology

The land in southern Louisiana, is like a huge, floating blanket, and erecting buildings here requires feats of engineering. Almost nowhere in the southernmost part of the state do the houses have basements; instead, they are set on concrete blocks, logs or other supports. The big buildings in New Orleans sit on foundations that plunge deep into the earth to the solid rock below the marshy terrain.

The highway linking New Orleans to Lafayette remains a masterpiece of ingenuity. Set on concrete piles, it runs over the series of swampy areas and bayous that stretch from New Orleans to Baton Rouge and from Maringouin to Lafayette. It spans a tiny portion of the enormous Atchafalaya basin, the largest stretch of swampland in America. Before the highway was built, travellers had to make a detour of several dozen kilometres to get to the districts of Breaux Bridge and Lafayette.

Numerous bayous wind their way through the countryside, cities and towns of Louisiana. There is water, water everywhere in this state, so don't be surprised when you see cemeteries with above-ground tombs in swampy areas. Eternal rest, fine, but not in the drink, thank you!

Flora

Thanks to the subtropical climate of southern Louisiana, New Orleans is full of flowers. The big avenues and boulevards are lined with majestic live oaks, magnolias whose blossoms give off a sweet, vanilla scent, and occasionally royal palms; Esplanade Avenue is the loveliest hands down. The inner courtyards in the French Quarter and the surrounding districts, often adorned with fountains and waterfalls, seem to be trying to outdo each other with their magnificent flowers.

Magnolia Blossom

And how to describe the finely worked wrought-iron balconies, each decked with more flowers than the last. Residential neighbourhoods like the Garden District boast splendid, meticulously tended gardens containing all sorts of subtropical species, from camellias and azaleas to begonias and fuchsias. New Orleans also has pleasant, shady squares. Audubon Park, laid out on the former site of Étienne Boré's grand plantation, and magnificent City Park are the pride of New Orleanians.

ARCHITECTURE

The architecture of New Orleans dazzles visitors. Both the city and the state of Louisiana deserve credit for how well they have preserved this architectural heritage, which is unique in North America. For Americans, the appeal of this fabulous port city on the Mississippi is so powerful that they gladly award it the title of "America's Most Interesting City". New Orleans' architecture as a whole reflects the influences and lifestyle of the French, African, Creole, Spanish, then English, American and Pan-European communities that have shaped the city over the past three centuries.

From the beginning of the 18th century until about 1860, French and Creole (a blend of Creole, French and Spanish styles shaped by the living conditions in the West Indies) influences marked the architecture in the French Quarter, along Esplanade Avenue and in the areas surrounding the city (Marigny, Central Business District, Tremé, Bayou St. John, Metairie, Pontchartrain, etc.). It should also be noted that none of the buildings in New Orleans (or anywhere else in southern Louisiana) have basements, as ground water lies less than a metre below the surface.

The changes in government and successive waves of immigrants had little effect on the architecture. When the original New Orleanians moved elsewhere, the freed slaves and new arrivals settled into the old French and Creole houses in the French Quarter and on its outskirts. Then, during the Spanish occupation, when the imposing Cabildo was erected on the Plaza de Armas (now Jackson Square) and St. Louis Cathedral was reconstructed, along with numerous other buildings and houses destroyed by the fire of 1788, the architecture continued to respect the French and Creole styles.

The Spaniards' great contribution to the architecture of New Orleans was the profusion of lacy wrought iron in all sorts of shapes that adorns the grilles, balconies, porches and fences of the city's residential and commercial buildings, and which visitors never tire of admiring.

The First Farmhouses in Louisiana

Though Robert Cavelier, Sieur de La Salle, founded Louisiana in 1682, it wasn't until 1699 that this addition to New France started to be colonized. That year, Pierre Le Moyne, Sieur d'Iberville, the "Father of Louisiana", brought several hundred colonists to Fort Maurepas (Biloxi, Mississippi), then others to Fort Louis-de-la-Mobile (Mobile, Alabama) in 1702. The first farmhouses were extremely rudimentary. In 1708, Louis Juchereau de Saint-Denis, who also founded Nachitoches in 1714, brought a number of colonists to the village of Bayou St. John, near the bayou (river) of the same name. Other settlers then moved onto a strip of land that stretched between Bayou St. John and Bayou Sauvage (Gentilly). It was there, and as far as Metairie, that the first "plantation houses" as such were built. In 1716, Jean-Baptiste Le Moyne de Bienville, brother of Pierre Le Moyne d'Iberville, ordered the construction of Fort Rosalie (Natchez) and established a community there. In the following years, other settlements developed. At that point, the farmhouses took on the now famous plantation-house style. It was in 1718, when Jean-Baptiste Le Moyne de Bienville founded New Orleans on the banks of the Mississippi (then known as the Missisipy or the Saint-Louis), that a distinctive kind of architecture truly emerged in southern New France, along with a style that would characterize Louisiana building for over a century and a half.

Three years after the founding of New Orleans, which already had some 470 inhabitants by 1721, a hurricane destroyed all the buildings in town. Aware that New Orleans would expand rapidly, Bienville commissioned the royal engineer, Pierre Le Blond de La Tour, to draw up the new plans for the city. The final plans for the Carré were completed in April 1722. With the help of Scotsman John Law, who was in the service of the French and also headed the Company of the West, and his assistants Adrien de Pauger and Ignace Broutin, Le Blond de La Tour designed a huge rectangle (the modern-day French

Ornamental Ironwork in New Orleans

Perhaps what most enchants visitors to the Crescent City is the profusion of wrought iron adorning the local houses, monuments and public buildings.

Wrought iron was often used to decorate railings, balconies, vertical supports, fences, front and garden gates, portals, etc. When thus embellishing houses built in the early days of New Orleans, only wrought iron, hammered by craftsmen on the anvil of a local forge, was used. Though most of the pieces executed during that period were made in New Orleans, better ones were imported from Spain. Unfortunately, the iron used for the Spanish pieces did not contain enough carbon and were thus more susceptible to rust.

American cast iron became very popular in the 1830s, and was molded in all sorts of patterns. Though many local foundries could make these pieces, New Orleanians preferred the ironwork produced by the Philadelphia company Wood & Perot. This factory created a large portion of the ironwork that can still be admired in all the neighbourhoods and cemeteries of New Orleans. One characteristic of this finely worked metal is that despite being very hard, it is brittle and tends to flake. For this reason, it must be painted to prevent it from rusting.

Visitors should make sure not to confuse wrought iron with cast iron: the former is hammered on an anvil, the latter cast in a factory. Though both are picturesque, wrought iron is more delicate and its lines are more graceful. Lacy cast iron is often used to decorate the fronts and supports of balconies, while wrought iron is always used sparingly.

The intricate ironwork of New Orleans comes in marvellous patterns to suit every taste and every fancy: oak leaves, vines, morning glories, ears of corn, roses, sheaves of wheat, pineapples, palm trees, fleur-de-lis — even, on storefronts and lavish homes, monograms.

Fine ironwork also figures prominently in the city's historic cemeteries. Many tombs are decorated with fences and gates illustrating the achievements of those buried inside. Here, a cherub carries a torch; there, a cast-iron gate around a tomb is topped by a delicate wrought-iron cross...

Throughout these old cemeteries, the cross, the symbol of Christianity; the lyre, that of music; the weeping willow, that of grief; and the lamb, that of innocence, are featured over and over again in these cast- and wrought-iron pieces.

Quarter) extending on either side of the Place d'Armes (Jackson Square), which faced the Fleuve Saint-Louis (the Mississippi), and reaching as far as Rue Bourgogne (present-day Burgundy Street), along the north part of the ramparts that surrounded the Carré in those days.

The Plantation House (1700-1800)

With the colonization of Louisiana in the early 18th century, the farming industry expanded rapidly. The first French colonists harvested cotton and indigo. Then, around 1730, planters from Santo Domingo (Haiti) introduced sugar cane to the area. A few miles from New Orleans, on vast stretches of farmland along the Mississippi, the plantation house, with its outbuildings and obligatory slave quarters, set the tone of the times. These plantation houses, with their sloped roofs studded with dormer windows, were very similar to those found in the French colonies in the West Indies in that era. The ground floor was used for storage and the area immediately outside it was shaded by the second-floor porch, which sometimes wrapped all the way around the house, or formed a "U" around it. The second floor served as living quarters for the plantation owners, whose bedrooms were at the back. The windows were equipped with jalousies, which, when closed, offered protection from the hot sun and the rain. The buildings already displayed a blend of French and Spanish architecture which was perfectly adapted to the South, and which soon shaped the Creole style of the region's farmhouses and townhouses.

The Creole Style (1788-1850)

In New Orleans, the French and Creole (revealing both French and Spanish influences) architectural styles soon emerged side by side in the French Quarter. The Creole townhouse of that era differed from the Creole farmhouse, whose style was introduced into New Orleans around 1790, when refugees fleeing the revolution on the island of Santo Domingo settled in Louisiana.

The Creole townhouse sits on a long, rectangular site. The building itself—freestanding, semi-detached or part of a row—is built entirely of brick and had two to four stories. At the back of the ground floor there is an inner courtyard accessible by a narrow corridor; this cramped passageway was widened in later buildings so that carriages could pass through it. The lower part of the structure has three arched openings: the entryway and two sets of French doors. The entryway is located on one side of the building and provides access to the corridor leading to the courtyard out back; the French doors open inwards, so the interior space opens directly onto the street. The second floor of the Creole townhouse has a balcony attractively decorated with wrought iron. Finally, the steeply sloping roof is punctuated by two dormer windows.

Originally designed as a farmhouse or village dwelling in the West Indies, the Creole farmhouse appeared in the French Quarter and in Faubourg Marigny when the refugees from Santo Domingo arrived. Smaller and squarer than the Creole townhouse, the Creole farmhouse appealed to less affluent New Orleanians. This type of house, which has only one floor and faces right onto the sidewalk, enjoyed tremedous popularity up until the middle of the previous century.

Other Styles of Homes (1800-1860)

Other types of homes inspired by Creole houses began appearing in New Orleans in the early 19th century. The façade of the *"porte-cochère"* or "carriage" house also has two windows (sometimes arched) and, for "modern" convenience, a carriage entrance on one side of the façade. This entrance gives access to a corridor leading to the courtyard, where the stables were located. The four windows on the second floor open onto a balcony adorned with wrought iron. The ground floor used to be used for business, while the four rooms on the upper floor served as living quarters for the merchant and his family. Finally, right beneath the pitched roof, there is an attic with two dormer windows.

Another distinctive trait of the "carriage" house and other houses dating from the same period is their outbuildings, located on one side of the courtyard. These started to appear in the early 19th century and continued to be built until around 1860. Smaller than the main house, they have one story fewer and open onto the inner courtyard. Their gently sloping roofs have no dormer windows, giving the building a more austere look. There are doors on either end of the ground floor and the second floor, whose balcony has wooden columns, since wrought iron was used only for façades; between the two doors are double windows. The outbuildings were usually servants' quarters, and also contained the kitchen for the main residence.

Also influenced by the Creole style, the "*entresol*" or "mezzanine" house conceals an inconspicuous middle floor between its lower and upper stories; this was used as storage space for the ground-floor business. The arched part of the ground-floor windows lets the daylight into these rooms. These houses also have pitched roofs, but with no dormer windows. The inhabitants lived in the rooms above the *entresol*; the four front windows of the house open onto a narrow balcony decorated with ironwork in a variety of motifs.

Other architectural styles can also be found in New Orleans. Between 1830 and 1870, the architecture of both the American cottage and the American townhouse were influenced by the Creole style. The former, with its central door flanked by two windows on either side, sits on a square base. There is a single window on each of the side walls of the upper floor, which is topped by a pitched roof with no dormer windows. Later, with the addition of another story, the Georgian house was born. The townhouse, for its part, is almost identical to the *porte-cochère* house, minus the dormer windows.

Architectural Curiosities

Shotgun houses are deep, narrow structures with a front porch. In fact, they are so narrow that a bullet fired from the front door will supposedly pass through all the rooms before exiting through the back door! The advantage of these corridor-like houses is that they allow for maximum ventilation during the long, damp period starting in June and sometimes lasting until October. Their occupants can create a draft by opening the windows and the front and back doors. There is also a double version of this kind of building—two shotgun houses set side by side, providing occupants with twice as much space.

The camelback house resembles both the Creole house and the double shotgun. It was very popular in New Orleans from 1860 to the early 20th century. The front part of the structure forms the ground floor, with a porch dominating the façade, while the back part rises up another story. This style of construction made it possible to circumvent an unpopular municipal tax determined by how much of a building fronted onto the street.

Another common style in New Orleans is the corner store. Both Creole and Georgian, these buildings, whose entrance is set at an angle facing the street corner, have a large, covered area in front. This shelter, which offers protection from both sun and rain, is supported by a series of wooden or cast-iron pillars and wraps around part of the ground floor. The shopkeeper can thus display his merchandise to passersby on both streets.

Finally, as in the French and Spanish West Indies, many houses in New Orleans have big verandas overlooking the sidewalk, all adorned with splendid ironwork.

New Orleans architecture attained new heights of extravagance with the development of the Garden District (see "Exploring", p 125).

The Cemeteries of New Orleans

Several of the 40 or so cemeteries in New Orleans are veritable mosaics of local history, and as such merit a visit. Because the ground is so swampy here, New Orleanians were (and still are) obliged to build above-ground, European-style (French and Spanish) vaults and stacked tombs; otherwise, a body buried just centimetres below the surface would be submerged in water.

Louisianians soon showed unlimited imagination in their efforts to honour the dead. In their cemeteries, you'll find everything from the grandiose to the pathetic, from Greco-Latin classicism to the most ornate baroque, from the ancient solemnity of the burial mound to audacious references to the Pharaohs, complete with abrupt shifts into Puritanism and scrupulous austerity.

The archives of 1724 make reference to the first cemetery (Saint-Pierre) in the French Quarter. In those days, New Orleanians buried their dead—except for a few wealthy, privileged individuals interred in the local churches—in this cemetery. In 1784, during the Spanish occupation, the authorities in the Cabildo instituted a public health measure prohibiting city residents from burying corpses and declared that church crypts would theretofore be used exclusively for heroes of the colony. In 1789, therefore, St. Louis Cemetery No. 1 was laid out on Basin Street, adjacent to the French Quarter. This cemetery contains the tombs of the pioneers of New Orleans, including the city's first mayor, Étienne Boré (1741-1820), who was the first planter to market granulated sugar.

The oldest legible inscription in the cemetery reads as follows: *"Ci-gît un malheureux qui fut victime de son imprudence. Verse une larme sur sa tombe, et un De profundis s'il vous plaît, pour son âme; il n'avait que 27 ans. 1798."* ("Here lies a poor wretch who was a victim of his own imprudence. Shed a tear on his tomb and please say a De profundis for his soul; he was only 27 years old. 1798."). Duelling was very much in fashion in the late 18th century; could this be a hapless loser?

St. Louis Cemetery No. 2 was inaugurated in 1823. To "escape the insalubrious miasmas", it was located 400 *toises*, or 2600 feet, outside the city limits. St. Louis Cemetery No. 3, laid out in 1854, is the burial place of a number of great restaurateurs, including Antoine Alciatore (Antoine's) and the Prudhommes.

In every cemetery in New Orleans, grieving families built private chapels and family vaults for their dear departed. Most of these are made of brick, since there is no stone in the area; some wealthy folk spent a fortune importing the finest marble to honour the memory of their dead. In addition, each community had at least one "prestige tomb". In 1848, the Société Française erected the most imposing one of all. An interesting Creole tradition made it possible for several generations to use the same tomb: when necessary, the remains of an old occupant would be deposited at the back of the tomb, and whatever was left of the coffin would be burned. This somewhat lugubrious practice could only be carried out after a year or more; otherwise the body might not be completely decomposed. In 1852, at the height of the yellow fever epidemic that wiped out a quarter of the population of New Orleans, wealthy families managed to secure additional places for their deceased, while less fortunate folk were buried in tiered vaults, often with three levels, along the back wall of the cemetery. These "ovens" (or *fours à pain* because they resemble bakers' ovens), a fine example of which can be seen at St. Louis Cemetery No. 3, were rented for periods of 364 days.

The magnificent Metairie Cemetery, laid out on the site of a former racetrack, covers 60 hectares and has 7,000 monuments. There are two interesting legends regarding this graveyard. One of its founders, Charles T. Howard, was offended that Metairie's exclusive Jockey Club had refused to make him a member and swore that he would turn the racecourse into a cemetery—and then did so. Howard had made a fortune with the Louisiana state lottery, which he owned, but the upper class considered him a boor. The mausoleum he had built for himself, oddly enough, shows an old man covering his lips with an accusing finger. The second legend has to do with the fact that in 1914, Josie Arlington, a local brothel-keeper, commissioned the renowned monument-maker Weiblen to build her tomb out of red granite. Supposedly, the red light from the tollgate shone on the plot before the famous madam's monument was even erected. When the heroine was interred, right-thinking people were appalled to discover that her final resting place, like her scandalous life, would be suffused with red light. Overnight, the news spread like wildfire, fueling the conversations of both the decadent and the virtuous of New Orleans. To avoid a permanent scandal, the cemetery administration promptly planted a row of trees to block the red light that so offended the modesty of the sanctimonious.

Every year on All Saints' Day, there is feverish activity in all the cemeteries of New Orleans. In the weeks leading up to November 1, families bustle about sprucing up, whitening and repairing the tombs. On All Saints' Day, the tombs are strewn with thousands of chrysanthemums.

Lafayette Cemetery No. 1, for its part, contains the remains of many victims of the yellow fever epidemic and the Civil War. Big magnolias line the lanes, shading the tombs in this graveyard, where members of various communities lie buried, including many people of Irish and German descent.

POPULATION

Between 1960, when the city of New Orleans had nearly 630,000 residents, and the 1990 census, when fewer than 500,000 people were counted, there has been a marked shift in population from the downtown to the suburbs. The present population of metropolitan New Orleans is about 1,200,000.

The Creoles

The word "Creole", from the Spanish *criollo*, was originally intended to designate whites born in the colonies in the southern part of North America, as well as those living in the West Indies. As in the French West Indies, the sons and daughters of French planters born in New Orleans became genuine Creoles. One of the most famous Creoles was Empress Josephine, born Marie-Josèphe Tascher de La Pagerie in Trois-Ilets, Martinique. The term later came to refer to people of French or Spanish descent or (popularly) to someone of mixed French or Spanish and African descent.

Baroness Micaela Almonester de Pontalba

When Micaela was born, her father, Don Andrés Almonester y Roxas, was already 70 years old. The widowed Almonester had married his second wife, a Creole named Louise de La Ronde, in 1787. An only child, Micaela married her 20-year-old cousin, Joseph Xavier Célestin Delfau de Pontalba, the son of a French baron, when she was 16. Both inherited huge fortunes. In the mid-19th century, after a long stay in France, Micaela had a lovely group of buildings, the Pontalba Buildings, erected on either side of the Place d'Armes (now Jackson Square). Each of these opulent buildings had elegant shops on its ground floor and 16 comfortable apartments on the upper floors. They are still standing today, a testimony to the baroness's taste and a precious architectural legacy for New Orleans.

In the course of its 38 years of Spanish rule (1762 to 1800), New Orleans never became hispanicized. During this period, Franco-Creole culture, education and traditions remained firmly intact throughout the city. The Spanish authorities left the cultural infrastructure in place and the soldiers, who had no choice but to marry Creoles, were rapidly assimilated into the dominant French culture.

The Germans

The Germans recruited by the French settled in an area that had been farmed by natives (Taensas) and said to be a beautiful spot with fine land. The census of November 24, 1721 shows that the German families lived 12 leagues upriver from New Orleans, on the left, on an excellent stretch of land formerly occupied by *"Champs Sauvages"*, which were uncultivated lands that were nevertheless easy to clear. The man in charge of the German colonization, Karl Friedrich d'Arensbourg, founded the village of Des Allemands, on land granted to De Meuse. Other German villages were also established: Mariental, Augsburg and Hoffen. Under the French Regime, the majority of Germans were Catholic, but there were also a number of Calvinists, Lutherans and other Protestants. These settlers were recruited in Alsace and Lorraine, as well as in various parts of Germany, Switzerland and even Hungary. In 1734, referring to a Swiss regiment, Governor Bienville stated that it would be better to relocate them here than to send them back to France: "These Swiss are much more hard-working than the French. Furthermore, they'll have an easy time marrying into German families." This German-speaking population, soon joined by French-speaking colonists from France and parts of what would become known as Canada (present-day Quebec, Acadia), ended up becoming bilingual and eventually assimilated into the francophone majority. It wasn't difficult to integrate them, since their were no German-speaking priests or teachers, and most of them were illiterate; even their names were Frenchified. Interracial marriages took care of the rest. The Germans were industrious colonists and played an active role in Louisiana's economic development. Their main crops were rice, corn and indigo, and they also grew all sorts of market garden produce, which they sold at the French Market in New Orleans. The Germans were also involved in the sugar industry, used slaves to harvest cotton, and were major stockbreeders for their time.

The Spanish

The French occupation lasted 60 years. Under the terms of the Treaty of Fountainbleau (1762), France ceded Louisiana to Spain. However, the Louisianians were only informed of this two years later. The news was greeted with displeasure. On March 5, 1766, Antonio de Ulloa came to take possession of Louisiana in the name of the King of Spain. The new governor was so unpopular that he had to enlist the help of the last French governor, Charles-Phillipe Aubrey, to assert his authority. After being summoned to show his credentials to the Creole leaders and refusing to do so, Ulloa fled to Cuba. For 10 months, starting on October 27, 1768, Louisianians revolted against the Spanish, thus becoming the first colony in the New World to protest its subjugation. On August 18, 1769, however, Don Alejandro O'Reilly, accompanied by 2,056 soldiers, succeeded in imposing Spanish authority and established the Cabildo.

At that point, Spanish law replaced French law, and Spanish supplanted French as the official language. The Cabildo was made up of six *regidors* (councillors), an attorney general and a clerk. It was under the Spanish regime of O'Reilly, regarded as the father of Spanish Louisiana, that slavery was abolished.

In 1770, O'Reilly was succeeded by Don Luis de Unzaga y Amezaga, who married a Creole. It was under his administration that the American Revolution began, and he lent his unconditional support to the republican rebels.

In 1777, Don Bernardo de Gálvez took over as governor. He, too, married a Creole, Félicie de Saint-Maxent d'Estrehan. Don Gálvez was of great help to the American revolutionaries. Today, a statue at the end of Canal Street commemorates this romantic hero of the Spanish colony.

In 1785, Don Gálvez was succeeded by Don Estebán Rodríguez Miró, who also married a Creole, Marie-Céleste Éléonore de McCarty. It was during his governorship that Louisiana welcomed the exiled Acadians wishing to join those who had

The Cabildo

The first Cabildo, the headquarters of the Spanish regime, was built in 1770, but was destroyed by fire in 1788, on Good Friday. The funds required for its reconstruction were provided by Don Andrés Almonester y Roxas, interred in St. Louis Cathedral, to which he was a generous donor. The present Cabildo dates from 1799 and is the fruit of a joint effort by the generous benefactor and Don Gilberto Guillermard, who was also responsible for rebuilding the cathedral, destroyed in the same fire.

The Cabildo was much more than a simple municipal government: it was the seat of the administration and a deliberative assembly with judicial powers. The entire jurisdiction of Louisiana was administered from the Cabildo. Civil and criminal cases were heard here, and the municipal government held its meetings here. It was in this same building, in the Sala Capitular, that Louisiana was officially transferred from Spain to France in 1830, and 20 days later from France to the United States. Nowadays, the Cabildo is used for various exhibitions. Visitors can see the "Iberville Stone", symbolizing the colony's foundation in 1699 as well as a death mask of Napoleon Bonaparte, a gift from one of the French emperor's many admirers.

arrived earlier. In 1788, Father Antonio de Sedella arrived in Louisiana as the representative of the Inquisition in New Orleans. Governor Miró had him arrested in the middle of the night and put on a boat back to Spain immediately. In a dispatch to the Spanish government, he wrote of how the thought of this Capuchin's mandate made him tremble and that the mere mention of the word Inquisition in New Orleans would be enough to drive off the people who were settling there. The same Father Antonio returned to Louisiana in 1795, this time as a clergyman. He spent the rest of his life in New Orleans, where he was known as Père Antoine and was mourned by all when he died there in 1829, at the age of 81. According to the 1788 census, Louisiana and western Florida had a total population of 19,500 whites, 1,700 persons of colour and 21,500 slaves — 10,000 more people than just three years before.

In 1791, Francisco Luis Hector, Baron de Carondelet, took over the governorship from Miró. He was responsible for installing a lighting system in New Orleans and creating a bilingual police force. He also ordered the construction of the canal, which provided a direct link between the Mississippi and Bayou St. John and Lake Ponchartrain, facilitating trade with the towns on the coast. He had forts, redoubts and batteries built, signed treaties with natives in the area, promoted free trade and founded the colony's first newspaper, *Le Moniteur de la Louisiane*. It was during his term, in 1795, that Étienne Boré began marketing granulated sugar.

In 1797, Carondelet was replaced by Brigadier General Manuel Luis Gayoso de Lemos, who died of yellow fever in 1799, and was the only governor to be buried in New Orleans.

The Marqués de Casa Calvo was governor until 1801, followed by Don Manuel de Salcedo, who remained in office until 1803, though Spain had returned Louisiana to France in 1800, under the secret Treaty of San Ildefonso.

The Clash of Cultures

For the first Americans who arrived in Louisiana after Napoleon sold the territory to the U.S. in 1803, everything—the French language that they didn't speak, the emancipated blacks (the only ones in America at the time), the pride of the Creoles and the Acadians—made them feel like fish out of water. This clash of cultures is perhaps best captured in Lyle Saxon's book *Fabulous New Orleans* where he describes an insidious air eating away at Puritanism.

In fact, the liberties enjoyed by Louisianians in general and New Orleanians in particular contrasted sharply with the strict moral standards prevalent elsewhere in the United States. Though New Orleans was a devout, Catholic city, the permissive atmosphere led to a proliferation of brothels, cafes and gaming houses. *Placage*—whites keeping quadroon mistresses—was common practice here. These women were ensconced in comfortable lodgings in the French Quarter and on Rampart Street.

Under Spanish rule, the export trade grew considerably. The land was so intensively cultivated that the colony was virtually self-sufficient. The population increased sixfold, reaching over 50,000 by around 1800. St. Louis Cathedral, the Cabildo and the Presbytère were all reconstructed under the Spanish regime, and Charity Hospital and the Ursuline Convent were built. It was a period of remarkable stability. The Spaniards rebuilt part of the Vieux-Carré, adorning it with splendid architecture, and erected elegant buildings with patios that delight admirers of beautifully laid-out spaces to this day.

The Slaves

The European settlers forced the natives to do arduous work, one of several reasons why entire populations perished. The new arrivals brought many illnesses to the so-called New World that the immune systems of the indigenous peoples could not fight off. Exhausted, weakened and drained by the demands of the European conquerors, these communities were then abandoned to their sad fate. Though huge numbers of natives died, the colonizers were more concerned about their shrunken work force than the death of these unfortunate and generally peaceable souls. The Europeans thus set their sights on Africa, and another kind of slavery emerged in the Americas.

Slave-trading was carried out in every European colony in the New World. The English, the Spanish, the French, the Dutch and the Portuguese purchased groups of Africans and installed them in slave quarters on their farmlands and plantations. According to a census taken in 1714, there were 111 whites, 134 natives and 10 blacks in Mobile (then part of French Louisiana) alone. And that was just the beginning...

Blacks started arriving in New Orleans as soon as it was founded in 1718. Two-thirds of the slaves the French brought to Louisiana came from Senegambia, in western Africa. They were transported to Louisiana and to the French colonies in the West Indies by the *Compagnie des Indes Occodentales* (Company of the West).

The *Code Noir*

In 1724, the French government instituted the *Code Noir*, which guaranteed certain rights to slaves and freed blacks. This code defined the responsibilities incumbent upon both slaves and masters, including, in the latter case, making sure that all slaves were baptized Catholic. Under its terms, slaves did not have to work on holidays or Sundays. The French *Code Noir* was decidedly more humane than those laws governing slavery in other Southern colonies (those under English and Spanish rule). This code remained in effect until the 1820s, after which the African-Americans were subject to the harsh laws prevalent in the Southern states.

Between 1726 and 1731, 13 slave ships came to the colony, and 5,987 Africans were unloaded. The archives mention their arrival at Pointe d'Alger (now Algiers or Algiers Point), across the Mississippi from the Vieux-Carré. There are two possible reasons why Bienville named the place Pointe d'Alger in 1719. Supposedly, before the French had even colonized Algeria, many ships hired to transport slaves would stop at Algiers before setting out on their long voyage across the Atlantic to the European colonies in America. The other, less plausible reason, which is nonetheless historically accurate, was that back when this shameful trade was being carried out, pirates from the coast of Algiers would often seize slave ships and sell off the human cargo to the highest bidder.

African-American Empowerment

In the 18th century, freed blacks began settling the Faubourg Tremé. This steady, gradual shift was of great historical importance, as these blacks became real landowners while slavery was still in full swing. This phenomenon had a profound impact on African-American culture. "Black" New Orleans was able to create a stable environment in which to celebrate its rich culture. Tremé was not only the first black suburb in the United States, but for the entire African-American community, it was a centre of economic, political, social and legal success. By 1850, just a decade after the start of the Civil War, freed slaves already owned $2,214,000.20 of real estate in the Faubourg Tremé.

At the time of the Civil War, there were 30,000 free blacks in the city of New Orleans alone—a larger number than anywhere else in the United States. In the *faubourgs* (districts) of New Orleans, blacks and whites had been living together since the French Regime, and they continued to do so after the Civil War, even when segregation laws were in effect.

The Americans

Well before France sold Louisiana to the United States in 1803, the Americans viewed the territory as the natural geographic continuation of their country. New Orleans lies at the mouth of the Mississippi, and this long river, which snakes its way from the north to the south, was rightly considered to be of strategic value. For reasons both military and economic, the young American republic coveted the region. As soon as the Louisiana Purchase had been concluded, the U.S. wasted no time encouraging a massive number of immigrants of Anglo-Saxon descent to settle in the region, first in the cities (New Orleans and Baton Rouge) and then gradually in the parishes along the Mississippi.

At the end of the first half of the 19th century, the "Anglos" continued moving into new regions—in St. Mary Parish, on the coast of the Gulf of Mexico and, in greater numbers, along the north part of the Atchafalaya River. "Sugar mania" prompted many other settlers to buy small farms from French farmers. The new arrivals replaced rustic buildings with immense agricultural facilities used for growing and processing sugar cane. The French farmers, for their part, moved to the prairies in the southwestern part of Louisiana. During the same period, many other immigrants arrived, though in fewer numbers than the Anglo-Saxons and Americans. Successive waves of German, Spanish, Irish, Italian and Slavic immigrants thus settled in American Louisiana.

In the years following the Civil War, there was a vast campaign to encourage new settlers to move to the prairies in the southwestern part of the state. Many German farmers from the American Midwest answered the call. These people were skilled at growing wheat and other grains; in Louisiana, they soon became expert rice-growers as well.

Another big wave of Anglo-Saxon immigration occured during the construction of the Southern Pacific railroad, in 1882. However, the preponderance of English-speakers became even more conspicuous after the discovery of oil in 1901, an upward trend that continued until after the Second World War.

POLITICS

The state capital, Baton Rouge, is the seat of the state legislature, which consists of the Senate and the House of Representatives. The state is divided into districts made up of one or more parishes.

The judiciary includes the state Supreme Court, five courts of appeal and a number of district courts. It is interesting to note that Louisiana is the only American state to follow civil law, derived from the Napoleonic Code.

Each state has a governor and a lieutenant governor. In Louisiana, these offices are presently held by Mike Foster and Kathleen Branco, respectively. The secretary of state and the attorney general are the two other most important figures in the state government.

In addition, each parish is governed by a board known as the Police Jury, whose members (the sheriff, coroner, clerk and assessor) are elected.

Finally, there are the state police, who monitor traffic on highways and major roads; the Sheriff's department, responsible for maintaining order and safety in the parishes, and the municipal or local police.

THE ECONOMY

When he decided to found New Orleans on the banks of the Mississippi in 1718, Jean-Baptiste Le Moyne de Bienville knew he had found the best spot. Thanks to the proximity of the Gulf of Mexico, the city soon became the veritable gateway to the Lower Mississippi and the hub of the Louisiana economy.

Under the French Regime, the city's port activities depended both on the lumber and fur trade and on the rich plantations near New Orleans, which produced indigo, sugar cane and cotton.

The economy of New Orleans went through a major crisis during the Civil War. The North's blockade prevented all shipping to the traditional cotton markets, and as the Union troops advanced, the slaves gradually fled the plantations. Consequently, real-estate values dropped dramatically and interest rates shot up. While industrialization had made some people rich in the North, the Southern planters could no longer meet their obligations. When slavery was abolished, they lost their labour force, and the economic structure of the South collapsed. It wasn't until several years later that the economy began showing signs of revival.

New Orleans enjoyed a period of economic strength during the Second World War, when local factories manufactured torpedoes, landing craft and other kinds of combat equipment for the U.S. army.

Petroleum, natural gas, the petrochemical and aerospace industries, sulphur, salt, canning and food processing, fishing and timber (forests still cover vast stretches of Louisiana) all contribute significantly to the state economy and the port activities in both New Orleans and Baton Rouge.

CULTURE

The Opéra Français

Louisiana's music scene was born on May 22, 1796, when the opera *Sylvain*, by André Grétry, was presented in a theatre on Rue St. Pierre (St. Peter St.) in New Orleans. For many years, this city was the opera centre of North America. By 1830, when operas were only occasionally presented in New York and Boston, there was a regular season here featuring singers and even entire companies from France. The performances took place at the Théâtre d'Orléans and then at the Opéra Français (Old French Opera House), which opened in 1859. American premieres of operas by Bellini, Donizetti, Halévy and Verdi were presented here. New Orleans remained a major centre for opera, especially French opera, until the Civil War broke out. Two New Orleans composers became world-famous: Louis Moreau Gottschalk (1829-1869) and Ernest Guiraud (1837-1892). These two prodigies studied in Paris. Guiraud returned to New Orleans briefly to attend the premiere of his opera, *Le Roi David*; he was only 17 at the time. He composed the musical accompaniment for the recitatives in Bizet's *Carmen* and completed the *Contes d'Hoffman*, which Offenbach had left unfinished. The Opéra Français, erected at the corner of Bourbon and Toulouse Streets in 1859, burned down in 1919.

The Petit Théâtre du Vieux-Carré Français

The Petit Théâtre du Vieux-Carré Français was founded in 1916 by an amateur theatre group. It is one of the oldest community theatres in the United States and the oldest theatre company in New Orleans. The company, originally housed in the Pontalba Building, moved to its present location at 616 St. Peter Street in 1922.

A building had been erected on this site in 1794, but it burned down the same year. Three years later, it was rebuilt for Don Manuel Cayoso de Limos, the last Spanish governor of Louisiana, who attended to the landscaping of the patio personally to make sure that it would be pretty for his young wife.

After the Louisiana Purchase in 1803, the building changed hands several times, then fell into disuse until the theatre company purchased it and restored it to its former glory.

Writers and Louisiana

Louisiana has been the birthplace of several writers, attracted a number of others and inspired many. African-American writers from Solomon Northup, author of *Twelve Years a Slave*, published in 1853, to contemporary novelist Ernest Gaines, have never overlooked the humiliation inflicted upon their

people. In another vein, a number of musicians have left behind
memoires or told others their recollections for publication; these
include Sidney Béchet, Jelly Roll Morton and Louis Armstrong,
whose book *Growing up in New Orleans* was published in
1952.

Without a doubt, it is Anne Rice, who, in her novels and short
stories (*The Feast of All Saints* and *The Vampire LeStat*), best
describes the characters encountered in everyday life in New
Orleans. A number of great white writers like Nobel Prize
winner William Faulkner and playwright Tennessee Williams,
born Thomas Lanier, have lived in New Orleans. It was here in
this Southern metropolis, where he was selling smuggled
whiskey that Faulkner started to write. Born on the other side
of the Mississippi, into a family that had been ruined by the
Civil War, he shared old-stock New Orleanians' distaste for
business-minded Yankees.

Tennessee Williams, who loved New Orleans more than any
other city in the world, was dumbstruck when he saw a
streetcar named Desire pass by his window. Thus was planted
the seed for his famous play, whose heroine, Blanche DuBois,
represents the dreamer, fragile and vulnerable amidst narrow-
minded realists.

Jazz and African-American Music

It all started in New Orleans. It was here that the traditional
African musical styles took root and evolved into jazz, blues
and gospel.

The oldest African-Americans still remembered the rhythms and
instruments used in the ceremonies and rituals they took part
in before being rounded up and sold into slavery in the white
world. On Congo Square, where they were permitted to gather
on Sundays, slaves would spend hours performing inspired
dances to the sounds of big cylindrical drums, tom-toms carved
out of tree trunks, square drums, castanets made out of bones,
calabashes, triangles, as we are told by jazz historian Arnaud
Bienville, whose name summons up the memory of the founder
of New Orleans. Though never written down, the music they
made was nonetheless coded; like all music it was based on a
specific rhythmic structure, and only within that structure did

imagination take over. This music would always retain these characteristics, which made it ideal for improvisation

Music, in general, played a big role in New Orleans, which had its own opera companies, symphony orchestras and even, toward the end of the 19th century, a Creole symphony orchestra made up entirely of black musicians; New Orleans was the birthplace of a phenomenon unknown elsewhere – that of the black Creole. Originally, the term "Creole" designated a white person born in the West Indian colonies. In French Louisiana, however, in spite of the *Code Noir* drawn up at Versailles in 1724, slave owners were not punished for their transgressions, and when they fathered mulatto children, they often had them baptized, assigned them less strenuous tasks and even freed them.

By around 1800, there were at least 2,000 of these freed black Creoles living in New Orleans, some of whom were able to take advantage of the same musical instruction available to whites.

Dixie

The word "Dixie", which evokes both a style of jazz (Dixieland) and all the Confederate States, has an interesting origin. After Louisiana was sold to the United States in 1803, a 10-dollar bill was issued in New Orleans. On one side, the word "*dix* "("ten" in French) was printed; on the other, the word "ten". The Americans pronounced *dix* according to English phonetics (the French pronounce it "dee"). As the bill was only in circulation in New Orleans, the city was nicknamed "Dixie".

In the middle of the previous century, New Orleans, with over 100,000 inhabitants, was by far the most populous city in the South and even the western part of the country. The port from which sugar and cotton were shipped was very busy, and money flowed freely. "Paris on the Mississippi" loved parties, parades and dancing and was lenient toward pleasure-seekers. Balls, nightclubs and bars abounded, and music filled the air, thanks to bands that seize any opportunity to parade through the streets. It was mainly in these parades that the local style of music developed. Behind the official band came the second line, made up of anonymous musicians who would get together to challenge the stars and often dethrone them. The spectators followed the bands, dancing all the way, and the band with the best beat would be declared the winner.

Funeral parades, a tradition imported from Africa that aimed at ensuring the dead a decent burial, also gave rise to veritable competitions. Many musicians started their careers—or at least started getting more lucrative bookings—at these parades. They would then move on to one of the city's numerous dance halls, which, eager to attract customers ready to pay what it took to have a good time, hired lots of musicians. Though originally looked down upon by the black Creole musicians who performed in chic nightclubs geared more to white tastes, the music played by African-Americans in popular dives gradually prevailed, thanks to its irresistible originality. The defeated Creoles simply ended up enriching the music of their brothers with traditional band instruments.

One of the first jazz musicians to be labelled as such was Buddy Bolden, who headed a seven- or eight-piece band around 1895. His bold approach enabled this style of music, which had not yet come into its own, to make a big leap forward. Sadly, he ended his days in an institution, worn-out from all sorts of excesses. Another pioneer, the black Creole Jelly Roll Morton, born Ferdinand La Menthe, made several recordings, thus leaving a more tangible legacy to posterity. His contemporary, Joe "King" Oliver, who would be followed by "Duke" Ellington and "Count" Basie, started out at the Aberdeen Club, at the corner of Marais and Bienville Streets. Oliver had a band until the early 1930s, when the Depression hit. It is he who gets the credit for discovering Louis Armstrong, both an instrumentalist and the first jazz musician to gain international renown. Another Creole, Sidney Béchet, closed the circle in a way by settling in France, where his talents as a melody-maker earned him a warm welcome.

In the 1920s, when New Orleans musicians, tempted to try their luck in the North, arrived in Chicago, bassist Pops Foster recalls that everyone, musicians from both east and west, tried to play like them. In France, the appearance of black musicians in the cabarets of Montmartre was greeted with enthusiasm by such major figures as Ravel, who was particularly enchanted by the saxophone, which came into its own in the hands of these men. He even wrote a sonata for piano and violin entitled *Blues*.

Blues... Many African-Americans in New Orleans didn't work on plantations, but they learned the soulful songs that would evolve into the blues from cotton pickers. This soulfulness, combined with the burning desire for rhythm that had remained fixed in the hearts of the African workers, took on another form as well, this time a religious one: gospel. Protestant ministers used hymns to teach African-Americans the rudiments of their religion and convert them.

Church singing was gradually adopted by the African-Americans and transformed into an art by powerful voices like New Orleanian Mahalia Jackson's.

Jazz, blues, gospel: in these three different forms, the music of these underpriviledged people from faraway lands became one of New Orleans's greatest treasures.

SPORTING EVENTS

Football

As in all big American cities, sporting events enjoy a special status in New Orleans.

The biggest sporting event to take place in New Orleans is still the Sugar Bowl, the classic annual football game. A major event, renowned for its famous parade through the city streets, it is held on New Year's Day. The Sugar Bowl, which is heavily covered by the media, is the final game between the two best college teams and is supposed to be the crowning event of the college football season. The kick-off takes place at the Louisiana Superdome, in front of a crowd of frenzied football fans.

New Orleans Trivia

At the corner of Carondelet and Gravier Streets, the Hibernia National Bank, built in 1920, was the tallest building in New Orleans for a while.

Factor Row, at the corner of Perdido and Carondelet Streets, was immortalized by French artist Edgar Degas in 1873, in a painting entitled *Le marché de coton à La Nouvelle-Orléans* (The Cotton Market in New Orleans).

Bourbon Street was not named after the whiskey, but rather the royal family, whose origins were half-French and half-Spanish.

From the early 1920s until 1968, it was prohibited to teach French in Louisiana schools and sometimes even to speak the language in public.

The construction of New Orleans' underground canal system lasted from 1927 to 1941. The city boasts one of the most renowned pump systems in the world.

Precipitation is a problem in New Orleans. From June to August, as much as 35 centimetres of rain can fall in two days.

The colour of a person's house used to be an indication of his or her wealth; the more colourful the house, the richer its owner.

Coliseum Park precedes the Lower Garden District. Nine of the streets here bear the name of Greek muses; the first street is dedicated to Terpsichore, the muse of dance and lyric poetry. This neighbourhood was subdivided in 1807 and used to be called the Faubourg de l'Annonciation.

Traditional African-American funerals in New Orleans, of the kind shown in films like *Harold and Maude* and *Live and Let Die*, take place only two or three times a year nowadays, and only for jazz musicians. Furthermore, gatherings or celebrations rarely take place when a Baptist is buried, regardless of his or her position in society.

Anne Rice, born in New Orleans on October 4, 1941, is one of Louisiana's most popular bestselling authors. Most of her books are set in New Orleans. Some of them have been made into movies, including *Interview with the Vampire*, starring Tom Cruise, and *Exit to Eden*, which is due out soon.

New Orleans: an "open city"? Having inherited a certain degree of permissiveness from its Creole and African-American communities, New Orleans remains an "open city"—just like Las Vegas has become. The 3,000 bars in New Orleans can thus decide for themselves when and how long to stay open.

Because of the geological characteristics of southern Louisiana, which has water just centimetres below its subsoil, New Orleans can never have a subway system.

Basketball

In the week leading up to the decisive college football game, another major sporting event is held in New Orleans: the Sugar Bowl Basketball Tournament. This game pits the two best college basketball teams against each other.

Baseball

Though New Orleans doesn't have a professional baseball team, fans can still take in a high-calibre game at the University of New Orleans stadium, where the local team, the Zephyrs, plays.

GASTRONOMY

New Orleanian gastronomy is a blend of French, Creole, African, Cajun and Spanish cuisine. Nowhere else in the United States does the food rival that of New Orleans and Cajun Louisiana.

New Orleans Recipes

Hurricane (aperitif)

This cocktail is an ancestor of planter's punch, that delicious mixture of tropical fruit juice and rum that is still very popular in the West Indies. The recipe is for one drink.

65 ml (1/4 cup) dark Martinican rum
7 ml (1/2 tablespoon) grenadine
185 ml (3/4 cup) pineapple juice
Juice of 1/2 lemon or lime
Ice
Garnishes: orange slices and maraschino cherries

Pour rum, grenadine, pineapple juice and lime juice into a mixing glass. Shake well. Moisten the rim of a glass with lemon juice and coat it with granulated sugar. Put some ice in the glass, add the mixture and garnish with a slice of orange and a maraschino cherry.

Oysters Rockefeller

This world-renowned recipe was created by Jules Alciatore for the famous New Orleans restaurant opened by his Marseillais father, Antoine. These oysters are still listed on the menu of the French Quarter restaurant, which is still run by Antoine's descendants. The name of the dish refers to the green and white of American dollars, which the fabulously wealthy Rockefeller, the founder of Standard Oil, certainly had lots of! The recipe is for six people.

36 cleaned oysters
2 cloves of garlic, finely chopped
60 ml (4 tablespoons) butter
30 ml (2 tablespoons) peanut oil
60 ml (4 tablespoons) flour
500 ml (2 cups) oyster juice and fish stock (fumet)
750 g (1 1/2 lbs) spinach, finely chopped
6 small green onions, finely chopped
60 ml (4 tablespoons) parsley, chopped
15 ml (1 tablespoon) Ricard or Pernod

Salt and freshly ground pepper, to taste
Tabasco sauce, to taste
Grated parmesan cheese
Cooking salt

Shuck the oysters, drain them and reserve the juice. Melt the butter with the oil in a saucepan with the chopped garlic; stir in the flour, the oyster juice and the stock (fumet) and allow to cook for a few minutes. Add the spinach, green onions and parsley and simmer, uncovered, for 10 minutes or until the sauce is fairly thick. Add the Ricard, the salt and pepper and the Tabasco.

Cover the bottom of a dripping-pan with 1 cm (1/2 inch) of cooking salt and put the oysters on top; pour the sauce over them sprinkle with parmesan then bake at 200° C (400° F) until they are lightly browned.

Soft-Shell Crab

Every spring, blue crabs shed their shell. For a few weeks, before the crabs' new armour has hardened, fishermen gather them up off the coast. The crabs are then savoured by New Orleanians, who prepare them in all kinds of ways—in salads, in sauces, grilled, breaded and fried.

Paul Prudhomme's Blackened Redfish

This dish was created by the famous Cajun chef from New Orleans. The recipe is for four people.

4 filets of redfish
60 ml (4 tablespoons) melted butter
15 ml (1 tablespoon) of each of the following ingredients: paprika, black pepper and salt
7 ml (1/2 tablespoon) of each of the following ingredients: Cayenne pepper, garlic powder, onion powder, dried oregano, white pepper and dried thyme

Heat a cast-iron skillet at high heat until it is hot enough that a drop of water evaporates instantly. Mix the herbs and spices in a bowl then coat the filets with the mixture. Put the filets in the hot skillet and cook for 2 to 3 minutes until they turn black.

Put 5 ml (1/2 teaspoon) melted butter on each filet; avoid getting butter on the skillet. Use a spatula to flip the filets and brush the blackened part of the fish with 5 ml (1/2 teaspoon) melted butter. Cook for 2 to 3 minutes more, until the fish is slightly blackened. Serve the fish on a heated dish.

Pecan Pralines

Pecan pralines are a traditional Creole treat, and New Orleanians have been enjoying them for generations.

375 ml (1 1/2 cups) granulated sugar
375 ml (1 1/2 cups) brown sugar
250 ml (1 cup) milk
30 ml (2 tablespoons) corn syrup
A pinch of salt
375 ml (1 1/2 cups) pecans, coarsely chopped
90 ml (6 tablespoons) unsalted butter
10 ml (2 teaspoons) vanilla

Cover a cookie sheet with buttered paper. In a saucepan, mix the granulated sugar, brown sugar, milk, corn syrup and salt together; bring to a boil at medium heat, stirring constantly. Add the nuts. Put a cooking thermometer at the edge of the pan and cook, uncovered, over medium heat, stirring regularly until the temperature reaches 115° C (236° F) or a small amount of the mixture dropped into ice water forms a soft ball. Remove immediately from the heat. Add the butter and vanilla and beat well until the mixture thickens. Quickly drop spoonfuls (about 5 cm/2 in in diameter) of the mixture onto the cookie sheet. If the mixture hardens, heat the saucepan over very low heat to soften. Let the pralines cool completely before removing them from the cookie sheet. Keep in an airtight container at room temperature.

Café Brûlot

This is another of restaurateur Jules Alciatore's creations that is now part of New Orleans's culinary heritage. Makes six cups of coffee.

750 ml (3 cups) of strong, hot coffee

8 cloves
1 cinnamon stick, broken in half
1 lemon: the zest cut in long strips 6 mm (1/4 in) wide
22 ml (1 1/2 tablespoons) granulated sugar
90 ml (6 tablespoons) cognac or brandy

In a saucepan placed over a live flame, mix the cloves, cinnamon, zest, sugar and cognac; stir for 3 minutes or until the mixture is hot. Remove from the flame. Flambé the mixture, allow to burn for a few minutes, then add the coffee. Ladle the coffee into six demitasses.

Gourmet Glossary

Andouille: Not comparable to the French *andouille*, which is prepared with pork chitterlings or tripe. The smoked, Louisianian *andouille* is made of pork meat and spices; it is used to spice up various dishes including the famous gumbo.

Beignet: Of French origin, this square-shaped doughnut is sprinkled with icing sugar and served hot and always with a *café au lait*.

Boudin: This is not a traditional *boudin* made with pig's blood, but rather is a sausage made of rice, onion, spices and herbs, among other ingredients.

Café au lait: Coffee with steamed milk, a favourite beverage of New Orleanians, which, like at the famous Café du Monde, is deliciously accompanied by *beignets*.

Calas: A fried pastry made of flour, rice and cinnamon, served with syrup at breakfast.

Court-bouillon: The Creole court-bouillon includes tomatoes, onion, garlic, pepper and hot peppers and is used to cook fish such as snapper, redfish, and red sea bream.

Creole: Probably of Spanish origin, this sauce has a base of tomatoes, garlic and sweet peppers. It is used in many culinary preparations including the famous Creole shrimp.

Papillote: A method called en papillote that consists of cooking – usually steaming – foods in parchment paper.

À l'étouffée: A method that consists of cooking foods in a sealed casserole dish.

Filé: Obtained by grinding sassafras leaves, this powder, similar to ground bay leaves, is used to season sauces and gumbos.

Gumbo: Traditional okra soup. To a spicy broth seasoned with a brown roux, are added *andouille*, crayfish, shrimp, oysters, crab and duck to taste. White rice is added to the soup bowl.

Gumbo z'herbes: Mustard greens and spinach are added to the usual okra gumbo.

Jambalaya: Similar to Spanish *paella*, it is composed of rice, sausage, seafood and tomatoes. The name jambalaya comes from the French *jambon*, which means ham, and the African *ya*, which means rice.

Maque-choux: A dish with a base of fresh corn and vegetables.

Mirliton: This vegetable from the squash family, called *chayotte* in Haiti and *christophine* in Guadeloupe and Martinique, is stuffed with ham or shrimp.

Muffaletta: An Italian sandwich-meal made of cold cuts, olives and cheese.

Pain perdu: As its French name suggests, this recipe uses slightly stale bread slices that are soaked in a mixture of milk, sugar and eggs and then browned on the stove (also known as French toast).

Po'boy: A contraction of "poor boy", this sandwich – or inexpensive meal – is made from a baguette of French bread stuffed with fried oysters, shrimp, soft-shell crab or crayfish and seasoned with hot pepper sauce.

Pralines: A favourite with New Orleanians, this candy is made of sugar, butter, cream and pecans.

Roux: Obtained by cooking flour in oil or butter, a roux heightens many Creole and Cajun dishes including the famous gumbo.

Sauce Piquante: A sauce made of a roux watered down with white wine to which are added tomatoes, hot peppers and a hint of vinegar.

Tasso: Smoked pork, sliced into thin strips and dried, tasso is often an ingredient in gumbo and is used to season myriad dishes.

PRACTICAL INFORMATION

Information in this section will help visitors from English-speaking countries better plan their trip to New Orleans.

ENTRANCE FORMALITIES

Travellers from Canada, the majority of western European countries, Australia and New Zealand do not need visas to enter the United States. A valid passport is sufficient for stays of up to three months. A return ticket and proof of sufficient funds to cover your stay may be required. For stays of more than three months, all travellers, except Canadians and citizens of the British Commonwealth, must obtain a visa ($120 US) from the American embassy in their country.

Caution: as medical expenses can be very high in the United States, travel health insurance is highly recommended. For more information, see the section entitled "Health" (p 78).

CUSTOMS

Foreigners may enter the United States with 200 cigarettes (or 100 cigars) and duty-free purchases not exceeding $400 US, including personal gifts and 1 litre of alcohol (you must be 21 years of age to drink alcohol). There is no limit on the amount of cash you are carrying, though you must fill out a special form if you are carrying the equivalent of more than $10,000 US. Prescription medication must be placed in containers clearly marked to that effect (you may have to produce a prescription or a written statement from your doctor to customs officials). Meat and its by-products, all kinds of food, seeds, plants, fruits and narcotics can not be brought into the United States.

For more ample information, contact:

United States Customs Service: 1301 Constitution Avenue Northwest, Washington, DC 20229, ☎ (202) 566-8195.

EMBASSIES AND CONSULATES

United States Embassies and Consulates Abroad

Australia
United States Embassy: Moonah Place, Canberra, ACT 2600, ☎ 270-5000.

Belgium
United States Embassy: 27 Boulevard du Régent, B-100 Brussels, ☎ (2) 513-3830, ≈ (2) 511-2725.

Canada
United States Embassy: 2 Wellington Street, Ottawa, Ontario, K1P 5T1, ☎ (613) 238-5335, ≈ (613) 238-5720.

United States Consulate: Place Félix-Martin, 1155 Rue Saint-Alexandre, Montréal, Québec, H2Z 1Z2, ☎ (514) 398-9695, ≈ (514) 398-9748.

United States Consulate: 360 University Avenue, Toronto, Ontario, M5G 1S4, ☎ (416) 595-1700, ⊷ (416) 595-0051.

United States Consulate: 1095 West Pender, Vancouver, British Columbia, V6E 2M6, ☎ (604) 685-4311.

Germany
United States Embassy: Deichmans Aue 29, 53170 Bonn, ☎ 228-3391.

Great Britain
United States Embassy: 24 Grosvenor Square, London W1A 1AE, ☎ (171) 499-9000.

Ireland
United States Embassy: 42 Elgin Road, Ballsbridge, Dublin 4, Ireland, ☎ 660-8922, 668-8085 or 668-8858.

Italy
United States Embassy: Via Veneto 121, 00187 Roma, ☎ (06) 46741, ⊷ (06) 46742217.

Netherlands
United States Embassy: Lange Voorhout 102, Den Haag, ☎ (70) 310-9209, ⊷ (70) 361-4688.

New Zealand
United States Embassy: 29 Fitzherbert Terrace, Thorndon, Wellington, ☎ 472-2068.

Spain
United States Embassy: C. Serrano 75, Madrid, 28006, ☎ (91) 577-4000, ⊷ (91) 587-2239.

Switzerland
United States Embassy: 95 Jubilaeumsstrasse, 3005 Berne, ☎ 31-43-70-11.

Foreign Consulates and Delegations in New Orleans

Belgium
There is no Belgian consulate in New Orleans; address inquiries to the consulate in Houston: 2929 Allen Parkway, Office 2222, Houston, Texas 77019, ☎ (713) 529-0775, ⚐ (713) 224-1120.

Canada
The Canadian consulate closest to New Orleans is located in Atlanta: 235 Peachtree Street, Northeast 100-Colony Square, Office   1700,   Atlanta,   Georgia,   30361-6205, ☎ (404) 255-8470, ⚐ (404) 532-2050.

Great Britain
British consulate: 321 St. Charles Ave., 10th floor, New Orleans, LA 70130, ☎ (504) 586-8300.

Netherlands
Dutch consulate: 643 Magazine Street, New Orleans, LA 70130, ☎ (504) 596-2838, ⚐ (504) 596-2800; mailing address: P.O. Box 60643, New Orleans, LA 70160-0643.

Spain
Spanish consulate: 2102 World Trade Center, 2 Canal Street, New   Orleans,   LA   70130,   ☎   (504)   525-4951, ⚐ (504) 525-4955.

Switzerland
Swiss consulate: 1620 Eighth Street, New Orleans, LA 70115, ☎ (504) 897-6510.

? TOURIST INFORMATION

Louisiana Office of Tourism: 666 Foster North Street, P.O. Box 94291, Baton Rouge, LA 70804, ☎ 1-800-334-8626.

New Orleans Metropolitan Convention and Visitors Bureau, Inc.: 11520 Sugar Bowl Drive, New Orleans, LA 70112, ☎ (504)-566-5031 or (504) 566-5011, www.nawlins.com.

New Orleans Tourist Information: ☎ 1-800-NEW-ORLEANS or ☎ 1-800-639-6753 *(24-hour service)*.

Welcome Center: 529 Saint Anne Street, New Orleans, LA 70112, ☎ (504) 568-5661 or (504) 566-5031.

Airport Hospitality Center: New Orleans International Airport, Baggage Claim area *(every day 10 am to 10pm)*.

Conventions and Other Events

Expo Emphasis! *(4429 Bienville Ave., 70119, ☎ 504-488-5825, ⇒504-488-5830)* specializes in the organization of conventions and expositions in New Orleans. Contact Bobby Bergeron directly; he organizes every aspect of the preparation and success of the event, from the stay to the lay out of the hall, transportation, meals, even guided tours of the city.

GUIDED TOURS AND EXCURSIONS

Greater New Orleans Black Tourism Network, Inc. *(Louisiana Superdome, 1520 Sugar Bowl Drive, New Orleans, LA 70112, ☎ 504-523-5652 or 1-800-725-5652, www.gnobtn.com)*. There is good reason for New Orleans to be identified with African-American culture and with jazz. With a black population that is 60% of the total population, New Orleans is the largest city of colour in the United States, a fact that is reflected at the administrative level. For 15 years, New Orleans has had black mayors, a mark of societal progress on the background of the cruel diaspora experienced by Africans brought to America.

The Greater New Orleans Black Tourism Network offers tours that emphasize the influence of African-American culture on the city. Famous the world over as the cradle of Jazz, New Orleans owes this distinction to a rather unique phenomenon that occurred in a wasteland northeast of the city known as the "plaines du Congo" that served as a fairground and a Native-American ball field during the week. On Sunday, the Lord's day, blacks were permitted to meet there, to dance and to play the African instruments that lived in their memories: tomtoms, calabash, triangles and the bamboo drum called "bamboula", in a dance phenomenon that was destined to progressively to lead to jazz. Jazz, the music of poor exiles as able to express explosive joy as melancholic languor, would leave profound marks not only on the places where we rejoice, but also on those where we commune with ourselves. Among the celebrated names of black music in New Orleans, are Louis Armstrong, the big band singer and trumpet-player, and the uncontested queen of gospel, Mahalia Jackson. Laughter and prayer, these two poles of the spectrum of human activity, show a strong African influence, one of the rich sources of the cultural originality of Americans.

Mythic Congo Square, now Louis Armstrong Park, is still a site of musical exchange and improvisation. The most important event in this sphere is still the New Orleans Jazz and Heritage Festival in April, a climactic point in the city's tourism calendar. For those that miss it, the many Social Aid & Pleasure Clubs organize annual fall parades with bands of all sorts and musicians of all ages.

The contribution of African-Americans is equally strong during Mardi Gras. This festival period that begins on Epiphany (January 6) and reaches its apogy in the days preceding Lent attracts visitors from the world over. The arrival of the Krewe of the Zulu King is among the festival's most important moments. It begins at dawn with the arrival of the "king", by barge on the Mississippi, and runs until dusk (St. Charles Ave. and Canal St.). There is also the parade of torch carriers and then the second line made up of all those who follow the procession, including musicians who go all out trying to attract more atention than the "official" paraders. The French Quarter, conceived by Pierre Le Blond de La Tour and built in 1718 by Adrien de Pauger, is the popular setting of good times with these thousands of celebrants, dancing to the rhythm of the festival that brings back so much French, African, native, Cajun and North American history.

Roots of New Orleans *(reservations: ☎ 504-596-6889 or 504-523-7818)*, a name reminiscent of Alex Haley's *Roots*, offers a half-day "discovery" tour that includes a creole lunch *(departure at 9am: adults $25, children $19, meal included; departure at 1:30pm: adults $19, children $15)*.

Global Resources, Inc. *(P.O. Box 50601, New Orleans, LA 70150; contact John Hankins, ☎ 504-861-0170)* specializes in cultural tourism.

Among the guided city tours, **Tours by Isabelle** ★★★ *($30 per person, departures at 9:30am and at 1:30pm, ☎ 391-3544)* are especially interesting. Most of the guides speak many languages which can simplify the understanding of certain anecdotes. In a minibus of about a dozen seats, the tour covers the entire French Quarter, the St. Louis No. 2 and Metairie cemeteries, Bayou St. John, City Park, the shores of Lake Pontchartrain, Tulane and Loyola universities, St. Charles Avenue, the Garden District and the Superdome. Not only are important historic sites covered, but the guides provide interesting and enthusiastic commentary on the city. For an additional five dollars, you can visit the Longue Vue House and Garden. The minibus picks up and returns passengers to their hotels.

Guided Tours and Walking Tours ★★★

The **National Parks Service** also offers various tours. Tickets for these walking tours are available the day of the tour beginning at 9am *(every day except Christmas and during Mardi Gras; 916 North Peters St., ☎ 589-2636)*. Check the weather forecast ahead of time since storms are particularly frequent during the summer.

The History of New Orleans *(10:30am; 90 min, including 1 hour of walking)*. A look at the historical events and the cultural diversity the union of which gave birth to New Orleans.

Tour of the Day *(11:30am; 90 min)*. More specialized than the "History of New Orleans", this walk features a different historical and cultural subject every day.

Garden District Tour *(2:30pm; 90 min; reservations required)* departs from the corner of First Street and St. Charles Avenue, in the Garden District. This tour proposes a circuit of the "Americans of the beautiful neighbourhoods", especially in the Uptown neighhourhood.

Exploring Delta Cultures *(3pm; 45 min)*. At the Jean Lafitte interpretive centre there is a presentation on the different aspects of the environment of the Mississippi Delta with various slide shows and recreational walks with different themes.

For over 200 years the Creoles of the Vieux-Carré have fashioned the history of New Orleans as much as that of Louisiana. A fascinating walking tour is offered by **Le Monde Créole French Quarter Tours ★★★** *($16; under 18 years of age and groups of more than 12 people 15 $; every day, except Mardi Gras; 10:30am and 2:30pm; 624 Royal St., French Quarter, ☎ 568-1801)*. This guided, two-hour tour is possible thanks to the anecdotal *Memoires de Laura* (*Memoirs of Laura Lecoul*, see also Laura Plantation in "Excursions Outside New Orleans", p 155), and exposes everything there is to know about Creole life in the period. The tour includes visits to the winter residence of Laura Locoul in New Orleans as well as to many other historic houses in the French Quarter. Tours are available in English, French, and, with a few weeks notice, in Spanish, German, Russian, and Japanese.

STEAMBOAT AND OTHER CRUISES

There are many guided river tours of the Mississippi and of the bayous around New Orleans.

The first paddleboats appeared in 1812 and made New Orleans the first stopover in the transportation of cotton. Later, they would serve as a mode of transportation of goods (furniture, French wine, books) and of famous passengers: artists, opera singers and actors.

From February to December, the **Delta Queen ★★★** *(☎ 586-0631 or toll free in North America 1-800-543-1949)*, the **Mississippi Queen ★★★** and the **American Queen ★★★** offer cruises of three to 11 days between New Orleans and Saint Paul, Minnesota, including plantation visits and stops in Natchez and Viksburg, Mississippi.

The **Natchez ★★** *(during the day, adults $14.75, children 6-12 years old $7.25; evenings, adults $18.75, children 6-12 years old $10.75, 3 and under free; 11:30am, 2:30pm and 7pm,* *departure from the Jax Brewery wharf,* ☎ *586-8777 or toll free in North America 1-800-233-2628)* makes two-hour cruises every day that include Creole buffets and jazz concerts *(adults $38.75, 6-12-year-olds $19.25)*.

The **Creole Queen** ★★ *(adults $14-$18, children $7-$10 depending on the time; 10:30am, 2pm and 7pm;* ☎ *524-0814 or toll free in North America 1-800-445-4109)* offers daily, guided tours leaving from the Canal Street Wharf on the historic site of the Battle of New Orleans in Chalmette. A Creole buffet is served at 7pm and there is also a two-hour cruise with a jazz concert *(adults $39, children $18)*.

The **Cajun Queen** ★★ *(adults $12, 2-12-year-olds $6; 10:30am and 2pm;* ☎ *524-0814 or toll free in North America 1-800-445-4109)*, a replica of a 19th-century paddle-wheel boat, leaves the wharf at the Aquarium of the Americas, on Poydras Street, for a one-and-a-half-hour cruise, that brings passengers to the French Quarter, the Chalmette Battlefield (site of the Battle of New Orleans), plantations and bayous.

The **Cotton Blossom** ★★ *(adults $14.50, children $7.25; every day 11am to 4pm; departure from Jackson Brewery, 1300 World Trade Center,* ☎ *586-8777 or toll free in North America 1-800-233-2628)* offers cruises on the Mississippi, the Intercoastal Waterway, and the Barataria-Lafitte bayou. Creole meals are available for a supplemental charge.

The **John James Audubon** ★★ *(10am, noon, 2pm and 4pm; departure from the wharf at the Aquarium of the Americas,* ☎*586-8777)* has eight departures daily to Audubon Zoo *(return trip including zoo admission: adults $16.50, children $8.25; aquarium visit additional $1; return trip adults $10.50, children $5.75; one way $8.50 and $4.50)*. The evening cruise include a visit to the Aquarium and a deluxe dinner *(adults $45.50, children $25; without meal adults $39.50, children $22; departures from the wharf at the Aquarium at 8pm and 10pm)*.

The **Crown Point Swamp Tour** ★★ includes transportation from your hotel to the wharf, located about 20 minutes from downtown New Orleans. The hour-and-a-half cruise meanders bayous, the natural habitiat of alligators, owls and racoons *($20, $35 with hotel pick-up; departure 10am and 2pm,* ☎ *592-0560)*.

R.V. River Charters offers barge cruises for tourists who want to use their recreational vehicles for stopovers *(10 to 12 days; $2,775 to $3,650 for two people; ☎ toll free in North America 1-800-256-6100)*. This formula is becoming increasingly popular. People board in their RV's and nonchalantly meander the great Mississippi River and its many bayous. The cruise crosses the Atchafalaya bassin and Cajun Country, stopping at the most interesting points to take stock of local culture: dance, music, cooking and other tourist attractions.

FINDING YOUR WAY AROUND

The area code for New Orleans and surroundings is 504, although it is not necessary to dial this prefix when you are calling from within the area. Numbers beginning with 1-800 are toll free.

New Orleans is very easy to reach. **New Orleans International Airport (Moisant)**, 16 kilometres (10 miles) west of the city, serves all of the major international airlines, while private planes and charters pass through the airport in the east on Lake Pontchartrain (**Lakefront Airport**). Highway I-10 and Interstates LA 61 and LA 90 cross the city, which is also accessible by train and national coach lines. New Orleans is also a port of call for cruiseships that navigate the Gulf of Mexico and the Caribbean Sea.

New Orleans is situated about 145 kilometres or 90 miles from the Gulf of Mexico and stretches along the Mississippi. The city is built around the French Quarter. Down the river, or "downtown", are Faubourg Marigny and the suburbs of Arabi and Chalmette, site of the famous Battle of New Orleans. Algiers Point and Gretna compose a suburb facing the French Quarter on the west bank of the Mississippi. West of the French Quarter and up the river, or "uptown", is the Central Buisiness District, which was once known as *Faubourg Sainte-Marie*. Further along is the Garden District and Tulane and Loyola Universities, Audubon Park and Zoo, and the residential neighbourhoods around Magazine Street and Carrollton Avenue (the area around Carrollton and St. Charles is called Riverbend). Next come the municipalities of Metairie and Kenner, in which is located New Orleans International Airport (Moisant). Between downtown and Lake Pontchartrain, the northern border of the city, are found the Faubourg Tremé and Mid-City, mainly African-American neighbourhoods.

From the I-10 the city can be reached via Exits 234A (Claiborne), 234B (Poydras) or 234C (Superdome), 235A (Vieux Carré-French Quarter and Orleans Avenue), 235B (Canal Street) and 236A (Esplanade Avenue).

Airports

Moisant Airport/New Orleans International Airport *(900 Airline Hwy., Exit 228 from the I-10, Kenner, ☎ 464-2650 or 464-3547)* is named for the famous New Orleans aviator and is the most important airport in Louisiana. It provides links with the major cities of North America, Central America and South America.

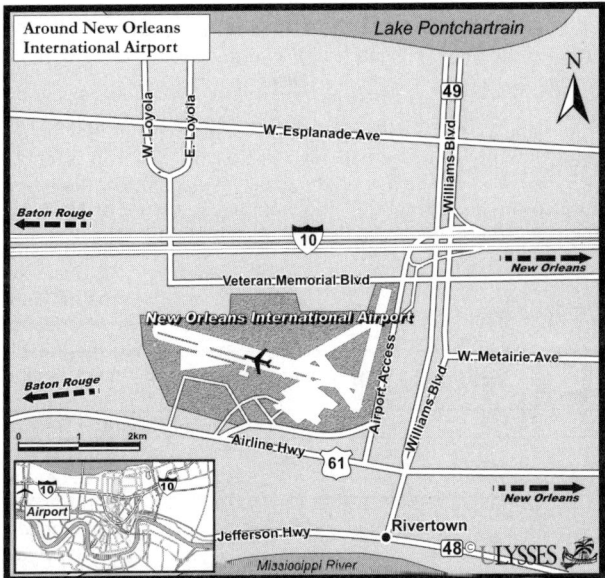

Around New Orleans International Airport

All essential services are found here: car rental, automatic teller machines, bars, restaurants, souvenir shops. There is also a New Orleans Tourist Office counter, a welcome centre for visitors and the Louisiana Tax Free Shopping counter, where out-of-state travellers can be reimbursed for sales tax paid during their stay.

Hospitality is a Louisiana tradition and is apparent from the moment of visitors' arrival.

The airport is 16 kilometres, or 10 miles, west of New Orlenas. The city centre can be reached via Exits 235B (Canal St.) and 235A (Vieux Carré-French Quarter) of Highway I-10. Buses, taxis and limousines transport tourists to hotels and convention centres. The **New Orleans Tour Airport Shuttle** takes passengers downtown from Moisant Airport in less than 45 minutes *($10; ☎ 522-3500 or 1-800-543-6332)*.

Lakefront Airport *(Exit 241 from the I-10, ☎ 242-4110)* receives charter and private flights.

Taxi fares are set by the city at $21 for a trip from the airport to most downtown locations for two people; for three or more passengers budget for about $8 per person.

Louisiana Transit provides public bus service linking the airport and downtown every half hour for $1.50 (the trip is about 45 min). The bus stop is on the upper level ramp. For the return trip to the airport, a stop is located at the corner of Elk Place and Tulane Avenue, facing the public library. The last bus leaves at 6:20pm.

Information: ☎ 737-9611

☞ FINDING YOUR WAY AROUND THE CITY

By Taxi

Taxi meters are regulated and the fare demanded for a trip is not negotiable. The regular fare is $2.10 plus $0.20 for every 1/5 mile or 40 seconds, plus $0.75 for every additional passenger. There is a small surcharge for luggage. Disputes can be addressed to the New Orleans taxi drivers' association.

United Cabs Inc.: 1630 Euterpe Street, New Orleans, ☎ 522-9771 or 1-800-323-3303.

Checker Yellow Cabs: ☎ 943-2411.

Liberty Bell Cabs: ☎ 822-5974.

By Public Transportation

New Orleans offers many types of public transit. Each requires exact change. The **Regional Transit Authority - RTA** *(☎ 248-3900)* offers a **Visitour Pass**, available in most hotels, for $4 per day or $8 for three days of unlimited bus and streetcar travel.

Regional Transit Authority (RTA): 6700 Plaza Drive, ☎ 248-3900 ou 569-2700.

The **Riverfront Streetcar ★** *($1.50 one way; Mon to Fri 6am to midnight, Sat and Sun 8am to midnight)* runs along the river for easy access to riverfront activities. Inaugurated in 1926, this nine-station circuit is the oldest in the city. Antique cars in rich gold and red colours, familiarly known as "the ladies in red", permit about 5,500 passengers per day to enjoy the cultural and commercial attractions of the riverfront. Here is a list of the stops:

1st stop:	Esplanade Avenue
2nd stop:	French Market (at the Halle des Légumes-Vegetable Market)
3rd stop:	French Market (at Decatur Street)
4th stop:	Jackson Square, St. Louis Cathedral and the Cabildo
5th stop:	Woldenberg Riverfront Park and Aquarium of the Americas
6th stop:	Aquarium of the Americas, Canal Street Wharf and Ferry
7th stop:	the *Creole Queen* paddle wheel boat and the Poydras Street entrance to Riverwalk

| 8th stop: | Julia Street entrance to Riverwalk and the New Orleans Convention Center |
| 9th stop: | historic Warehouse District |

St. Charles Streetcar ★★ *($1; 24-hour service)* follows St. Charles Avenue from Canal Street past Loyola University (run by Jesuits), Tulane University (home of the oldest business faculty in the United States), the Garden District and Audubon Park to Carrollton Avenue.

Public Buses serve the entire city *($1, $0.10 extra for transfers)* and take exact change or passes.

The **Central Business District Easy Rider** *($0.30; Mon to Sat 6:30am to 6pm)* stops along Poydras and Canal Streets, as well as at the Convention Center.

By Ferry

Three ferries shuttle between the shores of the Mississippi. The Canal Street Ferry is free for foot passengers and one dollar for cars. It docks at Canal Street, near the French Quarter and takes passengers to Algiers Point. A second ferry, on Jackson Avenue, south of the Garden District, serves Gretna. The third ferry leaves from Chalmette.

By Car

The good condition of the roads and the low price of gasoline compared to gas prices in Europe and Canada make driving an ideal mode of independent transportation in Louisiana. Excellent maps are available in travel book stores, or once arrived in Louisiana, at gas stations.

A few tips:

Driver's License: In general, European driver's licenses are valid, but it is preferable to obtain an international driver's license.

Canadian driver's licenses are completely valid in the United States. Take note that many states are linked to Canadian police forces by a computer network for the control of traffic infractions. A ticket remanded in the United States is automatically reported to a file in Canada.

Driving Code: Road signs at intersections indicate right of way. "Stop" signs are scrupulously respected. A "Stop" sign with a rectangular sign that reads, "4-way" indicates that every one must stop at the intersection and no particular lane has the right of way. Stops must be made even when there is no apparent danger. When two cars arrive at a "Stop" sign at the same time, the right of way on the right rule applies. In all other cases the car that arrived first has the right of wya.

Traffic lights are most often on the far side of the intersection. Be careful to stop before the intersection or the crosswalk.

In Louisiana it is permitted to make a right turn on a red light when the lane is clear (you must stop first, however). Intersections where this is not permitted are marked with a sign that reads, "No Turn on Red". When a (yellow) schoolbus stops with its flashing lights lit, it is obligatory to stop regardless of the direction you are travelling in. Failure to stop for a schoolbus is considered a serious offence.

Seat belts must be worn at all times.

Highways are free, except for most thruways. Interstate highways are designated by an "I" followed by a number.

The speed limit is 55 mph (88 kph) on most highways, and 65 mph (104 kph) on interstates.

The highway patrol is particularly zealous all over Louisiana. Be vigilant on the outskirts of towns and cities.

A triangular, yellow "Yield" sign means you must slow down and cede right of way to vehicles crossing your path.

A round, yellow sign with a black cross and the letter "R" on it indicates a level crossing.

Gas Stations: Gas is much cheaper in the United States than in Canada and Europe.

Table of Distances (km/mi)

Baton Rouge						
2548/1583	Boston					
1476/917	1584/984	Chicago				
127/79	2456/1526	1495/929	New Orleans			
1482/921	2388/1484	2210/1373	1390/864	Miami		
2729/1696	505/314	1371/852	2638/1639	2630/1634	Montréal	
2198/1366	352/219	1284/798	2107/1309	2039/1267	612/380	New York

Car Rental

The agency **HATA** (☎ 1-800-356-8392) is a free hotel and car rental reservation service (see "Accommodation", p 87).

Car-rental agencies are located at the airport and at various places in the city. To rent a car, you must have a valid driver's license and a major credit card. Rates start at about $30 per day and $150 per week for an economy class car wth unlimited mileage.

Alamo Rent A Car: 225 E Airline Highway, New Orleans, ☎ 469-0532 or 1-800-327-9633.

Avis Rent A Car: 2024 Canal Street, New Orleans, ☎ 523-4317 or 1-800-331-1212.

Budget Rent A Car: 1317 Canal Street, New Orleans, ☎ 467-2277 or 1-800-527-0700.

Dollar Rent A Car: 1910 Airlines Highway, Kenner, ☎ 467-2285 or 1-800-800-4000.

Hertz Rent A Car: 901 Convention Center Boulevard, Office 101, New Orleans, ☎ 568-1645 or 1-800-654-3131.

National Car Rental: 1020 Airline Highway, Kenner, ☎ 466-4335 or 1-800-227-7368.

Value Rent A Car: 1701 Airline Highway, Kenner, ☎ 469-2688.

Car Service and Assistance

American Automobile Association (AAA): 3445 North Causeway Boulevard, Metairie, New Orleans, ☎ 838-7500 or 1-800-222-4357.

CBD Chevron Services: 447 Rampart North, New Orleans, ☎ 568-1177.

Mardi Gras Truck Stop: 2401 Elysian Fields, New Orleans, ☎ 945-1000.

Parking

For any questions concerning parking downtown: ☎ 826-1854 or 826-1900.

In New Orleans, particularly in the French Quarter and the Central Business District, parking places are rare and precious. Restrictions are many, and some of the signs are easier to understand than others. If you have the misfortune of having your car towed, something authorities are quick to do, here is the address of the municipal pound:

Clairbourne Auto Pound, 400 North Clairborne Avenue, New Orleans, ☎ 565-7450 or 826-1900.

Parking Lots

Dixie Parking Service, Inc.: ☎ 523-4521.

Downtown Parking Service: ☎ 529-5708.

By Bus

Bus, along with automobile travel, is probably the best mode of transportation. Well organized and inexpensive, bus lines cover most of Louisiana.

On most bus lines smoking is forbidden. In general children five years of age and younger travel for free. People aged 60 years and over are eligible for significant discounts. Animals are forbidden.

Greyhound Bus Lines: 1001 Loyola Avenue, New Orleans, ☎ 525-6075 or 1-800-231-2222.

Hotard Coaches: 2838 Touro Street, New Orleans, ☎ 944-0253.

By Train

In the United States, the train is not always the least expensive way to travel, and it is certainly not the fastest. (It takes about 30 hours to travel from New York to New Orleans.) It can be interesting, however, for long distances as it is very comfortable (try to get a seat in a panoramic car to take advantage of the scenery). For schedules and destinations contact AMTRAK, the present owner of the rail network in the United States *(toll free in North America* ☎ *1-800-972-7245)*.

AMTRAK train station: Union Passenger Terminal, 1001 Loyola Avenue, New Orleans, ☎ 528-1610.

By Plane

By plane is certainly an expensive mode of transportation, but some airlines, especially regional ones, regularly offer special fares (low season, short stays). Be a smart shopper and compare prices. For precise details on various destinations, contact local tourist offices.

Many of the major airline companies fly to New Orleans International Airport (Moisant).

Aeromexico: ☎ 524-1245 or 1-800-237-6639.

American Airlines: ☎ 1-800-433-7300.

Aviateca Airlines: ☎ 1-800-327-9832.

Continental Airlines: ☎ 581-2965 or 1-800-525-0280.

Delta Airlines: ☎ 529-2431 or 1-800-221-1212.

Lacsa the Airlines of Costa Rica: ☎ 468-3948 or 1-800-225-2272.

Northwest Airlines Inc.: ☎ 1-800-225-2525.

Southwest Airlines: ☎ 834-2337 or 1-800-531-5601.

Trans World Airlines: ☎ 1-800-221-2000.

United Airlines: ☎ 466-1889 or 1-800-241-6522.

USAir: ☎ 454-2668 or 1-800-428-4322.

By Bicycle

The streets of New Orleans are particularly busy, so bicycling is much more pleasant in Audubon Park, City Park, and along the shores of Lake Pontchartrain. **Crescent City Cyclists** (☎ 276-2601) provides information on cycling activities.

Bicycle Rental

Some rental centres organize excursions in parks or in the Garden Dirstrict, outings to the bayous or to plantations in the environs of New Orleans. Rental rates vary, but budget for between $3.50 and $5 per hour, or between $12.50 and $15 per day.

French Quarter Bicycles: 522 Dumaine Street, French Quarter, New Orleans, ☎ 529-3136.

Joe's Bike Shop: 2501 Tulane Street, New Orleans, ☎ 821-2350.

Michael's: 618 Frenchmen Street, Faubourg Marigny, New Orleans, ☎ 945-9505.

Olympic Bike Rentals & Tours: 1618 Prytania Street, New Orleans, ☎ 523-1314 *(every day 8am to 7pm)*.

Hitchhiking

At your own risk! Hitchhiking in Louisiana is not recommended; motorists are very mistrustful of hitchhikers after so many horror stories. On the other hand, as a hitchhiker you never know what sort of person might pick you up. Basically the practice is to be avoided.

TELECOMMUNICATIONS

Recall that the **area code** for New Orleans and environs is **504**, but that when calling from within the calling area you need not dial the area code. Numbers beginning with 1-800 are toll free.

To reach an operator, dial 0. If you use the operator to make a local call, and you do not have a telephone card, it will cost $0.80.

A local call costs $0.25 from a public phone; keep change handy, although you can also use calling cards and credit cards.

For long-distance calls within North America, dial 1 + the area code + the local number.

For long-distance calls outside of North America, dial 011 + the country code + the area code + the local number.

Country Codes

Australia	61
Belgium	32
Germany	49
Great Britain	44
Holland	31
Italy	39
New Zealand	64
Spain	34
Switzerland	41

It is generally less expensive to use your own telephone company's direct service access number.

British Telecom Direct Access Numbers:
From a SPRINT phone: 1-800-825-4904
From an MCI phone: 1-800-854-4826
From an AT&T phone: 1-800-445-5688

INSURANCE

Cancellation Insurance

Your travel agent will usually offer you cancellation insurance when you buy your airline ticket or vacation package. This insurance allows you to be reimbursed for the ticket or package deal if your trip must be cancelled due to serious illness or death. Healthy people are unlikely to need this protection, which is therefore only of relative use.

Theft Insurance

Most residential insurance policies protect some of your goods from theft, even if the theft occurs in a foreign country. To make a claim, you must fill out a police report. It may not be necessary to take out further insurance, depending on the amount covered by your current home policy. As policies vary considerably, you are advised to check with your insurance company. European visitors should take out baggage insurance.

Life Insurance

Several airline companies offer a life insurance plan included in the price of the airplane ticket. However, many travellers already have this type of insurance and do not require additional coverage.

Health Insurance

This is the most useful kind of insurance for travellers, and should be purchased before your departure. Your insurance plan should be as complete as possible because health care costs add up quickly. When buying insurance, make sure it covers all types of medical costs, such as hospitalization, nursing services and doctor's fees. Make sure your limit is high enough, as these expenses can be costly. A repatriation clause is also vital in case the required care is not available on site. Furthermore, since you may have to pay immediately, check your policy to see what provisions it includes for such a situation. To avoid any problems during your vacation, always keep proof of your insurance policy on your person.

HEALTH

General Information

Vaccinations are not necessary for people coming from Europe or Canada. On the other hand, it is strongly suggested, particularly for medium or long-term stays, that visitors take out health and accident insurance. There are different types, so it is best to shop around. Bring along all medication, especially prescription medicine. Unless otherwise stated, the water is potable throughout Louisiana.

For Emergencies, dial ☎ 911

Snake and Insect Bites

The subtropical climate and the abundance of water and forest make Louisiana a preferred habitat of snakes, insects and mosquitoes.

The venimous water moccasin is quite common in marshy areas such as bayous, cypress groves, paddy fields and ditches. Like most reptiles, and wildlife generally, snakes fear humans. So as not to disturb snakes, one must walk carefully in areas such as those mentioned above. Walkers should wear good rubber boots when adventuring in the habitat of the famous water moccasin.

Mosquitoes, an insect well-known to Canadian readers, are abundant in summer. Wherever there is water you will find these annoying blood-sucking insects. A simple insect repellent is the best antidote to this annoyance.

When walking through woods, you must be on guard for ticks. Not only does this tiny insect bite, it also transmits disease. In case of tick bite, it is recommended to slip a few specimens into a hermetic container and take them immediately to the nearest pharmacy or clinic to be analysed. Wood ticks stick to the skin and must be cautiously removed with tweezers.

Do not get too close to alligators (or "cocodries", as they are called by Cajuns); despite their sleepy appearance, they are always on the look-out. If you are chased by an alligator, try not to run in a straight line, but rather zigzag; alligators charge straight at their prey and it is difficult for them to change directions.

In the city as well as in the countryside, there are red-ant hills. Avoid them, red ants can cause a skin irritation similar to a burn, hence their name, "fire ants".

A brochure on the particularities of Louisianian flora and fauna is available from the Acadiana Park Nature Station (☎ 318-261-8448).

In case of emergency, including snake bites and poisoning, see the telephone numbers below.

Hospitals

There are three hospitals located close to the French Quarter and downtown:

Touro Infirmary: 1401, Foucher Street, New Orleans, ☎ 897-7011 *(open 24 hours a day, emergency entrance on Delachaise Street, at the corner of Prytania Street)*. The centre is located near St. Charles Avenue. Credit cards are accepted.

Medical Center of Louisiana: 1532 Tulane Avenue, New Orleans, ☎ 568-2311.

Tulane University Medical Center: 1415 Tulane Avenue, New Orleans, ☎ 588-5268.

Pharmacies

Walgreen pharmacies *(open 24 hours a day)* sell, among other things, a product called "XS", which is particularly useful as a cure for that carnival hangover. There are Walgreen stores all over the city; here are a few addresses:

134 Royal Street.

4001 General De Gaulle Avenue, ☎ 368-8171.

1429 St. Charles Avenue, ☎ 561-8458.

3057 Gentilly Boulevard, ☎ 282-2621.

3311 Canal Street, ☎ 822-8073 or 822-8070.

9999 Lake Forest, ☎ 242-0981.

Safety

Unfortunately, American cities are not always the safest, this does not mean, however, that you should spend your trip barricaded in your hotel room.

Upon arriving, simply inquire about which neighbourhoods are to be avoided, no matter what the time of day. By taking the necessary precautions, there is no reason to worry about your safety. If, however, you are unlucky remember to dial **911** for all emergencies.

Safety Tips

Some sections of New Orleans are best avoided at night, and little recommended during the day for people who are alone. These include the northern part of the French Quarter and the streets around St. Louis Cemetery No. 1 and No. 2, as well as any poorly lit street in the French Quarter. The same thing goes for the area north of St. Charles Avenue between the West Bank Expressway and Audubon Park, but especially between Jackson and Louisiana Avenues, and for the area south of Magazine Street.

Emergencies

Police, Fire and Ambulance Emergency Number: ☎ **911**

Eighth District Police Station: 24 hours a day; 334 Royal Street, French Quarter, ☎ 822-2222.

Fire Department: ☎ 581-3473

New Orleans Dental Association: ☎ 834-6449

Travelers Aid Society: ☎ 525-8726

DISABLED TRAVELLERS

The rights of disabled people are protected by legislation enacted by the State of Louisiana.

There are parking zones reserved for disabled motorists with special parking permits. There is a $50 fine for parking in these reserved zones without a permit.

Accessibilty for people with limited mobility or in wheelchairs is a recognized requirement in all public spaces in Louisiana: hotels, motels, restaurants, museums, golf courses, parking lots, etc.

The following American organizations can also provide useful information for disabled travellers: **Society for the Advancement of Travel for the Handicapped** *(347 5th Avenue, Suite 610, New York, NY 10016,* ☎ *212-447-7284)*, **Travel Information SERVICE** *(Philadelphia, PA* ☎ *212-456-9600)*, **Mobility International USA** *(P.O. Box 10767, Eugene OR 97440,* ☎ *503-343-1284)* and **Flying Wheels Travel** *(P.O. Box 382, Owatonna, MN 55060,* ☎ *1-800-535-6790)*. **Travelin' Talk** *(P.O. Box 3534, Clarksville, TN 37043,* ☎ *615-552-6670)* regroups various networks offering similar information.

Services for Disabled People in Louisiana

Louisiana State Rehabilitation Services: ☎ 1-800-737-2875 *(24-hour service)*.

Resource for Independant Living: 1555 Poydras Street, New Orleans, ☎ 522-1955 *(Mon to Fri 8:30am to 5:30pm)*.

Advocacy Center for the Elderly and Disabled: 210 O'Keefe Avenue, Suite 700, New Orleans, LA 70112, ☎ 522-2337 or 1-800-960-7705.

Gray Lines *(*☎ *587-0861)* offers tours of New Orleans with adapted transportation.

Wheelchair Rental

Olympic Bike Rental and Tours *(*☎ *523-1314)*, as well as specializing in bicycle rental, rents wheelchairs. Free delivery.

CLIMATE

The climate encountered in Louisiana is essentially hot and humid during the summer, from the beginning of May to the end of September. It is ideal, if possible, to visit the region in the spring or fall when you will enjoy warm, sunny days and cool nights instead of the torrid heat waves and high humidity of summer. Winters are mild. Whatever the time of year you should pack a good raincoat.

Most public places in Louisiana, including hotels and restaurants are air-conditioned, sometimes too much so. A light sweater or jacket will come in handy.

Temperature

Average Maximum and Minimum Temperatures (°C/°F):

January:	19 and 9 / 66.2 and 48.2
February:	19 and 10 / 66.2 and 50
March:	22 and 13 / 71.6 and 55.4
April:	25 and 17 / 77 and 62.6
May:	29 and 20 / 84.2 and 68
June:	32 and 24 / 89.6 and 75.2
July:	32 and 24 / 89.6 and 75.2
August:	32 and 25 / 89.6 and 77
September:	31 and 23 / 87.8 and 73.4
October:	27 and 19 / 80.6 and 66.2
November:	21 and 13 / 69.8 and 55.4
December:	18 and 10 / 64.4 and 50

The best time to visit Louisiana is between October and May; June, July, August and September are very humid and sometimes uncomfortable.

MONEY AND BANKS

Money

The monetary unit is the dollar ($), which is divided into cents (¢). One dollar = 100 cents.

Bills come in one, five, 10, 20, 50 and 100 dollar denominations; and coins come in one- (penny), five- (nickel), 10- (dime) and 25-cent (quarter) pieces.

Dollar and fifty-cent coins exist, as does a two-dollar bill, but they are very rarely used. Virtually all purchases must be paid in American currency in the United States. Be sure to get your travellers' cheques in American dollars. You can also use any credit card affiliated with an American institution like Visa, MasterCard, American Express, Interbank, Barclay Bank, Diners' Club and Discovery. **Please note that all prices in this guide are in American dollars.**

Banks

Banks are open Monday to Friday from 9am to 3pm.

Banks can be found almost everywhere, and most offer the standard services to tourists. Most automatic teller machines (ATMs) accept foreign bank cards so that you can withdraw directly from your account (check before to make sure you have access) and avoid the potentially high charges of using a real teller. Most machines are open at all times. Cash advances on your credit card are another option, although interest charges accumulate quickly. Money orders are a final alternative for which no commission is charged. This option does, however, take more time. The easiest and safest way to carry your money, however, remains travellers' cheques.

First National Bank of Commerce: 210 Baronne Street, ☎ 561-1371 or 1-800-462-9511.

Hibernia National Bank: 313 Carondelet Street, ☎ 586-5552.

Shearson Lehman Brothers: 909 Poydras Street, Suite 1600, ☎ 506-3902.

Whitney National Bank: 228 St. Charles Avenue and 430 Chartres Street, ☎ 586-7272.

American Express Co.: 158 Baronne Street, ☎ 586-8201.

Automatic Teller Machines

First National Bank of Commerce (FNBC): 240 Royale Street and 801 Chartres Street.

Hibernia National Bank: 701 Poydras Street.

Whitney National Bank: 228 St. Charles Avenue.

Exchange Rates			
$1 CAN	= $0.71 US	$1 US =	$1.40 CAN
1 £	= $1.70 US	$1 US =	0.59 £
$1 Aust	= $0.71 US	$1 US =	$1.40 Aust
$1 NZ	= $0.63 US	$1 US =	$1.58 NZ
1 guilder	= $0.53 US	$1 US =	1.88 guilders
1 SF	= $0.72 US	$1 US =	1.38 SF
10 BF	= $0.29 US	$1 US =	35 BF
1 DM	= $0.60 US	$1 US =	1.66 DM
100 pesetas	= $0.71 US	$1 US =	140 pesetas
1000 lire	= $0.61 US	$1 US =	1650 lire

Exchanging Money

Several banks readily exchange foreign currency, but almost all charge a **commission**. There are exchange offices, on the other hand, that do not charge commission, but their rates are sometimes less competitive. These offices often have longer opening hours. It is a good idea to **shop around**.

At the airport: **Whitney National Bank** *(Mon to Thu 8:30am to 3pm, Fri 8:30 to 5:30pm)* and **Mutual of Omaha** *(every day 6am to 7pm)* are on the upper level of the main terminal.

Downtown: **Continental Currency Exchange Inc.** *(Mon to Sat 10am to 9pm, Sun 11am to 5pm)* is in Riverwalk Market; **Thomas Cook Currency Services** *(111 St. Charles Ave., ☎ 524-0700)* is one block from the French Quarter.

Credit Cards

Most credit cards are accepted at stores, restaurants and hotels. While the main advantage of credit cards is that they allow visitors to avoid carrying large sums of money, using a credit card also makes leaving a deposit for car rental much easier and some cards, gold cards for example, automatically insure you when you rent a car. In addition, the exchange rate with a credit card is generally better, and at many banks and some exchange bureaux you can get cash advances with your credit cards. The most commonly accepted credit cards are Visa, MasterCard, and American Express. Visa International has a 24-hour telephone service in case of loss or theft of your credit card.

Visa International: ☎ 1-800-847-2911 or 1-800-336-8472.

American Express: ☎ 1-800-528-5200.

MasterCard: ☎ 1-800-826-2181.

🛏 | ACCOMMODATIONS

Types of Accommodation

Hotels: A few luxury establishments, large international chains such as Le Meridien, Holiday Inn, Crown Plaza, with restaurants for various budgets. Many downtown and along highways. International-style service.

Motels: Located on access roads. Separate room for two to four people, with television, private bath, and parking.

Bed and Breakfasts: Lodging in host's home, either in a detached building or in a charming plantation house. Furnishings are often antique. Light breakfast, or American-style breakfast (eggs, bacon, sausages, etc.), is graciously served.

Cabins: These individual cottages with kitchenettes are still available, but harder and harder to find.

Campgrounds: They are numerous. Budget for $5 and less for state-run campgrounds and about $12 for private ones.

Youth Hostels: Members of the American Federation of Youth Hostels.

Reservations and Rental

The HATA agency, open every day from 8:30am to 10:30pm, makes hotel and motel reservations and can take care of car rental.

If you are interested in a particular area, HATA can suggest hotels and take care of the reservations.

HATA *(☎ 1-800-356-8392, toll free all over North America)*.

SHOPPING

Ask shopkeepers if they are members of Louisiana Tax Free Shopping, a state-run program by which tourists can be reimbursed sales tax paid during their visit.

Louisiana is the only state with such a program. The simplest strategy is to pick up the directory of participating stores and establishments (there are over one thousand of them) at:

Louisiana Tax Free Shopping: 2 Canal Street, New Orleans, LA 70130, ☎ 568-5323.

At the time of purchase, you will be given a form to fill out which you hand in, with your receipts, before you leave Louisiana. Refunds of less than $500 are made immediately, in cash, at the Refund Center of New Orleans International Airport; amounts of more than $500 are paid by cheque and sent by mail to visitors' homes.

Business Hours

Post Offices: Monday to Friday, 8:30am to 4:30pm, and Saturday, 8:30am to noon.

Main Post Office: 701 Loyola Avenue, ☎ 589-1111 or 589-1112.

Stores

Stores are generally open Monday through Saturday, from 9:30am to 5:30pm or 6pm. Supermarkets, on the other hand, are open later, and in some cases are open 24 hours a day, 7 days a week.

What to Buy

New Orleans offers many Mardi Gras souvenir shops, art galleries and antique stores.

Taxes

Unlike in Europe, prices do not include sales tax. Keep this in mind when planning your budget, as in New Orleans added sales tax can be as much as 9% of the price of the item. See the explanation of Louisiana Tax Free Shopping, above.

Tipping

In general, tipping applies to all table service (no tipping in fast-food restaurants), as well as service in bars and nightclubs, and taxi service. The tip is usually about 15% of the bill before tax, but varies, of course, depending on the quality of service. The tip is not included in the bill; you must calculate it yourself and leave it on the table for the waiter or waitress.

PUBLIC HOLIDAYS

Public Holidays

The following is a list of public holidays in the United States. Most stores, administrative offices and banks are closed on these days. **In addition to these holidays, Mardi Gras is a public holiday in Louisiana.**

New Year's Day (January 1)
Martin Luther King, Jr.'s Birthday (third Monday in January)
President's Day (third Monday in February)
St. Patrick's Day (March 17)
Patriots Day (April 19)
Memorial Day (last Monday in May)
Independence Day (July 4)
Labor Day (first Monday in September)
Columbus Day (second Monday in October)
Veterans' Day (November 11)
Thanksgiving (fourth Thursday in November)
Christmas (December 25)

TRAVELLING WITH CHILDREN

All sorts of family adventures await you in New Orleans. Here is some advice to help you make the most of it.

Make your reservations early and make sure that children are welcome where you plan on staying. If you need a crib or extra cot be sure to request it when reserving. A good travel agent can be indispensable when it comes to this, and also for planning your various excursions.

If you are travelling by plane, ask for seats facing a partition, you will have more room. Bring diapers, extra clothes, snacks toys and small games in your carry-on luggage. If you are travelling by car, the same articles will be equally indispensable. Also be sure to bring enough water and juice to avoid dehydration.

Never travel without a first-aid kit. Besides adhesive bandages, antiseptic cream and diaper rash ointment, don't forget doctor-recommended allergy, cold and diarrhea medication.

If you plan on spending a lot of time outdoors, be careful on the first few days. Children's skin is much more sensitive than adults', and a sunburn can occur much faster than you think. Slather your children with sunscreen and make them wear a hat.

When its time for a night out, many hotels can provide you with a list of reliable babysitters. You can also use the services of a daycare; check the phone book and make sure that it is a licensed establishment.

Child Care

In addition to child care services, these agencies offer tourist activities and entertainment options specially designed for children:

Accent Arrangements: ☎ 524-1222.

Dependable Kid Care: ☎ 486-4001.

The **New Orleans Metropolitan Convention and Visitors Bureau, Inc.** (see p 60) *(☎ 566-5031 ou 566-5011)* sells a five-dollar booklet of suggestions for activities and sights that are of interest to children.

SENIOR CITIZENS

In New Orleans, those aged 65 and older can take advantage of substantial reductions on admission prices to museums and other attractions, as well as special rates in hotels, restaurants, etc. These special prices are often not advertised, so be sure to enquire.

The **American Association of Retired Persons (AARP)** *(601 E. Street NW, Washington, DC 20049, ☎ 202-434-2277)* accepts as members anyone over 50 who makes a request. This association offers several benefits to its members, including reduction on trips organized by various companies. Cruises and guided tours are available from the **AARP Travel Service** *(400 Pinnacle Way, Suite 450, Norcross, GA 30071, ☎ 1-800-927-0111)*.

When it comes to your health, be particularly careful. Besides your regular medications, also bring along your prescription in case you need to renew it. You might also consider bringing along your medical file, along with the name, address and telephone number of your doctor. Finally, make sure that your health insurance covers you while abroad.

MISCELLANEOUS

Bars and Nightclubs

Some establishments charge an entrance fee, especially when there is a band. Tipping is not obligatory, but it is appreciated; if you do decide to tip, 10% to 15% is the norm.

Note that the legal drinking age is 21.

Time Difference

New Orleans is in the Central Time Zone, six hours behind Greenwich Mean Time. When it is noon in New Orleans, it is 1pm in Montreal and New York, 6pm in London, 7pm in Paris, and 10am in Los Angeles.

Drugs

The United States has a strict "zero tolerance" policy on drugs (even "soft" drugs). Drug users and dealers caught with drugs in their possession risk severe consequences.

Electricity

Voltage is 110 volts throughout the United States, as in Canada. Electrical plugs are two-pinned and flat. Visitors from outside North America will need a transformer and a plug adapter. These are available here.

Radio Stations

WWOZ - 90.7 FM
1201 St. Philip Street, ☎ 568-1239.
Traditional jazz and rhythm and blues.

KMEZ (Big Easy 102.9 FM)
1450 Poydras Street, Suite 440, ☎ 593-6376.
Soul music and classics from the sixties and seventies.

WWNO - 89.9 FM
University of New Orleans, ☎ 280-7000 or 286-7000.
Classical and jazz.

Weights and Measures

The United States uses the imperial system:

Weights
1 pound (lb) = 454 grams (g)
1 kilogram (kg) = 2.2 pounds (lbs)

Linear Measure
1 inch = 2.2 centimetres (cm)
1 foot (ft) = 30 centimetres (cm)
1 mile = 1.6 kilometres (km)
1 kilometres (km) = 0.63 miles
1 metre (m) = 39.37 inches

Land Measure
1 acre = 0.4 hectare
1 hectare = 2.471 acres

Volume Measure
1 U.S. gallon (gal) = 3.79 litres
1 U.S. gallon (gal) = 0.83 imperial gallon

Temperature
To convert °F into °C: subtract 32, divide by 9, multiply by 5
To convert °C into °F: multiply by 9, divide by 5, add 32

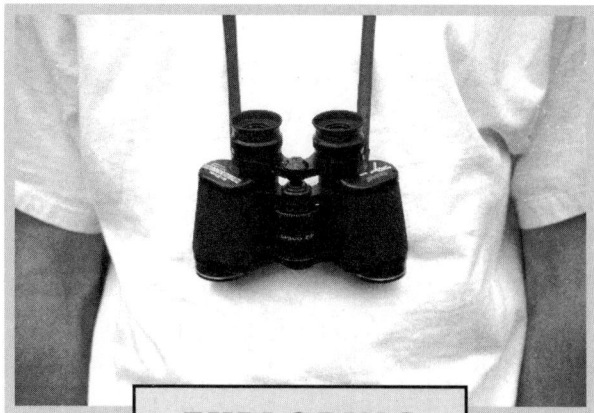

EXPLORING

New Orleans' unique cachet is simply one of a kind. Despite the numerous cataclysms, such as fires, hurricanes and floods, that have ravaged or affected several of its districts over the centuries, there has always been a constant, meticulous concern for maintaining the integrity of the "Creole City's" period architecture and urban development and for respecting its splendid reputation. This is why so many of its neighbourhoods, districts and suburbs are so interesting to visit, indeed to explore, and why it remains one of the most vibrant cities in North America.

★ THE FRENCH QUARTER (VIEUX CARRÉ) ★★★

The French Quarter (Vieux-Carré Français) boasts an impressively rich architectural heritage. From its elaborate balconies and blooming courtyards, the quarter displays its charms, at once French, Spanish and Creole; one cannot help but compare this cultural mosaic to that of the French- and Spanish-speaking Caribbean islands. In Jackson Square (the old Place d'Armes), the spires of elegant St. Louis Cathedral dominate the landscape. From the square to the middle of the park, painters at their easels confer a certain *je ne sais quoi* to the area, with its evocative street names like Decatur, Conti, Dauphine, Bienville, Bourbon, Ursulines, Chartres, Toulouse,

Typical house in the French Quarter

Dumaine, etc. Situated on the banks of the Mississippi River, the **French Quarter** combines past and present in a peaceful, verdant setting. In its midst is **Jackson Square**, a former military parade site, in front of **St. Louis Cathedral** with its tall steeples and white façade, which now watch an endless procession of musicians, artists and horse-drawn-carriage drivers stream by. The **equestrian statue of Andrew Jackson**, the general who saved New Orleans from British invaders during the War of 1812, also stands before the Cathedral. To the right and left (respectively) of the Cathedral, visitors can admire the **Presbytère** and the **Cabildo**, an old guardroom that later became the seat of the Spanish Colonial government, and the site of the signing of the Louisiana Purchase in 1803. These two buildings are now part of the Louisiana State Museum, as are the **Lower Pontalba Building** and the **Upper Pontalba Building**, red brick structures, adorned with quintessential cast-iron balustrades, that were the first apartment buildings built in the United States.

This very particular type of nineteenth-century architecture is characteristic of New Orleans. The buildings' façades are decorated with delicate balustrades, veritable cast-iron

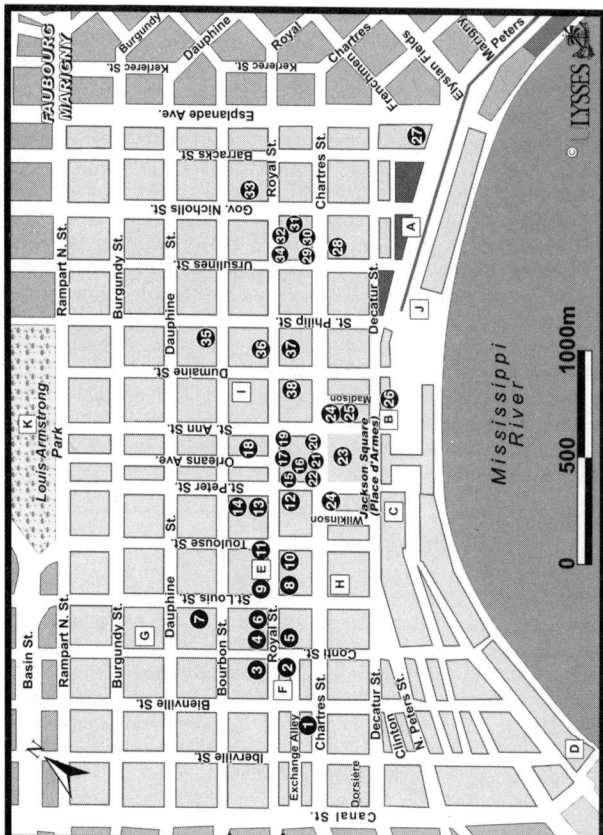

The French Quarter (Vieux Carré)

Attractions

1. Kolly Residence
2. Old Banque de la Louisiane
3. Old Bank of the United States
4. Louisiana State Bank
5. New Orleans Court Building
6. Casa Faurie
7. Hermann-Grima House
8. Seignouret House
9. Ménieult House
10. Casa de Comercio
11. Court of the Two Lions
12. First Skyscraper
13. Thierry House
14. Monnier House
15. Louisiana State Arsenal
16. Pirate Alley
17. Cathedral Garden Houses
18. Quadroon Ballroom
19. Père Antoine Alley
20. Presbytère
21. St. Louis Cathedral
22. The Cabildo
23. Jackson Square (Place d'Armes)
24. Pontalba Building
25. 1850 House
26. French Market
27. Old U.S. Mint
28. First Ursuline Convent
29. Beauregard-Keyes House
30. Soniat House
31. Clay House
32. Haunted House
33. Thierry House
34. Galier House
35. Lafitte's Blacksmith Shop
36. Cornstalk Fence
37. Miltenberger Houses
38. Jean Pascal House

A. French Market
B. Café du Monde
C. Jackson Brewery
D. Aquarium of the Americas
E. Historic New Orleans Collection
F. Gallery for Fine Photography
G. Wax Museum
H. New Orleans Pharmacy Museum
I. New Orleans Historic Voodoo Museum
J. Jean Lafitte National Historical Park
K. Louis Armstrong Park

Mississippi River

500   1000m
0   500

LYSSES

embroideries in which complex designs harmoniously intermingle. This fashion was initiated by the Spanish after the fire that ravaged the city in 1788.

On that score, the famous and imposing **Labranche Building** (Édifice La Branche) *(700 Royal Street)* should not be overlooked. Also worth seeing is **Lafitte's Blacksmith Shop** (La Forge Lafitte) *(941 Bourbon St.)*, a typical example of the brick-and-post cottage, and the Greek Revival **Beauregard-Keyes House** *(1113 Chartres St.)*, two examples of typical eighteenth-century Louisiana architecture and masonry.

Another interesting building in the French Quarter is the **Hermann-Grima House** *(320 St. Louis St.)*. Built in the Georgian style in 1831, which was then much in fashion along the Louisiana coastline, it opens its doors to visitors for whom demonstrations of Creole cooking are held from October to May. Reservations are required.

The French Market (Le Marché Français)

The French Market has always been known as such, even though it was first a Native American trading post. Under the Spanish regime, in 1791, it was transformed into an indoor market. German/Creole market gardeners – Germans who came during the French regime – were the first to supply the public market with food; they were later followed by Italians. As early as 1831, a train skirting the Elysian Fields (Champs Élysées) from the French Market (Marché Français) ran all the way to Lake Pontchartrain. Thanks to President Roosevelt, the old French Market was restored in 1936. With its Old Butcher's Market (Halle des Boucheries), built in 1813, its Vegetable Market (Halle des Légumes) in 1822, its Red House (Maison Rouge), encompassing the original bazaar, and its new Kitchen Market (Halle des Cuisines), the French Market makes up a fascinating whole. The French Market also houses the Flea Market, where local hand-crafted wares can be purchased. Cafés set themselves up here in 1860. The Café du Monde is its oldest tenant. Delicious *beignets* and its popular *café au lait*, a robust chicory-flavoured coffee, can be savoured here. The French Market extends over several blocks between Decatur Street and North Peters Street.

The **French Market** ★★★ (Le Marché Français) spreads over five blocks of houses along Decatur Street and North Peters Street; here, visitors will find secondhand shops, restaurants and, a most remarkable place, a two-hundred year old market that displays fresh meats, incredibly aromatic spices as well as fresh fruits and vegetables 24 hours a day. Visitors will also find the venerable **Café du Monde** here, a place where you can treat yourself to a full-flavoured coffee and a *beignet* (French sugar doughnut) any time of day or night.

Right nearby stands the **Jackson Brewery** *(620 Decatur St.)*, commonly known as **Jax**. This old factory converted into a picturesque shopping arcade has about one hundred shops and boutiques under its roof.

The **Aquarium of the Americas** ★★★ *(adults $9,75, seniors $7,50, children 2 to 12 years of age $5; every day 9:30am to 5pm; Canal St., ☎ 861-2537)*. Over 100,000 species of birds, fish and reptiles, in their natural habitats, can be admired here.

This beautiful, resolutely modern facility is very popular and is close to Woldenberg Riverfront Park and its promenade, which follows along the banks of the Mississippi River. Here, visitors mingle with families and hundreds of school children from neighbouring states arriving by school bus. The place is certainly worth a visit, but be forewarned, the cost of parking in the adjacent lot proves to be almost as high as the price of admission itself! It is therefore preferable to use the tram skirting the river (the Riverfront Streetcar), which can be taken from the French Market.

From its very entrance (upon passing through the turnstile), the Aquarium of the Americas offers explorers the planet's wondrous submarine worlds. On the ground floor, visitors first pass beneath a huge vaulted aquarium in which the moray eel, the skate, the boxfish and the shark swim about above visitors' heads and on either side of the glass arch. The visit continues through different oceanographic ecosystems and climatic microcosms, set up in order to accommodate species from the "coralline" waters of the Caribbean and the Pacific, as well as those from the polar oceans of the Arctic and the Antarctic.

Upstairs, two parrots greet visitors in the Amazon River Basin exhibit, a recreation of the moist, humid environment of this

South American region. The sturgeon catfish, the arapaima, the *pacu*, the boxfish, the carnivorous piranha in their own special tank (their scales are a veritable mosaic of gold and silver nuggets) and finally the black-and-white-spotted leopard ray are all to be found here. Farther along, visitors encounter Arctic and Antarctic species such as affable, child-pleasing penguins with their little tufts of yellow hair. Other areas reproduce the sea bed of the Gulf of Mexico. In one tank, between the pillars of a replica of an oil rig, metal rods are completely encrusted with coral. The astonishing saw shark and the giant sea turtle swim in its waters. In other aquariums, blue jellyfish, unquestionably the most magnificent of their kind, fluttering their colourful umbrellas, while other tanks recreate the murky ocean depths, enabling visitors to better observe certain species of phosphorescent fish.

The Aquarium of the Americas shelters many other residents such as spiders, snakes (terrestrial and aquatic), tortoises and turtles, as well as a rare albino alligator. Under a guard's vigilant eye, young and old alike can gently pet a harmless baby shark raised in an aquarium built especially for this purpose!

The **Historic New Orleans Collection** ★★ *($2; Tue to Sat 10am to 4:45pm; 533 Royal St., ☎ 523-4662)*. Historic site, museum and research centre on the history of the state and the city itself. Guided tours of the gallery and the residence.

The **Gallery for Fine Photography** ★★ *(free admission; Mon to Sat 10am to 6pm, Sun 11am to 6pm; 322 Royal St., ☎ 568-1313)* displays a very beautiful collection of photographs from the late 1800s to the present. Works by Lartigue and by Henri Cartier-Bresson as well as those by jazz portraitist Herman Leonard and photos of Mardi Gras can all be viewed here, among others. Practically every theme is tackled and a new exhibit is presented every month.

The **Louisiana State Museum** ★★★ *(for each museum: adults $4, seniors and students $3, free for children under 12; for the museum complex: $10 and $7.50, Tue to Sun 10am to 5pm; 701 Chartres St., ☎ 568-6968)*. This museum occupies a certain number of historic buildings in the French Quarter. The **Old United States Mint** *(400 Esplanade Ave.)* is dedicated to jazz and Mardi Gras; the **Presbytère** *(701 Chartres St.)* presents exhibitions pertaining to the history of Louisiana; the **1850**

House (Maison 1850) *(523 St. Ann St.)* specializes in the period preceding and following the American Civil War. (See also "Walking Tour of the French Quarter", p 103)

The **Musée Conti Wax Museum** ★ *(adults $5,75, seniors and students $5,25, children $3,50; every day 10am to 5pm; 917 Conti St., ☎ 525-2605 or, from the US, 1-800-233-5405)*. Heroes, villains and celebrities such as the humanist and writer Mark Twain and the naturalist painter John James Audubon are in effigy here, not to mention great mock-ups of historic events: Napoleon signing the Louisiana Purchase, Lafayette visiting the city in 1825 and the Battle of New Orleans, to name but a few.

The **New Orleans Pharmacy Museum** ★★ *(adults $2, seniors and students $1, free for children under 12; Tue to Sun 10am to 5pm; 514 Chartres St., ☎ 524-9077)*. Founded in 1950, this museum is a replica of the first chemist shop built here in 1823. The dispensary and carved rosewood counters are filled with retorts and huge blown-glass jars whose contents sometimes prove disturbing: virtually unidentifiable multicoloured fluids, grigris and roots of all kinds.

The **New Orleans Historic Voodoo Museum** ★★ *(adults $5, seniors and students $4, guided French Quarter tour $18, guided cemetery tour $10; every day 10am till dusk; 724 Dumaine St., ☎ 523-7685)*. In this unique museum, all the secrets of this mysterious religious practice, which originated in Africa, are disclosed. Here, visitors will see the most mysterious of objects, age-old evidence of good and evil spells... (see also p 116).

The **Jean Lafitte National Historical Park and Preserve - French Quarter Folklore Center** ★★★ (Le Parc national et réserve historique Jean-Lafitte - Centre de folklore du Quartier Français) *(every day 8am to 5pm; 916 North Peters St., ☎ 589-2636)*. Exhibitions and shows are presented here as are demonstrations of all kinds. This is also the point of departure for guided tours of the French Quarter - the oldest district in New Orleans, classified as a National Historical Landmark - and of the Mississippi Delta region.

Louis Armstrong Park ★★★ *(north of the French Quarter, between St. Peter and St. Philip Streets)*, dedicated to this great jazz musician and inaugurated by his widow in 1980, lies on the former Congo Square. The **Municipal Auditorium** and the **New Orleans Theater for the Performing Arts** are also here.

Piazza d'Italia ★, near the river, is easily identified by its fountain shaped like Italy.

Near the World Trade Center, **Plaza de España** ★ *(adjacent to the French Quarter, southwest side, close to the Mississippi)*, for its part, symbolizes the timeless link that exists between Spain and New Orleans.

Historic Street Names in the French Quarter

Just as the French Quarter's precious architectural heritage is scrupulously preserved by the State, as are its other neighbourhoods and districts, so are street names maintained with equal resolve by the city of New Orleans. On each of the street signs, the original French name appears above the more recent appellation. Some streets and squares have commemorative name plates bearing Spanish appellations; these names, such as Calle Real for Royal Street and Plaza de Armas for Place d'Armes (now Jackson Square), were added during the Spanish occupation of Louisiana. The following list offers such examples; historical and modern appellations of a few streets, squares, places and districts.

Current names	Original French names
Exchange Passage	place des Échanges
Esplanade Avenue	avenue de l'Esplanade
Elysian Fields	avenue des Champs-Élysées
St. Louis Cemetery No. One	cimetière Saint-Louis no. 1
Central Business District	Faubourg Sainte-Marie or Ville Gravier
Pirate Alley	passage des Pirates
Père Antoine Alley	passage du Père Antoine
Jackson Square	Place d'Armes
Bourbon Street	rue de Bourbon
Love Street	rue d'Amour
Burgundy Street	rue de Bourgogne
Chartres Street	rue de Chartres
Iberville Street	rue de la Douane

Governor Nicholls Street	rue de l'Hôpital
Decatur Street	rue de la Levée
Piety Street	rue de la Piété
Victory Street	rue de la Victoire
Good Children Street	rue des Bons-Enfants
Greatmen Street	rue des Grands-Hommes
Felicity Street	rue Félicité
Barracks Street	rue du Quartier
Rampart Street	rue du Rempart
Royal Street	rue Royale
St. Andrew Street	rue Saint-André
St. Philip Street	rue Saint-Phillipe
St. Peter Street	rue Saint-Pierre
St. Ann Street	rue Sainte-Anne
St. Mary Street	rue Saint-Marie
French Quarter	Vieux-Carré Français

Walking Tour of the French Quarter ★★★

Visiting the French Quarter or Vieux Carré on foot is much more enjoyable than doing so by car. By strolling along its main boulevards, through its streets and alleys, visitors will discover the charms of New Orleans' historic district, also known as "The Crescent City" on account of its location around a bend in the Mississippi. Put aside at least three hours for this stroll, and more if you wish to take your time and window shop, or have something to eat or drink in one of the many cafés in the area. The numbers will enable you to locate places worth visiting on the French Quarter map.

The Kolly Townhouse - The First Ursulines Convent - Charity Hospital (1) *(301 Chartres St., at Bienville)*. Jean-Daniel Kolly, the Elector of Bavaria's financial adviser and one of the investors in the *Compagnie des Indes Occidentales*, had this *hôtel particulier* built in 1718, soon after the founding of New Orleans. Kolly resided here for about ten years. It was then home to the Ursulines, until 1749 when they took possession of their new convent on Chartres Street. The building's final occupant was the Charity Hospital, New Orleans' first hospital.

Go back up Bienville Street to Royal Street; take a right and stop at no. 334.

The **Banque de la Louisiane (2)** *(334 Royal St.)*. This magnificent building was built in 1826, in what was then the financial district, to house the Banque de la Louisiane. It has since been used as the seat of the government of the State of Louisiana, by the American Legion and, more recently, as the French Quarter police station.

Cross Royal Street to no. 343.

The **Old Bank of the United States (3)** *(343 Royal St.)*. It is in this edifice, built in 1800, that the first Bank of the United States opened. The building is adorned with magnificent windows and lacy wrought-iron balconies, attesting to the talent of artisans in that era.

Continue along Royal Street to Conti Street.

The **Louisiana State Bank (4)** *(403 Royal St.)*. The bank's monogram, LSB, is still visible in the balconies' wrought ironwork. The building was erected in 1821 according to the plans of the Frenchman Benjamin Larobe, one of the architects of Washington's Capitol.

Cross Royal Street to no. 400.

The **New Orleans Court Building (5)** *(400 Royal St.)*. This white marble edifice dates from the beginning of the century. It once housed the State Supreme Court and is now occupied in part by the Wildlife Museum as well as by the U.S.'s fifth judicial district court of appeal. The building was entirely renovated in 1997.

Cross Royal Street again to no. 417.

Casa Faurie also know as **Morphy House (6)** *(417 Royal St.)*. This *hôtel particulier* was erected in 1801 for the maternal grandfather of the Impressionist painter Edgar Degas. Purchased four years later by the Banque de la Louisiane, it was resold in 1819 to David Gordon, who was to make it the centre of New Orleans high-society. General Andrew Jackson was the guest of honour at lavish parties thrown here during his second passage through the city, in 1828. By 1841, Gordon was ruined and the building, sold at auction, was to become the property of Judge Alonzo Morphy. Today, it houses the famous Brennan's restaurant. See "Restaurants", p 195.

Turn left on St.Louis Street and head to no. 820.

The **Hermann-Grima House** ★ **(7)** *(adults $5, seniors and students $4, 8 to 18 years of age $3, free for children under 8; Mon to Sat 10am to 4pm; 820 St. Louis St.)*. The house was built in 1831 by architect William Brand for the wealthy merchant Samuel Hermann; it is a rare example of American architecture in the French Quarter. Thirteen years later, it fell into the hands of the lawyer and notary Felix Grima, who added the outbuildings. The house and stunning horse stables are well preserved. Another original detail is its Creole-style open kitchen. Today, cooking classes and Creole culinary demonstrations are held here on Thursdays, from October to May. The building now billets a women's religious association.

Go back to Royal Street and turn left.

The **Seignouret House** (Maison Seignouret) **(8)** *(520 Royal St.)*. It was François Seignouret, a wealthy wine merchant originating from Bordeaux, who had this splendid residence built in 1816. A skilled cabinet maker, Seignouret also built a few pieces of furniture on which he discreetly added an S, his last initial. One such example can be discerned in the frieze of the wrought-iron balcony upstairs. A radio and television station now occupies the space.

Cross the street.

The **Merieult House** (Maison Mérieult) **(9)** *($2; Mon to Fri 9am to 5pm; 533 Royal St.)*. Here stands the oldest house on Royal Street, built in 1792 for the merchant Jean-François Mérieult. The Merieult House was one of the few to survive the fire that ravaged the city two years after its construction.

Apparently, during a stay in Europe, Jean-François Mérieult's bride, Catherine McNamara, received an offer for a large sum of money from Napoleon in exchange for her beautiful naturally-red hair. The Emperor wished to offer it as a gift to the Turkish Sultan, whose beloved wanted desperately to be admired as a redhead. But the lovely Catherine did not let herself to be swayed, and returned to Louisiana with a full head of hair.

In the rear courtyard of the Merieult House is another beautiful building, the **Williams Residence**, built in 1888.

The Merieult House, now the property of the Kemper and Leila Williams Foundation, contains a magnificent collection of prints, old maps and other documents relating to the history of New Orleans.

Cross Royal Street once again.

Casa de Comercio (10) *(536 Royal St.).* This building, built soon after the December 1794 fire, which destroyed the city's core, is a significant example of Spanish architecture in New Orleans.

Head to the intersection of Toulouse Street.

The Court of Two Lions (11) *(537 Royal St. and 710 Toulouse St.).* The building derives its name from the two stone lions supporting the high portal from which Toulouse Street can be seen.

Continue along Royal Street.

The **First Skyscraper** (Le Monnier House, La Maison Le Monnier) ★ **(12)** *(640 Royal St.).* The first house built in 1811 by Dr. Le Monnier had three floors, making it more or less "Louisiana's first skyscraper". The doctor's consulting room, on the top floor, is considered one of New Orleans' architectural gems.

Turn left on St. Peter Street.

Le Monnier House (13) *(714 St. Peter St.).* Constructed in 1829 for Dr. Yvos Le Monnier, it was then purchased in 1860 by Antoine Alciatore, who converted it into a boarding house. Gastronome and *cordon bleu* chef, Alciatore offered such an exquisite *table d'hôte* that New Orleans' upper crust flocked to his place in droves, so much so he decided to open a restaurant. Success was immediate and Antoine's quickly achieved international renown.

Antoine's is still in existence, only a stone's throw from here, and Antoine Alciatore's descendants now run it. See "Restaurants", p 194.

Continue on to 718 St. Peter Street.

The **Flechier House** (Maison de Flechier, Garnier House) ★ **(14)** *(718 St. Peter St.)*. This house was built soon after the 1794 fire, for the planter Étienne-Marie de Flechier. A bar now occupies the premises. French and Spanish interior courtyards abound in the French Quarter; the one in the Flechier House is truly magnificent and well worth a visit.

Head back toward and cross Royal Street.

The **Louisiana State Arsenal** ★★ **(15)** *(adults $4, seniors and students $3, free for children under 12; Tue to Sun 9am to 5pm; 615 St. Peter St.)*. This structure was the prison *(calabozo)* at the time of the Spanish occupation. In the early 1800s, the State of Louisiana set it up as an arsenal and military academy, attended by the sons of the best Creole and American families. The building, which has aged fairly well, now houses the Louisiana State Museum (see p 100).

Take a few steps back up to Royal Street and turn right on Cabildo Alley, which leads to Pirate Alley.

Pirate Alley (16) was originally called Ruelle d'Orléans, Sud. It is here that General Jackson supposedly arranged to meet the buccaneer brothers Pierre and Jean Lafitte to discuss the city's plan of defence against British troops. The present alley dates from 1831. The great novelist William Faulkner lived there as a youth.

Head toward Royal Street and stop at Orleans Street.

The **Cathedral Garden (17)** *(at Royal St. and Orleans St.)* lies behind a wrought-iron gate. Inside visitors will see the monument erected in honour of the sailors who died after volunteering to fight a yellow fever epidemic.

Head for no. 717 on Orleans Street.

The **Quadroon Ballroom** (Salle de Bal D'Orléans) **(18)** *(717 Orleans St.)*. A small village founded in 1718 under the French regime, New Orleans has since become one of the U.S.'s principal cities. The opening of the Théâtre Français in 1817 marks an important date in its history. Its director, Davis, intended to add a lavish opera house, a restaurant and a casino, which could compete with the best European establishments. However, the Civil War, which ruined the New Orleanian aristocracy, put an end to these lavish designs. In 1881, the nuns of the Holy Family Order made this their mother house and opened a school there as well. And in 1964, another sign of the times, the "ballroom", as it has always been called, was sold to a hotel complex. Despite the transformations it has sustained, the historic ballroom still stands, though it is now shorn of its original decor.

Return to Royal Street, turn left; at the edge of Cathedral Garden is Père Antoine Alley.

Père Antoine Alley (19) *(between the Cathedral and the Presbytère)*. This alley was laid out in 1831. No one here ever refers to it as Orleans Alley (its official name), but rather, as Père Antoine Alley: in memory of the beloved Spanish monk. The same holds true for the Cathedral Garden, better known to its users as "Père Antoine's garden".

Continue on to Chartres Street and Jackson Square. When facing the Cathedral, the Presbytère (the grey building) is on the right.

The **Presbytère ★★ (20)** *(adults $4, seniors and students $3, free for children under 12; Tue to Sun 9am to 5pm)*. The Spanish Capuchins' monastery erected on this site did not escape the fire that ravaged the city in 1788. In 1791, Don Andrès Almonester y Roxas had El Casa Curial ("the Presbytère") built on its foundations, as a residence for the priests of the neighbouring St. Louis Cathedral. Construction work was not finished until 1810, that is seven years after the colony became American.

Despite its name, "the Presbytère" has never been used as such, and when local authorities acquired it in 1853, it was to house the courthouse. It is now part of the Louisiana State Museum complex (see p 100). Though the Presbytère's artisans were mainly Spanish and American, a French influence clearly predominates.

St. Louis Cathedral ★ (21), the oldest cathedral in the United States, was built between 1849 and 1851, according to plans by J.N.B. de Pouilly; Pope Paul VI granted it the status of minor basilica in 1964, and Pope John Paul II celebrated mass there during his visit to the United States in 1987. The St. Louis Cathedral is the third church to be erected on this site. The first was swept away by a hurricane in 1722, and the second destroyed by a fire.

St. Louis Cathedral

To the left is the Cabildo.

The **Cabildo** (Spanish Governing Council) ★★ **(22)** *(adults $4, seniors and students $3, free for children under 12; Tue to Sun 9am to 5pm)*. Under the Spanish regime, the Cabildo's buildings served as the home of the Spanish colonial government, until they were destroyed by the fire that ravaged the city in 1788. Don Andrès Almonester y Roxas had them rebuilt before the end of the century, and a magnificent, quintessentially Spanish wrought-iron balustrade, created by Marcelino Hernández, still graces the historic Cabildo.

This building has seen many governments file through its doors. The French, who had preceded the Spanish, returned; the United States government gave it up to the Confederates for a time, before also returning. The deed by which France sold Louisiana to the United States of America (the Louisiana Purchase) was signed here, in the Sala Capitular. The "Iberville Stone" symbolizing the colony in 1699 as well as a death mask of the Emperor Napoleon can also be admired here.

The park and the square are known as Jackson Square.

Jackson Square (Place d'Armes) ★★ **(23)**. It was called "Place d'Armes" under the French; it was "Plaza de Armas" to the Spanish and, toward the middle of the nineteenth century, it was officially transformed, with the usual attendant ceremonies, into **Jackson Square**. The equestrian statue of General Jackson, which has dominated the square since 1856, was the work of sculptor Clark Mills. It commemorates Jackson's victory over the British during the famous Battle of New Orleans in 1815, which took place in Chalmette, about 10 kilometres from here.

From here, you can see the two imposing buildings on either side of Jackson Square.

The **Pontalba Buildings** ★ (24) *(bordering Jackson Square on each side)*. The wealthy merchant Don Andrés Almonester y Roxas was one of the most important figures of the time when Louisiana was a Spanish colony. In 1849, his daughter, the baroness Micaela Almonester de Pontalba, had the edifice built. With its ground floor giving out on Jackson Square (then known as Place d'Armes), it was designed to house luxury boutiques with the aim of attracting the local wealthy clientele. Forsaking their old-fashioned stalls in the French Quarter, shopkeepers responded to the proposition with enthusiasm, and visitors from all across Louisiana and even from other states soon flocked there.

You'll spot the 1850 House, on St. Ann Street, in the centre of the Pontalba Buildings.

The **1850 House** ★ (25) *(adults $4, seniors and students $3, free for children under 12; Tue to Sun 10am to 5pm; 525 St. Ann St.).* The central part of one of the Pontalba Buildings has been entirely restored on its three floors. Its refined decor and period furniture allow visitors to get a fair idea of how the New Orleanian upper crust lived in the mid-18th century.

Upon exiting the 1850 House, turn left on St. Ann Street. At Decatur Street, head straight to the narrow building adjoining the French Market.

The **French Market** (Le Marché Français) ★★★ **(26)**, see p 99.

Continue your stroll to Esplanade Avenue and stop at no. 400.

The **Old United States Mint** ★★ (27) (Le Vieil Hôtel de la Monnaie des États-Unis) *(adults $4, seniors and students $3, free for children under 12; Tue to Sun 9am to 5pm; in the 400 block of Esplanade Ave.).* Fuerte San Carlos stood here in the 18th century. In 1839, the U.S. government had the US Mint built. The building is now part of the Louisiana State Museum complex. The great moments of jazz and Mardi Gras are illustrated in a permanent exhibition (see p 100).

Head back via Decatur Street and turn right at Ursulines Street. Chartres Street is one block away.

The **Old Ursuline Convent** (L'Ancien Couvent des Ursulines) ★★ **(28)** (see also no. (1) 301 Chartres St.) *(adults $4; seniors and students $2; free for children under 8; Tue to Fri guided tour at 10am, 11am, 1pm, 2pm and 3pm, Sat and Sun at 11:15am, 1pm and 2pm; 1114 Chartres St.).* This is one of the oldest buildings in the Mississippi Valley. The Ursulines, who arrived in New Orleans in 1727, had it built in 1749. The convent became the city's first Catholic school, the

The Statuary of New Orleans

Like all great cities in the world, New Orleans has wished to pay homage to its heroes and heroines by erecting monuments in their honour.

The one raised in memory of **Jean-Baptiste Le Moyne, Sieur de Bienville**, stands in the heart of the French Quarter, in the little triangular park bordered by North Peters, Conti and Decatur Streets. The memorial recalls the fact that the man who founded New Orleans in 1718 was "Born in Montreal (Quebec) on February 23rd, 1680 - Died in Paris (France) on March 7th, 1767".

The equestrian statue of the democrat **Andrew Jackson**, hero of the Battle of New Orleans in Chalmette and president of the United States of America from 1829 to 1837, stands in Jackson Square. The monument is adjacent to a group of sculptures representing the four seasons, a somewhat unexpected subject matter in a city that knows but one: perpetual summer. Near Lafayette Square are the statues of **Benjamin Franklin** and the former head of Congress **Henry Clay**. Another statue, depicting **Molly Marine**, cast in concrete in 1943 (the only material that could be spared in this time of war) and now covered in bronze, stands on the corner of Canal Street and Elk Place. This monument is an homage to the female pioneers of the American Army. At City Park's entrance, visitors can see the equestrian statue of **General Pierre-Gustave Toutant Beauregard**. Lee Circle *(1000 St. Charles Ave.)* is dominated by a high column surmounted by the bronze statue of the "unfortunate" Confederate leader **General Robert E. Lee**. This monument, weighing some three tons, is the work of sculptor Alexander Doyle.

The sizeable African-American population forms the majority in New Orleans and has not forgotten the righteous fight lead by the Reverend Martin Luther King Jr. for the civil rights and integration of blacks. A monument to **Martin Luther King Jr.** therefore graces the intersection of the main thoroughfare bearing his name and Claiborne Avenue. It was also an absolute must to honour he who proved one of the most prestigious ambassadors of New Orleans and the true originator of classic jazz, **Louis "Satchmo" Armstrong**. This luminary, for his part, has his statue in the park bearing his name (formerly Congo Square), which is situated on Rampart Street, between St. Ann and St. Peter Streets.

In New Orleans, as in all other cities of multiple origins, monuments and public squares also testify to ties woven throughout history. Near the International Trade Mart, for instance, is the gilded bronze statue of **Joan of Arc**, given by the French government. Other tokens of international friendships include the statue of **Sir Winston Churchill**, set up in British Place and, on the central median of Basin Street, those of Latin American heros **Simón Bolívar** (Don of Venezuela), **Benito Juárez** (Don of Mexico) and **General Francisco Morazón** (Don of Honduras).

first orphanage and the first institution to welcome Native Americans and African Americans. The Ursulines occupied the building until 1827. The Louisiana State Legislature succeeded them from 1831 to 1834, and in 1846, the convent was reattached to St. Mary's Italian church.

The **Beauregard-Keyes House** (Maison Le Carpentier - Maison Beauregard) ★★ **(29)** *(adults $4, seniors and students $3, $1,50 for children under 12; Mon to Sat 10am to 5pm; 1113 Chartres St., ☎ 523-6722)*. After having purchased the land from the Ursulines, Joseph Le Carpentier built this house in 1827 for his daughter and her husband, the notary Alonzo Morphy.

General of the Confederate Army, Pierre-Gustave Toutant Beauregard, affectionately nicknamed "the great Creole", as much for his military prowess as for his capricious disposition, spent the rough winter of 1866 that followed the South's defeat and the end of the Civil War in a small room in this house. The novelist Frances Parkinson-Keyes, author of several works inspired by life in Louisiana and the tribulations experienced in this very place by the celebrated General, lived here in the late 1800s.

Continue along Chartres Street.

Soniat House (Maison Soniat du Fossat) ★ **(30)** *(1133 Chartres St.)*. This *hôtel particulier* was erected in 1829 for the Louisiana planter Joseph Soniat du Fossat, a full-fledged member of the New Orleanian aristocracy. Around 1860, a face-lift to the building had the original wrought-iron gates replaced by the wonderful filigree work seen today. The Soniat House now houses a charming little hotel of the same name (see "Accommodations", p 168).

Head toward Governor Nicholls Street and, from there, turn left.

The **Clay House (31)** *(618-620 Governor Nicholls St.)*. John Clay had this residence built in 1828 to house his family. John was the brother of Henry Clay, the fierce supporter of American protectionism who presided over Congress from 1810 to 1820. The building at the end of the garden was added in 1871 and served as a school as of 1890.

Head to the corner of Governor Nicholls and Royal Streets, where you will find a "haunted" house promising customary chills and thrills for fans of this genre.

The **La Laurie House**, also known as **"The Haunted House" (32)** *(1140 Royal St.)*. Edmond du Fossat innocently had this house built in 1830, then sold it to Barthélemy de Macarty (also called Maccarty or McCarty on old documents), who bequeathed it to his daughter Delphine. After marrying de La Laurie, Delphine threw very popular parties here and all of New Orleans praised her as an excellent hostess. But, in 1833, one of the servants brought a complaint against her mistress, claiming she had been severely lashed. That a slave's complaint was heeded is extraordinary in itself, and Delphine was, at the very least, fined. Had the magistrates suspected something? The following year, a fire broke out on the premises. All the neighbours rushed over to help the inhabitants of the house. They yelled, they hammered at doors and windows, but to no avail. Could the La Lauries have already succumbed? Or were they simply away? This was not the time to speculate, however, and the rescuers broke down the double-locked door. A ghastly scene met their eyes. In the smoke-filled room, seven miserable servants were found chained and horribly mutilated.

In the next day's paper, Madame La Laurie was openly suspected of having set fire to the house herself. A roaring mob gathered around the house of the torturer couple, determined to hang them high and raze this accursed place to the ground. At that very moment, a carriage carrying the La Lauries suddenly appeared from the courtyard. They fled the city to avoid public condemnation and were never seen again.

It is said that Delphine La Laurie died in Europe a few years later, and that her body was brought back to New Orleans to be buried here in secret.

Though the house was later entirely renovated, it is still said to be haunted. To this day, more than one New Orleanian affirms having heard the moaning and yelling of the torture victims along with the clanging of chains and the snapping of whips. Better to abstain from prowling about this house at the stroke of midnight, or at any time of night for that matter!

Fellow visitor... Take a deep breath, be careful crossing Royal Street and return to Governor Nicholls Street.

Thierry House (Maison Thierry) **(33)** *(721 Governor Nicholls St.)*. This house dates from 1814 and once belonged to Jean-Baptiste Thierry, the editor of the newspaper the *Courrier de la Louisiane*. Greek Revival in style, it is the first and one of the most interesting constructions of this style in Louisiana.

Return to Royal Street.

Gallier House ★★ **(34)** *(adults $5, seniors and students $4, children $3; Mon to Sat 10am to 4pm; 1132 Royal St., ☎ 523-6722)*. The son of a highly renowned architect who, moreover, left behind interesting memoirs, James Gallier Jr. was also to mark New Orleanian architecture during the whole period preceding the Civil War. We are indebted to this father and son for several buildings, including St. Patrick's Cathedral *(724 Camp St.)*, Gallier Hall *(545 St. Charles Ave.)*, the Pontalba Buildings and the St. Charles Hotel. The house has been restored, decorated and furnished in the style of the 1860s. Its balconies are made of wrought iron with a pattern of lovely roses.

New Orleans' Mysterious Side

Cities of the Dead ★★★

Parts of New Orleans are situated about 1.5 metres below sea level. This characteristic used to cause distressing problems for citizens who wished to bury their loved ones, for as Archimedes' old principle dictates, the mass of subterranean water pushed the deceased back up to the surface, which prevented any possibility of a decent burial. "Cities of the Dead" were thus created, where one now finds tombs of all styles built above ground.

There are 42 cemeteries in New Orleans and its surrounding area. Among the most noteworthy is **St. Louis Cemetery No. 1** *(400 Basin St., just outside the French Quarter)*. It is the oldest and most visited one, for it holds the tombs of notable people as well as almost mythic characters from the early days of New Orleans. **St. Louis Cemetery No. 2** *(visits organized by the Parks Service, ☎ 589-2636)* is divided into two parts. A third cemetery was isolated by the community and devoted to the burial of Catholic African Americans, who were largely responsible for the wrought-iron gates and ornamentations that decorate the premises. Finally, the **Metairie Cemetery** is a unique place in the world as much for the variety of its monuments as for their ostentatiousness.

Voodoo

Voodoo was introduced to New Orleans by African and Haitian slaves at the beginning of the 19th century, and soon became a trend, not unlike New Age today. Originating from Dahomey (now the Republic of Benin), this belief was an amalgamation of African and Catholic rites, and its original god was a snake known as Zombi.

By 1700, the Dahomey had sold about 20,000 slaves to the Europeans, several of whom ended up in Martinique, Guadeloupe and Haiti (then called Sainte-Domingue). In 1717, close to 3,000 Africans were brought to Louisiana, after having transited by the French West Indies (the

Caribbean islands). Following the bloody uprisings in Haiti, the French planters, accompanied by their slaves, retreated to Southern Louisiana. Several among them settled in New Orleans, and this is how voodoo came to the city in the early 1800s.

Voodoo was, above all, a matriarchal institution. Only women were allowed to preside over the ceremonies to which all slaves were invited. Participation in these ceremonies became so widespread that, in 1817, the local Council, fearing uprisings, limited these gathering to Sundays, and to a place under close surveillance, Congo Square.

For adherents of voodoo, June 23rd, St. John's Eve, was the biggest day of the year. Great bonfires on which live animals (hens, frogs, cats, snakes) were sacrificed were prepared and the crowd chanted incantations while the "queen" performed a ritual dance.

The two most well-known figures in New Orleans' voodoo history are Docteur Jean and Marie Laveau. The former, a giant with ebony skin marked with hideous tattoos, claimed to be a Senegalese prince and held considerable power over Creoles, who he supplied with amulets and other cultic objects.

Marie Laveau, for her part, was a tall and seductive woman with a copper-coloured complexion and a mean countenance. At first, a fervent Catholic, she married someone by the name of Jacques Paris in 1819... who mysteriously disappeared soon after. Marie Laveau then went by the name of "the widow Paris", before becoming the mistress of a certain Louis-Christophe Duminy de Glapion, with whom she had 15 children.

No link was ever officially established between the disappearance of Marie Laveau's first husband and her subsequent adherence to voodoo, in 1830. She reigned for 30 years on the shores of Lake Pontchartrain, enjoying enormous power and never hesitating, it is said, to eliminate potential queens by means of powerful *gris-gris* (African charms). She retired in 1869, and it was her daughter, born in 1827, who succeeded her, attaining a notoriety that exceeded that of her mother's. Marie Laveau-De Glapion is buried in St. Louis Cemetery No. 1, near the Basin Street entrance. Her tomb is always decorated with candles, flowers and offerings.

Today, voodoo's influence is practically nonexistent. However, there are still boutiques selling drops, powders and amulets with such evocative names as "Follow Me" and "Courting Powder", as well as the famous root called "Johnny the Conqueror" or "High John", which is often mentioned in the blues.

The **New Orleans Historic Voodoo Museum** ★★ *(adults $5, seniors and students $4, French Quarter tour $18, cemetery tour $10; every day 10am till dusk; 724 Dumaine St., ☎ 523-7685)*. This museum – the only one of its kind in the world – displays the most mysterious of objects, age-old evidence of good and evil spells...

Take Ursulines Street and turn left on Bourbon Street to the intersection of St. Philip Street.

Lafitte's Blacksmith Shop (35) *(941 Bourbon St.)*. The first notarized deed relating to this house dates back to 1772. The Lafitte brothers had opened this shop as a cover for their much more profitable activities as privateers in the neighbouring waters of the Gulf of Mexico, or more precisely, in swampy Barataria Bay. They attempted to redeem themselves by participating in the famous Battle of New Orleans, doing so with a courage that actually was to their credit.

Continue along Royal Street.

The **Cornstalk Fence** ★ **(36)** *(915 Royal St.)* stands before the hotel of the same name. The first house built on this site dates at least as far back as 1731, for it appears on a city map drawn up by Gonochon that year. It was replaced by a residence to be occupied from 1816 to 1826 by François Xavier Martin, first Chief Justice of the State Supreme Court. This magistrate was to be the author of the very first history book on Louisiana. The group of Victorian buildings seen today were built in 1850. The wrought-iron portal at the entrance gate, with motifs of cornstalks and ears of corn entangled with morning glories, is magnificent.

The **Miltenberger Houses [900-906-910 Royal Street) (37)**. The three houses built in 1838 for Mrs. Miltenberger were meant for her three sons. In 1910, it was her great-granddaughter Alice Heine who occupied them all. This interesting heiress first wed the Duke of Richelieu, before becoming a princess, through her second marriage to Prince Louis of Monaco.

Take Dumaine Street and head to no. 632.

Madame John's Legacy - Jean Pascal House (38) *(632 Dumaine St.)* Is a lovely raised house, with a recessed balcony. The first construction dates back to 1726. After the great fire on Good Friday of 1788, which razed almost the whole of New Orleans to the ground, Madame John entrusted the rebuilding to Robert Jones, a renowned artisan. The Spanish officer Manuel de Lanzos was its first tenant. This house (much like the Old Ursuline Convent) is rightly considered one of the most beautiful examples of Creole architecture in the entire Mississippi Valley; this style, developed in the French West Indies, was to influence many Louisiana architects. The building is now the property of the State of Louisiana, which had it transformed into a museum. Unfortunately, access to the museum is strictly reserved for student groups and community groups. These privileged few can admire a magnificent collection of period furniture (see "The Louisiana State Museum", p 100).

Here ends our stroll through the French Quarter (Vieux Carré), but by all means continue exploring the streets and alleyways on your own...

★ **CENTRAL BUSINESS DISTRICT AND WAREHOUSE DISTRICT ★**

West of the French Quarter is the Central Business District, a downtown area that is often associated with Canal Street. Just south of the Central Business District, the Warehouse District, whose industrial buildings were until recently in disuse, has become home to artists and galleries.

Piazza d'Italia (1) (p 102), **Plaza de España (2)** (p 102), **Gallier Hall (3)** (p 137), **Lafayette Square (4)** (p 137) and **Julia Row (5)** (p 137).

The **Contemporary Arts Center ★★ (6)** *(adults $5; Mon to Sat 10am to 5pm, Sun 11am to 5pm; 900 Camp St., ☎ 523-1216).* The Center exhibits contemporary art in all its forms: alternative theatre, music, visual arts, and more.

The **Virlane Foundation Collection ★★ (7)** *(free admission; 1055 St. Charles Ave., at Lee Circle).* This private organization has made it its objective to spur public interest in the arts and, more particularly, in contemporary sculpture. The collection consists of works from universally-known artists from all over the world; these works are exhibited in the square around the K&B Building and in the building itself. Explanatory booklets and detailed maps are distributed free of charge. In addition to a sculpture by British artist Henry Moore *(Reclining Mother and Child)*, visitors can take pleasure in observing the movement of the helicoidal piece *Flight* by the American Lin Emery (to whom we owe a similar work in front of the New Orleans Museum of Art), *The Virlane Tower* by Kenneth Snelson, a structure whose metal bars are supported and joined together by a steel cable that seems to defy gravity, or again, *Bus Stop Lady*, a life-size woman waiting for the bus, whom we cannot help but greet. In short, over 70 creations can be viewed here.

The **Confederate Museum ★★★ (8)** *(adults $4, children under 12 $2; Mon to Sat 10am to 4pm; 929 Camp St., ☎ 523-4522).* Built in 1891, this is the oldest museum in Louisiana. Thousands of priceless mementos can be seen here: weapons, uniforms, flags dating back to the Civil War and even the personal effects of Northern heroes.

Louisiana Children's Museum ★★ (9) *($5; Tue to Sat 9:30am to 5pm, Sun noon to 5pm; 420 Julia St., ☎ 523-1357).* Educational museum for children. Good news, the museum features hands-on, participatory exhibits!

Louisiana Superdome ★★ (10) *($6; seniors $5, 5-10 years old $4; guided tours 10am, noon, 2pm and 4pm; Sugar Bowl Drive, 1500 Poydras St., ☎ 587-3808 or 587-3810).* Built in 1975, it can accommodate up to 80,000 people; it is the largest

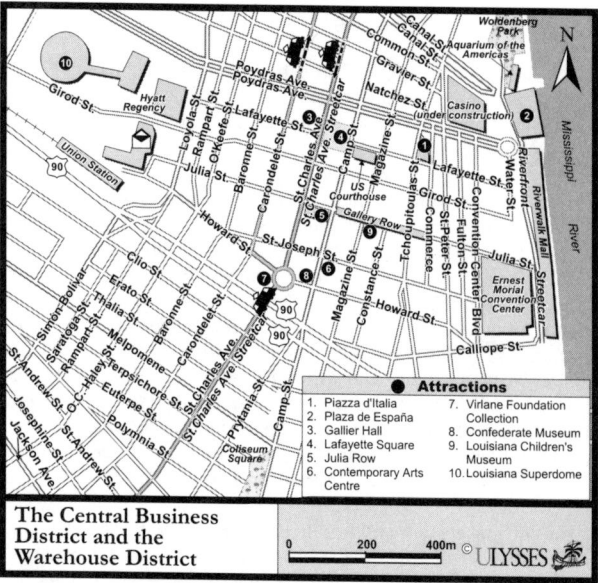

The Central Business District and the Warehouse District

	Attractions	
1. Piazza d'Italia		7. Virlane Foundation Collection
2. Plaza de España		8. Confederate Museum
3. Gallier Hall		9. Louisiana Children's Museum
4. Lafayette Square		10. Louisiana Superdome
5. Julia Row		
6. Contemporary Arts Centre		

0   200   400m © ULYSSES

building of its kind in the world. This is where big sports events, mega-concerts and more take place.

⭐ MID-CITY ★★★

North of the French Quarter and the Central Business District is the Mid-City area, stretching, from east to west, between City Park and Metairie Cemetery, which leads to the suburb of the same name.

The **Sun Oak ★ (1)** *($5; by appointment; 2020 Burgundy St., ☎ 945-0322)* in the historic Faubourg Marigny. Creole cottage with neoclassical ornamentation. Beautiful collection of French, Creole and Cajun furniture. Decorative arts. Large park; accommodations.

Esplanade Avenue - Bayou St. John - Lakefront ★★★. If the Garden District of St. Charles Avenue is the architectural

Edgar Degas in New Orleans

In 1872, Edgar Degas came to New Orleans, whence his mother, née Musson, originated and where his brothers, Achille and René, had established themselves as cotton merchants.

The place enchanted him. *"Nothing pleases me more than the black women of all shades, holding little white babies that are oh so white in their arms, in white houses with fluted wooden columns and in orange-tree gardens and the ladies in muslin in front of their little houses and the steamboats with two smokestacks, as high as the twin chimneys of factories, and the fruit merchants with full and overflowing shops, and the contrast between the bustling and so affluent offices and the huge brute strength of the black population, ... etc. And the lovely pure blooded ladies and the lovely quadroons and the black women who are so well built!"*, he wrote to a Parisian friend.

His letters are generally written on paper with the *de Gas Brothers* letterhead, his brothers having kept the original name to make a good impression in the elegant circles in which they moved. The painter, for his part, renounced it. *"Those among the nobility are not in the habit of working. Since I wish to work, I will therefore retain a common name"*, he explained.

His correspondence aptly reflects high society in New Orleans, which was rather shaken up after the Civil War. In a letter to his friend Rouart dated December 5th, he deplores the absence of the traditional opera season in speaking of his blind cousin, Estelle, who had married his brother René and who was pregnant. *"Poor Estella who is a musician was counting on it. We would have rented her a ground-floor box where she would never have missed a performance until the time she was to give birth."* He goes on to emphasize how, *"In its place, we have a comedy, drama, vaudeville troupe, where there are many fairly talented performers from Montmartre"*.

Degas was to take several family "scenes" from his stay home with him. These scenes inspired major paintings such as *Portrait dans un Bureau (Portrait in an Office)*, more commonly known as *Le Bureau de Coton à La Nouvelle-Orléans (The Cotton Office in New Orleans)*, his first work to make it into a French museum, the one in Pau, to which it still belongs. In this painting, we see the brothers loafing, René nonchalantly reading the paper as his associate Achille leans against a wall staring off into space, while the merchants bustle about. The two brothers ultimately went bankrupt and it was, ironically, Edgar the successful artist who assumed their debts in order to save the honour of their family name.

expression of New Orleanians of American origin, the district that stretches from the French Quarter to the Bayou St. John is in large part made up of the magnificent residences of old French families. At 2306 Esplanade Avenue, you'll see what was, for a brief period during the winter of 1872, the residence of the Impressionist painter Edgar Degas, who had come to visit his financier brothers in New Orleans.

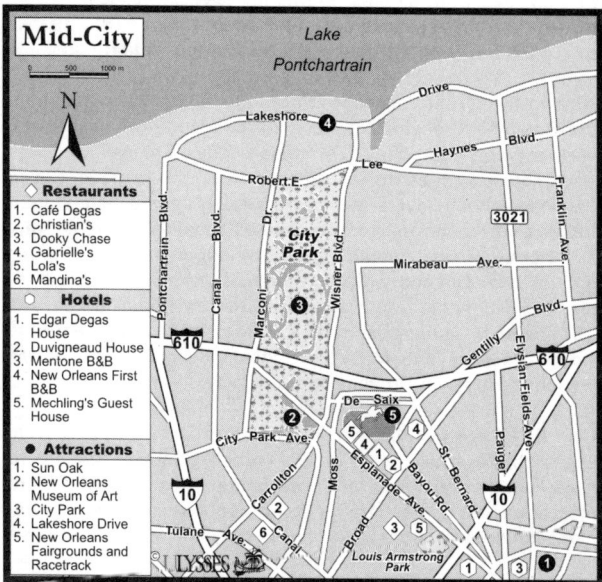

Mid-City

Lake Pontchartrain

◇ **Restaurants**
1. Café Degas
2. Christian's
3. Dooky Chase
4. Gabrielle's
5. Lola's
6. Mandina's

○ **Hotels**
1. Edgar Degas House
2. Duvigneaud House
3. Mentone B&B
4. New Orleans First B&B
5. Mechling's Guest House

● **Attractions**
1. Sun Oak
2. New Orleans Museum of Art
3. City Park
4. Lakeshore Drive
5. New Orleans Fairgrounds and Racetrack

ULYSSES

New Orleans Museum of Art ★★★ (2) *(adults $6, seniors $5, 3-17 years old $3; Tue to Sun 10am to 5pm; 1 Lelong Drive, City Park, ☎ 488-2631)*. The New Orleans Museum of Art (NOMA) owes its existence to a generous patron. Son of a rich family of planters from Jamaica, Isaac Delgado, born in 1837, left his native island at the age of 14. He came to join his uncle Samuel in New Orleans, who was making a fortune in the sugar industry. Having become rich in his turn, Isaac Delgado showed great generosity toward his adopted city. At the beginning of the century, he made large donations to charitable organizations, and in 1905, remitted $180,000 to the Charity Hospital. A true art lover, Delgado handed over a sum of $150,000 in 1910 so that a fine arts museum worthy of the city he was so fond of could be built in City Park.

The imposing building, whose lobby is flooded with daylight, is the work of Samuel A. Marx. This architect has lent this structure, whose architrave is supported by four huge columns, a Greek style adapted to the subtropical climes. As for the collection, it is distributed according to theme throughout the many rooms on both levels. The museum boasts an abundance of treasures from all eras and all continents, including a rich collection of Renaissance art, obtained in October 1952 thanks to a donation from the Samuel H. Kress Foundation.

Among the pieces museum visitors can enjoy are magnificent pre-Columbian sculptures; a rich collection of glass and earthenware; European, American and Chinese pottery; remarkable 17th-century paintings from the famous Cuzco Peruvian school; several works from the great Flemish, Dutch, Italian and French masters as well as those of contemporary American painting; works painted by Edgar Degas during his stay in New Orleans with his maternal uncle Michel Musson; bronzes from this same artist as well as Rodin; 18th- and 19th-century furniture; and more. The museum also boasts the Courtyard Café and Museum Shop. An amusing aside: the museum uses *Van Go* vans to transport its works.

City Park ★★★ (3). This 750-hectare park stretches from Esplanade Avenue, north of the French Quarter, right up to Lake Pontchartrain. This land was once part of the Louis Allard plantation. It is a choice spot for all outdoor sports. Eight-hundred-year-old oak trees surround lagoons where visitors can abandon themselves to the pleasures of fishing. Other activities here include horseback riding and golf.

Lakeshore Drive ★★ (4) skirts New Orleans' sizeable lake: Lake Pontchartrain, which is 60 kilometres long and 40 kilometres wide. The **Lake Pontchartrain Causeway ★** spans this large body of water.

The **New Orleans Fairgrounds and Racetrack (5)** *(admission fee; Wed to Sun from Nov to Apr; 1751 Gentilly Blvd., ☎ 944-5515)* has been open since 1872, which makes it one of the oldest in the U.S. Its entrance, the work of architect James Gallier, was built in 1859 for an agricultural fair. It is here that the Louisiana Derby takes place. Bets are placed on thoroughbred horses racing at this track and others; all of these races are simultaneously broadcast. No children under 6 years of age allowed.

Longue Vue House and Gardens ★★ *(adults $7, seniors $6, students and children $3; Mon to Sat 10am to 4pm, last guided tour 3:45pm; Sun 1pm to 4:15pm, last guided tour 4:15pm; 7 Bamboo Road, ☎ 488-5488 or 486-7015)*. Built in 1942 by the wealthy New Orleanian Edgar Stern, this Greek-Revival estate has a Spanish patio surrounded by English gardens, thus showing the historical course of the city in its own way. It contains a beautiful collection of French and English 18th- and 19th-century furniture.

★ THE GARDEN DISTRICT

The walking tour of the Garden District begins on Washington Avenue.

Take the time to stroll about the Garden District, with its sumptuous residences and beautiful gardens. Some of the distinctive features of certain residences and historic sites in this part of New Orleans have already been discussed elsewhere. A complete tour should take about two hours.

Lafayette Cemetery No. 1 ★★ (1) *(1400 Washington Ave.)* has been in existence since 1833 and was then the property of the City of Lafayette before it's annexation to New Orleans. Because the interment of "Americans" in the cemeteries near the French Quarter was less desirable, many people of German (not the descendants of colonists who came to settle in Louisiana in the eighteenth century but, rather, immigrants who came to New Orleans much later) and Irish origin were buried here. In 1852, yellow fever was raging and over 2,000 victims were then interred in this single cemetery. Most of the tombs are fairly modest monuments. In 1970, the City of New Orleans undertook to restore some tombs and, with the aim of making the place more attractive, had a lovely row of magnolias planted along a path at the cemetery's entrance.

From the cemetery's exit, on Washington Avenue, head for Prytania Street, then to Fourth Street. Turn right...

Colonel Short's Villa (2) *(1448 Fourth St.)* was built in 1859. Four years later, at the height of the Civil War, the house was seized by Federals while its rebel owner was away. The structure is graced with lacy wrought-iron balconies and a railing whose distinctive motifs are reminiscent of cornstalks. It is said that the colonel's wife so greatly missed Kentucky that her husband procured this gate for her, evoking the corn fields from her distant land. This lovely portal, forged by the Wood and Perot Foundry in Philadelphia, brings the one at the 915 Royal Street house, in the French Quarter, to mind.

Return to Prytania Street and cross the street.

The **Villeré-Carr House (3)** *(2621 Prytania St.)* was built around 1870 in typical Greek Revival style for one of the members of the prominent New Orleanian Villeré family. Its porch and angular windows harmoniously blend with this lovely architectural whole, particularly sought-after at the time.

Continue your stroll along Prytania Street.

The **Briggs-Staub House (4)** *(2605 Prytania St.)* is one of the rare Gothic constructions in the city. It was erected in 1849, and its architecture shows the European influences of the time.

Take Third Street and head to no. 1331.

The **Musson-Bell House (5)** *(1331 Third St.)*, erected in 1850, was commissioned by the wealthy cotton merchant Michel Musson, the celebrated painter Edgar Degas' uncle. The house

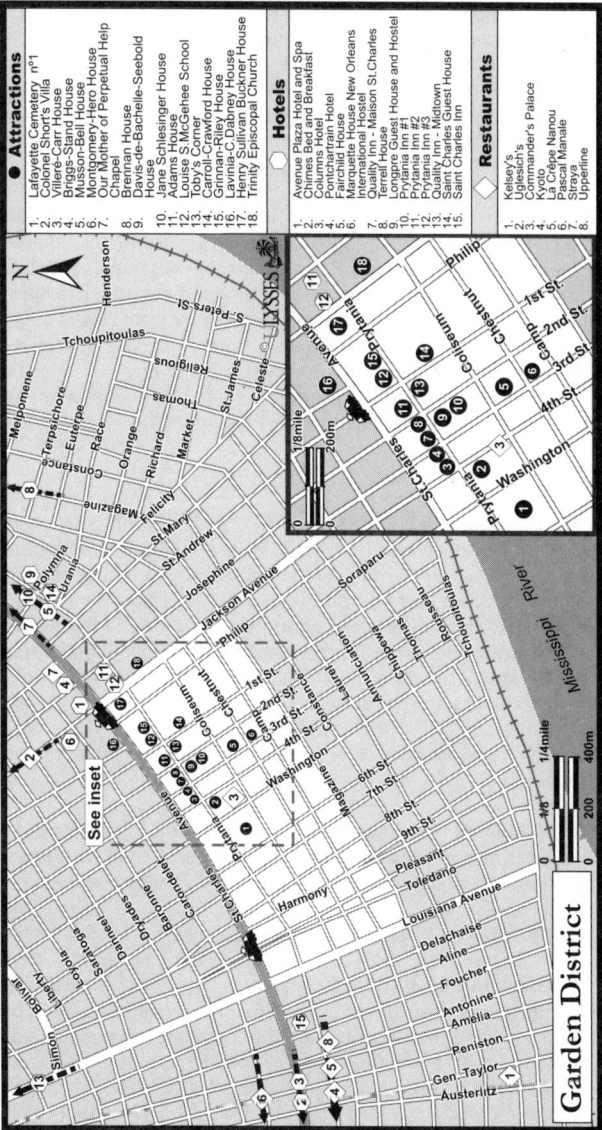

● **Attractions**

1. Lafayette Cemetery n°1
2. Colonel Short's Villa
3. Villere-Carr House
4. Briggs-Stand House
5. Musson-Bell House
6. Montgomery-Hero House
7. Our Mother of Perpetual Help Chapel
8. Berein House
9. Davis-de-Bachelle-Seebold House
10. Jane Schlesinger House
11. Adams House
12. Louise S.McGehee School
13. Toby's Corner
14. Carroll-Crawford House
15. Grinnan-Riley House
16. Lavinia-C.Dabney House
17. Henry Sullivan Buckner House
18. Trinity Episcopal Church

◯ **Hotels**

1. Avenue Plaza Hotel and Spa
2. Chimes Bed and Breakfast
3. Columns Hotel
4. Pontchartrain Hotel
5. Fairchild House
6. Marquette House New Orleans
   International Hostel
7. Quality Inn - Maison St.Charles
8. Terrell House
9. Longpre Guest House and Hostel
10. Prytania Inn #1
11. Prytania Inn #2
12. Prytania Inn #3
13. Quality Inn - Midtown
14. Saint Charles Guest House
15. Saint Charles Inn

◇ **Restaurants**

1. Kelsey's
2. Joleschi's
3. Commander's Palace
4. Kyoto
5. La Crêpe Nanou
6. Pascal Manale
7. Straya
8. Upperline

Garden District

is magnificently girdled by elaborate wrought-iron balconies. This place was witness to a particularly tragic conjugal story. In 1872, Edgar and his brother René arrived from France to visit their maternal family. René fell madly in love with his cousin Estelle, sadly blind since the age of 12. Because they were first cousins, René and Estelle obtained a papal dispensation to live out their happiness without religious constraint. Four children were born of their union. Every afternoon, a friend of Estelle's came by to read to her and took advantage of her visits to court René. Succumbing to her charms, René abandoned Estelle and his children. Beside himself with rage, Estelle's father disowned his son-in-law and adopted his grandchildren, giving them the name of Musson, and crossed the Degas name from his family for good. Estelle's name and likeness were, however, immortalized in a painting by Edgar entitled *Le Portrait d'Estelle (Estelle's Portrait)*, which can still be admired in the New Orleans Museum of Art (see p 124).

Continue to no. 1213.

The **Montgomery-Hero House (6)** *(1213 Third St.)*. This splendid residence was built around 1868, perhaps even before the Civil War, by Archibald Montgomery. From the time of Montgomery's death in 1885 until 1977, the house belonged to the Hero family. Its green shutters as well as the fine white columns rising from the front and side porches distinguish this lovely home, restored in all the elegance of its era by the Reynoirs, its last proprietors.

Retrace your steps back to Prytania Street and head to the Chapel.

Our Mother of Perpetual Help Chapel (7) *(2521 Prytania St.)*, first built as a private residence in 1856, was then converted into a chapel to cater to the needs of the Redemptorist priests.

Continue along Prytania Street.

The **Brennan House (8)** *(2507 Prytania St.)*, with its stunning Corinthian columns, dates from 1852. The wealthy owners of the time turned to a Viennese artist to decorate the magnificent ball room, their pride and joy, in gold leaf.

Go back across Prytania Street.

The **Davis-De Bachelle Seebold House - Women's Guild of the New Orleans Opera Association (9)** *(2504 Prytania St.)* was first home to Edward Davis, who had commissioned its construction in 1858. Dr. Hermann de Bachelle Seebold and his wife, music lovers and patrons of the arts, acquired it in 1944. Upon Mrs. Seebold's demise, the opera association inherited this residence flanked by an octagonal turret, one of the few to be opened to the public (reservations are required). Every piece of furniture dates from the time of the original owners.

Continue along Prytania Street. Turn right at Second Street.

Part of the **Jane Schlesinger House (10)** *(1427 Second St.)* was once attached to the residence of a large plantation. The annex was moved and joined to the building under construction in the 1850s. The four-metre-high French doors giving directly onto the balcony and almost reaching the ceiling are one of its distinctive features.

Retrace your steps to Prytania Street and turn right.

The **Adams House (11)** *(2423 Prytania St.)*. Having acquired a piece of land on François de Livaudais' plantation in 1860, the merchant John I. Adams had this residence built there, and lived in it as of 1896. The two (front and side) porches are lined with a series of white colonnades.

Cross Prytania Street once again.

The **Louise McGehee School (12)** *(2343 Prytania St.)*, also known as Bradish-Johnson House, is the work of architect James Freret. It displays lines highly influenced by the French *École des Beaux-arts*, where the master studied from 1860 to 1862. Freret built this residence in 1872 for the wealthy sugar-cane planter Bradish Johnson. In 1929, it was converted into a private school for girls.

Across the street is **Toby's Corner (13)** *(2340 Prytania St.)*, also called the Toby-Westfeldt House. It is said to be one of the oldest residences in the Garden District. Its style is inspired by Creole cottages in the Caribbean. During its construction in 1838, its owner, an affluent businessman originally from Philadelphia, took great care to have his house raised in order to protect it from floods, which are all too common in New Orleans.

Head toward First Street and turn right.

The **Carroll-Crawford House (14)** *(1315 First St.)*, erected in 1869 in the Italianate style by its first owner Samuel Jamison, later housed Joseph Carroll, a cotton magnate who came from his native Virginia to acquire more wealth in New Orleans. Magnificent balconies and a wrought-iron railing adorn this beautiful pastel residence.

Return to Prytania Street.

The **Grinnan-Riley House (15)** *(2221 Prytania St.)*. It is to architect Henry Howard, who designed a great number of buildings in New Orleans, that the Englishman Robert A. Grinnan entrusted the construction plans of his *hôtel particulier*. Also of interest is that the coat of arms on the front door is similar to that at the Nottoway plantation (situated in White Castle), also designed by Howard.

Go back up First Street to St. Charles Avenue.

The **Lavinia C. Dabney House (16)** *(2265 St. Charles Ave.)*, erected in 1856-57, is the work of the architectural firm Gallier, Turpin & Associates. As of 1893, the Dabrey residence was inhabited by Jonas O. Rosenthal's family, who occupied it until 1952. That same year, it became the see of the Episcopal Church until 1972.

Continue your stroll along St. Charles Avenue until you reach Jackson Avenue.

The **Henry Sullivan Buckner House (17)** *(1410 Jackson Ave.)* was built in 1856 by the famous architect Lewis E. Reynolds. With its grandiose balconies graced with colonnades girdled by elaborate ironwork, it is one of the most majestic residences in the Garden District. Soulé College, a private school, occupied this beautiful property until 1983.

Trinity Episcopal Church (18) *(1329 Jackson Ave.)*. Construction work on this imposing church in the Gothic style, commissioned to architect George Purves, began in 1852. In

1873, major alterations were made to the church's actual façade, steeple and portal, the joint work of architect Charles L. Hilger and the building contractor Middlemiss.

★ WALKING TOUR OF
THE UPTOWN DISTRICT

The length of your stroll depends on how much time you spend in Audubon Park and Zoological Gardens. Put aside approximately half a day, that is two or three hours, to visit the zoo. You will be able to freshen up and eat at the zoological gardens or, then again, enjoy a picnic in Audubon Park. Bring bottled water along in order to avoid the long lineups at drinking fountains, which inevitably form on school-field-trip and summer-heat-wave days.

The **Garden District** ★★★ *(between St. Charles and Magazines Streets and Jackson and Louisiana Avenues)*, which can be visited in part by streetcar for a pittance, is one of the historic neighbourhoods on the outskirts of New Orleans. Here, visitors can admire most architectural styles – be they of Victorian, French or Spanish influence – that have marked Louisiana.

The **Audubon Zoological Gardens** ★★★ *(adults $7.75, seniors and students $3.75; every day 9:30am to 5pm; 6500 Magazine St., ☎ 861-2537)*. This zoological garden is one of the top five in the United States and houses over 1,500 animal species on 24 hectares of greenery and centuries-old trees. The site also boasts a vast collection of reconstituted, full-scale prehistoric animals (see also p 135).

Audubon Park ★★★ *(every day, from sunrise to sunset; 6400 and 6900 St. Charles Ave.)*. This magnificent 300-hectare park bears the name of the celebrated naturalist and artist John James Audubon; the zoological park of the same name is here.

The **Milton H. Latter Memorial Library** *(Mon to Sat 10am to 5pm, Sun 12:30pm to 4:30pm; 5120 St. Charles Ave., ☎ 596-2625)*. Built in 1907, it was first the residence of the silent film actress Marguerite Clark. The Latter family then bought the house and donated it to the city in 1948, in memory of their son who died in World War II. The library is open to the public and is worth a visit.

Head to the intersection of St. Charles Avenue and Walnut Street.

Tulane University - Gibson Hall *(6823 St. Charles Ave.)* was erected in 1893-94. The plans were drawn up by architects Harrod and Andry, and came in first in a contest held throughout the State of Louisiana. The winners were also awarded the task of creating the other campus pavilions, namely Tillton Hall *(left of Gibson Hall)*, built in 1901, and Dinwiddie Hall *(right of Gibson Hall)* in 1936. The University was founded in 1834 and was then called the Medical College of Louisiana before becoming the University of Louisiana. In 1884, it was renamed once again, this time after Paul Tulane, one of its principal benefactors. That same year, the State of Louisiana chose not to maintain the university as a public institution, and Tulane University thus became private.

The **Amistad Research Center** *(Mon to Sat 8:30am to 5pm; Tillton Hall, Tulane University, ☎ 865-5535)* is a large archive on the history of ethnic minorities in the U.S., dealing with, among other things, race relations and the civil rights movement.

The **Middle American Research Institute & Art Gallery** ★★ *(free admission; Mon to Fri 8:30am to 4:30pm; Tulane University, 6823 St. Charles Ave., ☎ 865-5110)* has been around since 1924 and presents an exhibition on the pre-Columbian and Hispano-American eras. An interesting collection of Mayan and Guatemalan art is featured here, and visitors are free to consult the books and documents in the impressive library dedicated to Central America.

Continue along St. Charles Avenue.

With the exception of its Law Faculty, located on St. Charles Avenue at Broadway Street, the **Loyola University campus** *(6363 St. Charles)* borders Tulane University's and stretches out thus to Calhoun Street. In the middle of the campus stands the imposing Gothic-style Holy Name of Jesus Church. Since its foundation by the Jesuits in 1911, the University has distinguished itself with its law and communications programs. The latter faculty is housed in the Louis J. Roussel pavilion.

Cross St. Charles Avenue toward Audubon Park.

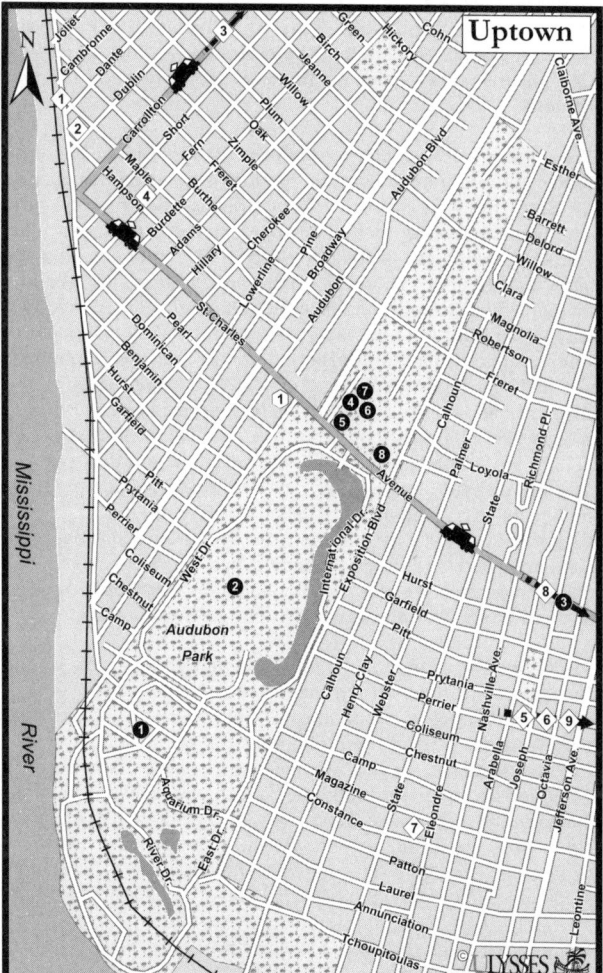

Uptown

○ Hotels	◇ Restaurants	● Attractions
1. Park View Guest House	1. Brigtsen's	1. Audubon Zoological Gardens
	2. Café Volage	2. Audubon Park
	3. Piccadilly Cafeteria	3. Milton H. Latter Memorial Library
	4. Figaro's Pizzeria	4. Middle American Research Institute
	5. Kyoto	& Art Gallery
	6. La Crêpe Nanou	5. Tulane University
	7. Martinique Bistro	6. Amistad Research Centre
	8. Pascal Manale	T. Middle American Research Institute
	9. Upperline	8. Loyola University

0   1/8   1/4mile

0   200   400m

ULYSSES

Audubon Park is across the street from both Tulane and Loyola Universities. It stretches from St. Charles Street to the Mississippi's north shore, encompassing the zoological gardens of the same name, which are bordered by Walnut and Calhoun Streets.

This land once belonged to Jean-Baptiste Le Moyne Sieur de Bienville, before becoming the property of the planter Étienne de Boré, the first mayor of New Orleans and the man who discovered how to granulate sugar in industrial quantities, changing the Louisiana industry forever. The city acquired the land in 1871. In 1884-85, plans to organize the World's Industrial and Cotton Centennial Exhibition got underway. This was to highlight the hundred-year anniversary of this industry. The megalomaniac pretensions of this event's organizers seemed to know no bounds and they had, most notably, the largest building in the world built for the occasion, a building whose exhibition hall had a surface area of 14 hectares. The ridiculous amounts of money disbursed made the event a financial disaster. Nothing remains of these buildings today. A few years later, Frederick Law Olmsted (the creator of Central Park in New York City and Mont-Royal Park in Montreal) was entrusted with the task of planning this magnificent park. Its name commemorates the famous John James Audubon, artist and ornithologist, and his contribution to New Orleans.

Audubon Park is one of the largest urban parks in the United States, not to mention one of the most famous. The park is dotted with lagoons and fountains, and several of its oaks date back from the time of the de Boré plantation. Besides the visit to the Audubon Zoological Gardens (see below), many outdoor activities can be practised here: golf, tennis, cycling, running, walking and horseback riding. One of the running tracks has signs at every fifteenth post or so, indicating the warm-up exercises to do during this activity. The park also offers picnic areas, a swimming pool, children's playgrounds, and more.

Visitors can reach the Audubon Zoological Gardens by walking across Audubon Park and following the golf course on the right, when facing the park on St. Charles Avenue. Count on a 45 minute to one-hour walk. Using the shuttle service that runs from St. Charles Avenue to the Zoological Gardens is another option.

John James Audubon (1785-1851)

Celebrated naturalist and artist John James Audubon has been honoured time and again in the place names of Louisiana. Born Jean-Jacques in 1785 in Santo Domingo, now Haiti and the Dominican Republic, he is of French origin. After studying in France, Audubon made his first trip to the United States in 1805. The following year, he returned and became a naturalized American by marrying Lucy Bakewell whom he had met in Pennsylvania during his first trip, and became a naturalized American. Audubon settled in Louisiana in 1821, first in New Orleans, then in St. Francisville, at the Oakley plantation where he worked for four months as a tutor to the three sisters of Mrs. Percy, a naval officer's widow. Here, John James Audubon did 82 of the 435 watercolours of his famous "The Birds of America" series. The remainder of the drawings were done while travelling through a vast territory stretching from Florida (he bought a house for himself in Key West and resided there as of 1832) all the way to Quebec. He produced a great number of drawings, sketches and paintings all through his life. His most famous work, *The Birds of America*, in four volumes and containing 435 plates, is most certainly the most expensive collection in the world since it was auctioned in London for several million pounds in 1984.

The **Audubon Zoological Gardens** was once considered one of the vilest of its kind in the U.S. The deplorable conditions in which its inmates lived aroused outraged protests from animal lovers. Fortunately, this situation has since radically changed, and the zoological gardens now enjoys an excellent reputation. The zoo pays special attention to natural habitats, thereby encouraging reproduction. Over 1,800 different species can be observed here, including white alligators in an exhibit named the "Louisiana Swamp". Other areas reproduce the environment of a Cajun bayou with its flora and fauna. In this exhibit, visitors learn, among other things, how the famous Spanish moss is gathered and used as stuffing for furniture; the zoo also boasts a mock-up of a fishing camp, equipped with shrimping nets and crayfish traps, as well as a dredger used to collect oysters from the Gulf of Mexico. Farther along, for those who are so inclined, is the wonderful world of reptiles.

The largest snake species in the world, from the giant cobra, which can reach up to six metres in length, to the green anaconda, sometimes measuring up to 12 metres, wow 'em at the Reptile Encounter. A brand new exhibition entitled *Butterflies in Flight* presents a video on the metamorphosis and the migrations of butterflies. Visitors then enter a hothouse (or aviary) in which thousands of exotic butterflies flutter freely. In proximity of the hothouse, under the shade of centuries-old trees, the statue of John James Audubon watches over his friends from the animal kingdom and their visitors.

★ THE ST. CHARLES AVENUE STREETCAR ★★★

Following the sale of Louisiana in 1803, many of the city's inhabitants did not appreciate the massive influx of "Americans". Those who lived in the French Quarter (Vieux Carré) jealously guarded the exclusivity of their neighbourhood – these same Creoles had however lived with the Spanish – even enlarging their territory toward Faubourg Marigny. So, the Americans settled in Faubourg Sainte-Marie, now the Central Business District. The newcomers prospered in the business district and then developed the residential areas of Uptown and the Garden District. These rich merchants had their opulent houses built, not at the edge of the street like those in the French Quarter, but further back, allowing for magnificent gardens at the front as well as at the back of their houses.

Definitely one of the best ways to see the Lower Garden District, the Garden District and Uptown is from the St. Charles Streetcar from Canal Street *(at Carondelet)*. For the modest price of $1, the route and the reduced speed allow you to discover this wonderful part of the city in less than two hours. For a more in-depth visit, we suggest walking. The streetcar has existed since 1835 (run by electricity since 1893) and has contributed greatly to the rapid development of this area of the city, particularly to the expansion of St. Charles Avenue.

A Few Points of Interest from the Streetcar

The streetcar terminal is located on Canal Street at St. Charles Avenue, at the west end of the French Quarter. Work is in progress to extend the line from Canal Street to City Park. The route starts in the business district. There are a few high-rise buildings along the road from Poydras Street. The perspective from this street is interesting with the Superdome in the background.

After the Poydras intersection, on the right you will notice a large neoclassical-style building with a white marble portico. This is **Gallier Hall** *(545 St. Charles Ave.)*, among the first constructions of this type in the United States, considered one of the most remarkable masterpieces by the architect James Gallier. The building, New Orleans' old city hall, now houses a theatre and a reception hall for the city's social and cultural events.

Gallier Hall

Across the street in the garden of **Lafayette Square**, are statues of Henry Clay, Head of Congress from 1810 to 1820, Benjamin Franklin, one of the fathers of confederation, inventor of the lightening rod and prestigious American ambassador to France, as well as the notable John McDonogh, who is responsible for a number of measures that advanced education in New Orleans.

Two blocks further on Julia Street, to the south of St. Charles, is **Julia Row** *(600 to 648 Julia St.)*. These thirteen identical brick houses were erected in 1833. The New Orleans

Preservation Resource Center is located at no. 604. (☎ 581-7032).

The **Lower Garden District** starts at Lee Circle. At the centre of the circle is a monument in honour of General Robert E. Lee, head of the Confederate armies during the American Civil War. On the left is the **Zion Lutheran Church** *(1924 St. Charles Ave.)*, built out of wood in 1871. On the right, the K&B Plaza houses the Virlane Foundation Collection (see p 120).

At the Josephine intersection, **Eiffel Tower Catering** is a recent, rather unusual, restaurant. All the original pieces of the Eiffel Tower restaurant were sent from Paris to New Orleans and assembled here in 1986.

The large and reputable **Pontchartrain Hotel** *(2031 St. Charles Ave.)*, built in 1927, is on the right.

Jackson Avenue is the boundary of the Garden District which extends to Louisiana Street.

A few blocks further, at Fourth Street, on the right, is **Christ Church Cathedral** *(2919 St. Charles Ave.)*. The tomb of Reverend Leonidas Pold, the first Episcopal bishop of Louisiana and a Confederate general, was placed in the crypt of this church which was built in 1886.

Beyond the Episcopal cathedral is **Elms House** *(3029 St. Charles Ave.)*, erected around 1869. This was the site of Germany's Consulate General from 1931 to 1941. John Elms acquired the property in 1951.

On the left, close to Louisiana Street, the **Bultman Funeral Home** *(3338 St. Charles Ave.)* is where Tennessee Williams' play *Suddenly Last Summer* takes place.

Past Louisiana Street, on the right, is the prestigious **Columns Hotel** *(3811 St. Charles Ave.)*. It was erected in 1883 as a private residence.

On the left, the red-brick **Rayne Memorial Methodist Church** *(3900 St. Charles Ave.)* dates from the end of the last century.

A few streets further, still on the left, you will notice the **Touro** synagogue *(1501 General Pershing St.)*, built in 1909.

The **Napoleon Avenue** intersection marks the starting point for a number of Mardi Gras parades that proceed along St. Charles to Canal Street.

Sacred Heart Academy *(4521 St. Charles Ave.)* is a private school, created in 1899 for young girls. The wings of the huge building are connected by wide covered walkways surrounding a flowering garden. Above the entrance gate, in wrought iron, is the French inscription "Sacré-Coeur".

After Upperline Street, on the left, is the **Milton H. Latter Memorial Library** *(5120 St. Charles Ave.)*, built in 1906. The tile roof of neo-Italian inspiration is of interest.

After that, **Benjamin House** *(5500 St. Charles Ave., between Octavia and Joseph Streets)* is built entirely out of limestone, an uncommon and expensive construction material in New Orleans.

On the right, you will see the **Rose Park** residences which are among the most admired in New Orleans, particularly the Victorian **"Wedding Cake House"**.

At the State Street intersection, on the left, is **Saint Charles Presbyterian Church** *(1545 State St.)*, erected in 1930. Its stained-glass windows were imported from Germany.

On the left, past State Street, **Castle House** draws much of its inspiration from the Wedding Cake House.

The red-brick buildings on the right constitute **Loyola University of the South**. In 1911, the college, founded in 1904 by the Jesuits, acquired the necessary accreditation to become a university. It is the largest Catholic university in the southern states. The campus church, **Holy Name Church**, dating from 1918, is the only Catholic church on St. Charles Avenue.

After that, extending over 39 hectares, is **Tulane University**, founded in 1883. Across from the two campuses, on the left, is the splendid **Audubon Park**. After the park you will come across **Greenville Hall**, constructed in 1882, which is now a part of the Loyola University campus.

A large part of New Orleans' wealth resides on **Audubon Street**. There is a guard posted limiting access. Tom Cruise and Nicole Kidman stayed in one of the houses here when they were in New Orleans to shoot a film.

Zemurray House, presently the Tulane University Rector's residence, was initially the property of Sam Zemurray, president of the United Fruit company.

On Broadway Street, on the left, is the **Law Faculty of Loyola University**. This building of Italian inspiration was the original home of the Congregation of Dominican Nuns.

The streetcar continues along **Carrollton Avenue**, a much more modest area. Many of the houses are camelback style. There are also a few so-called shotgun houses (see "Architectural Curiosities" p 30).

The streetcar ends a few blocks from here. It's better to get off here and take the streetcar heading in the opposite direction. If, however, you feel like taking a stroll, there are many cafés, restaurants and shops in the area.

To explore on foot on the way back, get off at Washington Avenue.

★ A DRIVING TOUR OF NEW ORLEANS ★★★

The tour begins in the Faubourg Marigny, where Esplanade Avenue starts.

440 Esplanade Avenue - The Old United States Mint ★★, close to the French Market, is one of five forts built by the French Regime in the 18th century to protect the city; this one was called Fort Saint Charles (San Carlos). The American government bought the property in 1815 and undertook the construction of the mint in 1834-35. The work of architect William Strickland was completed in 1839. By request of General Beauregard, significant restoration was done in the 1850s. The mint was operational from 1838 to 1862 and from

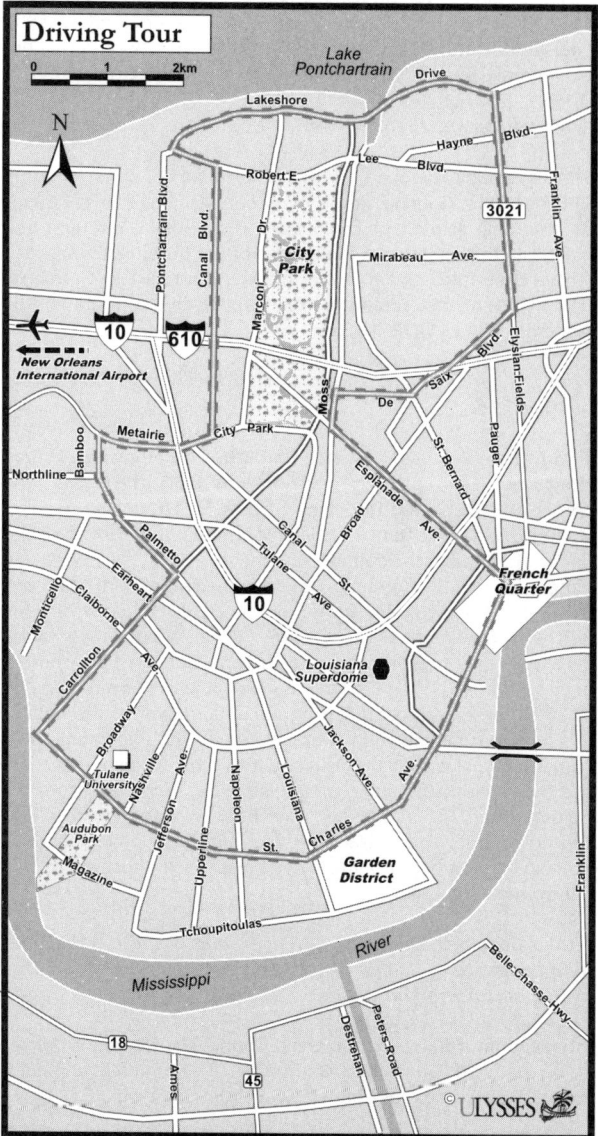

Driving Tour

0 1 2km

N

Lake Pontchartrain

Lakeshore Drive

Hayne Blvd.

Robert E. Lee Blvd.

Franklin Ave.

3021

Pontchartrain Blvd.

Canal Blvd.

Marconi Dr.

City Park

Mirabeau Ave.

10

610

New Orleans International Airport

Moss

De Saix Blvd.

Elysian Fields

Metairie

City Park

Pauger

Bamboo

St. Bernard

Northline

Esplanade Ave.

Palmetto

Canal St.

Broad

Tulane Ave.

French Quarter

Earheart

Montcello

Claiborne

10

Carrollton Ave.

Louisiana Superdome

Broadway

Nashville Ave.

Jackson Ave.

Tulane University

Napoleon Ave.

Louisiana Ave.

St. Charles Ave.

Audubon Park

Jefferson

Upperline St.

Garden District

Magazine

Tchoupitoulas

Mississippi River

Belle Chasse Hwy.

18

Ames

45

Destrehan

Peters Road

Franklin

©ULYSSES

1879 to 1910. Production reached its peak at a total value of $5,000,000 worth of coins. Today, under the guidance of the Louisiana State Museum, the old mint houses two permanent exhibitions, one on jazz and the other on Mardi Gras.

Drive up Esplanade to...

704 Esplanade Avenue - The Gauche House ★, constructed in 1856 by John Gauche, is the most ostentatious of the houses on this chic stretch of Esplanade. The unusual wrought-iron balconies that go around three sides of the building are adorned with a cheerful *Dancing Cupid*, made in Sarrebruck, Germany. It is said that this sculpture was inspired by an engraving by Albrecht Dürer (1471-1528).

Turn left on Dauphine Street toward the French Quarter, to number 716.

716 Dauphine Street - Doctor Gardette Residence - Le Prêtes House ★. This spacious mansion was built in 1835 at the corner of Orleans and Dauphine Streets for Dr. Joseph Coulon Gardette, a dentist from Philadelphia who came to New Orleans under the Spanish Regime. In June of 1861, following his victory at Fort Sumter, General Pierre-Gustave Toutant Beauregard forwarded some of the flags taken from his northern adversaries to this residence where they were ceremoniously presented to the Orleans Guards. For a period beginning in 1870 the Citizen's Bank occupied this site. Finally, in 1892, an extremely rich Turk became master of the house. It is said that he enjoyed inviting New Orleans' high society to sumptuous galas. Rumour also had it that his fortune as well as the five beautiful women of the family were stolen from his Sultan brother. Then one day, after being woken by screaming, the neighbours found the Turk and his five women dead. A Turkish servant had disappeared, as well as the fortune of this controversial character.

Follow Dauphine Street and turn right onto Bienville Street, the third street; go to Rampart North then turn right again and stop at Rampart North and Conti.

Intersection of Rampart North and Conti - The Mortuary Chapel - Our Lady of Guadalupe Church ★. This chapel, originally called Saint Antoine Chapel, was built near the St. Louis number 1 and 2 cemeteries in 1826-27 for funeral services of deceased relatives of devoted Catholics who had previously sought these services from St. Louis Cathedral on Jackson Square. The chapel became known as the mortuary chapel in the years 1832 and 1833 during the terrifying fever epidemic that decimated thousands of New Orleanians and when mortuary services in the heart of the city were banned. The ban lasted until 1860. After the Civil War, the chapel took on the name of the celebrated Mexican Virgin and thus became Our Lady of Guadalupe Church.

Amusing anecdote: the church houses a statue of a non-existent saint. The story has it that the crate containing the famous statue destined for the New Orleans chapel only had "Expedite" written on it. Those who received it didn't worry about the sender's mistake and inscribed, at the bottom of the statue, Saint Expedite!

Get back on Esplanade and continue until Bayou St. John. You will travel through the Marigny, Tremé and Mid-City districts.

At **2306 Esplanade Avenue ★** you can see what was, for a short period in the winter of 1872, the **residence of impressionist painter Edgar Degas**, who had come to visit his brother living in New Orleans.

Continue to Moss Street, which intersects Esplanade just before the Bayou St. John bridge, turn left and stay alongside the water.

1440 Moss Street - Ducayet House (Maison Ducayet) **★★** *(adults $3, seniors $2, under 12 yrs $1; Wed to Sun 10am to 3pm; ☎ 482-0312)*, a plantation house in the Caribbean colonial style, was constructed around 1800 by the aristocratic Ducayet family. The property was later acquired by the second mayor of New Orleans, James Pitot.

1342 Moss Street - The Blanc House ★, another plantation house, was modified in a neoclassical-inspired style. It was erected by Evariste Blanc and now serves as the rectory of the Our Lady of Rosary School.

Return to Esplanade Avenue, cross the bridge, and continue on Lelong Drive which runs behind the equestrian statue of General Paul-Gustave Toutant Beauregard.

The **New Orleans Museum of Art** ★★★. A majestic row of oaks and magnolias in City Park leads directly to the museum. The museum's collection boasts important pre-Columbian works of art, as well as impressionist and contemporary paintings (see also p 124).

City Park ★★. A part of this park was originally occupied by the property of the rich Creole plantation owner Louis Allard. Between the 18th century and the first half of the 19th century, a number of duels, which were quite common at the time, were fought here. These duels were fought under the shade of the century-old oaks that can still be seen on the left (south side) of the museum. The park's 750 hectares are used for outdoor activities such as sailing, tennis, cycling and horseback riding, or you can go fishing in one of the lovely lagoons or just have a picnic. There is also an 18-hole golf course, a magnificent rose garden and, for the kids, merry-go-rounds, a miniature train and various games.

Behind the museum, take Franklin D. Roosevelt and then turn left on the second street, Stadium Drive.

The **New Orleans Botanical Garden** ★★ *(adults $3, 5-12 yrs $1, guided tour by reservation; ☎ 483-9386)* is adorned with statues and fountains reminiscent of the Art Deco era. Next to the oaks and magnolia trees, the park is home to splendid azalea and camellia gardens as well as a pond with water-lilies.

Return to where you entered the park, turn left onto Wisner Boulevard. Take the first bridge crossing the Bayou St. John, where De Saix Boulevard leads to Gentilly Boulevard.

2601 Gentilly Boulevard - Dillard University. In 1835, New Orleans University, founded in 1869, combined with Straight University to create Dillard University. The campus, covering 300 hectares, is one of the most beautiful in the South.

Continue along Gentilly to Elysian Fields. Turn left and head toward Lake Pontchartrain. Approaching Lakeshore Drive, you *will notice the **University of New Orleans** campus on your left. At the roundabout go west (left) on Lakeshore Drive.*

Lakeshore Drive ★★ is a panoramic route hugging the Lake Pontchartrain shoreline. The lake is 60 kilometres long and 40 kilometres wide. You can cross over the lake via the longest bridge in the world: the **Pontchartrain Causeway** ★. The Mardi Gras Fountain, which is lit up at night, is visible from the bridge, on your left.

The **Southern Yacht Club** *(West End Lakefront)* is the second oldest sailing club in the United States (1849).

*Follow this route until Robert E. Lee Boulevard. (After the club, if you take Robert E. Lee Boulevard east, you will get to **Bucktown** ★★, an old fishing village now annexed by the city of Metairie.)*

Go left, east, until you reach Canal Boulevard, turn right onto it, and go south, for about four kilometres. At City Park Avenue, turn right. This becomes Metairie Road further on.

Along this route you will come across **Greenwood, St. Patrick** and **Metairie Cemeteries** ★★★.

Take the first street on the right after Metairie Cemetery.

Along the cemetery, **Fairway Drive** ★ is bordered by sumptuous oaks its whole length on both sides.

A bit further along Metairie Road, you will see a sign indicating the entrance to the Longue Vue House.

7 Bamboo Road - Longue Vue House and Gardens ★★ *(adults $7, seniors $6, children & students $3; Mon to Fri 10am to 4:30pm, Sun 1pm to 5pm; ☎ 488-5488 or 486-7015)*, one of the most prestigious private properties in the United States, belonged to Edgar B. Stern and his wife. The neoclassical-style mansion, with Palladian details, was constructed from 1939 to 1942. The French and English furnishings date from the 18th and 19th centuries. The English and Spanish-style gardens cover more than three hectares.

Follow Bamboo Road to Palmetto. Take Palmetto to Carrollton Avenue.

7325 Palmetto Street - Xavier University of Louisiana, serving 3,400 students, was founded in 1915 by The Blessed Katherine Drexel and the Sisters of the Blessed Sacrement: it is the only black Catholic university in the United States. Moved to this site in 1929, the old campus at 5116 Magazine Street now houses Xavier Loans. This African-American university is known for its teaching in medicine and pharmacology; 25% of black pharmacists in the U.S. are Xavier alumni. More than 40% of graduates pursue post-graduate studies here since Xavier offers no less than 36 programs.

Continue along South Carrollton Avenue.

2901 South Carrollton Avenue - Notre Dame Seminary, an institution for instructing priests, is also the Episcopal diocese of the Archbishop of New Orleans.

719 South Carrollton Avenue - The Old Carrollton Courthouse ★. The Lusher school, built in 1855, was previously the administrative centre of the city of Carrollton and Jefferson parish. Carrollton was annexed by New Orleans in 1874.

At the end of Carrollton, St. Charles Avenue starts; take St. Charles.

7214 St. Charles Avenue - St. Mary's Dominican College, a girls' college founded in the 1860s, closed in 1985. The Victorian part of this attractive wood building with a slate roof was erected in 1872.

Continue for three more blocks.

Audubon Park ★★★, a 160-hectare park, was named in honour of the great naturalist and painter John James Audubon, who did his most outstanding work while in Louisiana. The park has a golf course, a zoo and tennis courts. You can have a picnic, go horseback riding, go for a bike ride (horse and bike rental on site), or go for a morning jog or a simple walk along the paths. There's a mini-train that offers a tour of the site. Vehicles are allowed and from the park you can also reach the zoo on Magazine Street (parallel to St. Charles, further south). Panoramic views of the river can be enjoyed from the back of the park.

After the park, on the other side of the street, there are two universities next to each other.

6823 and 6363 St. Charles Avenue - Tulane University and Loyola University. Tulane was created by the Jesuits in 1834 as the Medical College of Louisiana; now it offers various other disciplines such as engineering, social sciences, art, architecture, business administration (the first to offer this in the U.S.) as well as law with specialties in civil law and the Napoleonic Code, still in effect in Louisiana. In 1840, the Jesuits opened the College of the Immaculate Conception downtown and, in 1904, on its present site, Loyola College. In 1911, Loyola College and Immaculate Conception College joined to form Loyola University, which remains the largest Catholic university in the South.

5100 St. Charles Avenue - The Milton H. Latter Memorial Library ★★ is now a branch of the New Orleans public library. This beautiful residence was built in 1907 for Marguerite Clark, a silent-film star.

Continue along St. Charles Avenue.

4521 St. Charles Avenue - Sacred Heart Academy. The French name is set in the wrought ironwork above the entrance gate. The academy, inaugurated in 1899 by the Sisters of the Sacred Heart, is the oldest private school in the city.

Go to Fourth Street, which is parallel to Washington:

In the Garden District be careful about one-way streets. On Prytania Street and St. Charles Avenue the traffic is heavy. Also, watch for the streetcars!

Turn right at Washington, pass two streets, turn left onto Coliseum and go back up Fourth Street.

1448 Fourth Street - Colonel Short's Villa ★ has a superb wrought-iron fence with corn and morning-glory designs. This imposing residence with its attractive jagged-shaped wrought-iron balconies, was built in 1859 for Kentuckian Colonel Robert H. Short. Four years later, during the Civil War, the house was seized by the Northern forces in the absence of its Rebel owner. Apparently, the corn adorning the fence was a gift from the colonel to his wife who missed Kentucky and its cornfields. Made in Philadelphia at the Wood and Perot Foundry, the ironwork is similar to that of the Cornstalk Hotel at 915 Royal Street in the French Quarter (see no. 35 of the French Quarter walking tour).

Continue to a lower parallel street, Third Street; at the corner of Prytania turn right then right again.

1415 Third Street - Robinson House, one of the biggest houses in the Garden District, was constructed for Walter Robinson, who lived here until 1865. It was the first house in New Orleans to be equipped with modern plumbing.

Continue further along.

1331 Third Street - Musson House - Bell House ★★. The finely worked wrought-iron balconies of this house are absolutely remarkable. Michel Musson, the maternal uncle of famous impressionist painter Edgar Degas had the house built in 1850.

Go to the same street number but two streets down, on First Street: Turn left at the next corner, go left up the next street, right at the next and then right again.

1331 First Street - Morris-Israel House was erected in 1869 and completely renovated not long ago. This house is one of the most beautiful examples of Garden District architecture.

Continue one block further.

1239 First Street - Brevard House. This house, made for Albert Hamilton Brevard in 1857, offers another attractive example of exceptional artistic ironwork with its rose-patterned gates.

Continue for another block.

1134 First Street - Payne-Strachan House. Judge Jacob U. Payne had this house built by court slaves in 1849-50. On this site on December 6, 1889, Jefferson Davis, ex-officer of the

U.S. army, senator, minister and president of the Confederate States died.

At the next intersection, Magazine Street, turn left. Go to the next block, Philip Street. Turn left again and go four blocks to Prytania.

2343 Prytania Street - Bradish Johnson House is better known as the Louise S. McGehee School for Girls, established here in 1929. Originally, the mansion belonged to Bradish Johnson, a rich sugar-cane-plantation owner, who had it built in 1870.

Go back to St. Charles Avenue and continue for 1.5 kilometres (one mile).

1000 St. Charles Avenue - Lee Circle. This roundabout is named after the most famous Civil War hero: General Robert E. Lee. The bronze statue of Lee, weighing more than 3,000 kilograms, was made by New York sculptor Alexander Doyle. It was symbolically placed facing north.

Take the right off the roundabout and turn left at the next street.

929 Camp Street - The Confederate Museum ★★, open since 1891, is still one of the best of its kind and houses thousands of mementos of the Civil War. It is run by the Louisiana Historical Association.

Continue two blocks further on Camp.

724 Camp Street - St. Patrick's Church ★★ was for a long time the tallest building in Uptown and is also the second oldest parish church in New Orleans (1838).

Continue on the same street.

500 Camp Street - Lafayette Square. After the purchase of Louisiana in 1803, Americans started arriving in great numbers. The Creole population, opposed to the sale of Louisiana, refused to co-exist with the newcomers so Americans had to create their own neighbourhood outside the French Quarter. The downtown of this new area was located at Lafayette

Square, named in honour of the Marquis de Lafayette, one of the great heros of the American Revolution.

Go to the other side of the park.

524 St. Charles Avenue - Gallier Hall. Completed in 1850, this masterpiece by architect James Gallier, Sr. is considered to be the most beautiful Greek-Revival building in the country. Before bearing the name of its architect, the building was the city hall.

Continue along Camp Street and turn right at Poydras; go down Poydras to Convention Center Boulevard and turn right.

900 Convention Center Boulevard - The Ernest N. Morial Convention Center was the site of a world exposition in 1984. It was transformed the following year into a convention centre. Recent expansion has allowed the centre to increase its exhibition surface area by 67,500 square metres.

Return to, and go left up Poydras.

1500 Poydras Street - The Louisiana Superdome ★★ *(adults $6, seniors and students $5, 5-10 yrs $4; guided tour 10am, noon, 2pm and 4pm)*, completed in 1975, can accommodate 80,000 spectators.

Stay on Poydras and take South Claiborne to the right; continue until Canal Street, turn right and drive until you reach the grey granite building on the left.

423 Canal Street - The Customs House. On the site of Fort Saint Louis (San Luis), construction of this building started in 1848 but wasn't completed until 65 years later, in 1913. When it was being built the Customs House was right on the Mississippi; now the river is four streets over. The wall recesses that you can see from Decatur Street will never be occupied by the statues that were originally meant to go there.

Go to the end of Canal Street.

2 Canal Street - The World Trade Center, a tall building, is home to most of the city's maritime industries as well as New Orleans consulates. The top of the observation tower offers a far-reaching view of the city and the port of New Orleans; a panoramic (glass-enclosed) elevator on the outside takes you there. There's a rotating bar-lounge at the top of the tower. **Plaza de España** is at the foot of the tower, beside the river.

Woldenberg Riverfront Park and The Aquarium of the Americas ★★★. The aquarium houses 7,500 marine species, and uses no less than 4,500,000 litres of fresh and salt water to maintain them. It is also an important conservation and environmental-research centre. Programs that are both educational and enjoyable are offered to the public (see p 99).

The **Canal Street Ferry ★★★** *(free for pedestrians, cars $1; 6am to midnight, departures every 30 min)*. Operated by the Louisiana department of transport, the ferry takes pedestrians and drivers to Algiers Point on the west bank of the Mississippi. This service has been offered without interruption since 1827.

A Fine View ★★★

The observation tower of the **World Trade Center** *(adults $2, 6-12 yrs $1; every day 9am to 5pm; 2 Canal St., ☎ 535-2851)* provides a new perspective on the city and the port; the tower has a rotating bar. Another place to admire the city is the terrace of the **Omni Royal Orleans** Hotel *(535 Gravier St., at Camp St.)*.

The **Canal Street Ferry** *(free for pedestrians, cars $1; 6am to midnight, departures every 30 min)* offers a unique view and the chance to float along the Mississippi.

Go to the other side of the Mississippi.

Algiers Point ★★★. In 1719, Bienville, the founder of New Orleans, was assigned this region, which is adjacent to the Vieux Carré on the other side of the Mississippi. Algiers Point was originally a landing site for slaves arriving from Africa. A suburb built here between 1840 and 1900, and due to its particular character, in 1978 it was classified an American historical heritage site. Additional tourist information is available on site. A walking tour of the area is particularly interesting.

This is the end of the driving tour of New Orleans. It's now up to you to make your own discoveries in the streets, avenues and boulevards of the fabulous "Crescent City".

★ EXCURSIONS OUTSIDE NEW ORLEANS

Would you like to admire the wonderful Crescent City from way up in the air? Or spend a few hours on the tranquil waters of a bayou or swamp? It is in fact possible to fly over New Orleans and take a day-long excursion less than an hour away from the bustling city. Most hotels in New Orleans have a lot of information about these "air-land" excursions.

The **Air Reldan ★★** company *(starting at $25 per person; 8227 Lloyd Steaman Drive, suite 120, ☎ 241-9400)* offers flights over New Orleans during the day or night. Since there are no beaches in Louisiana, the company offers charter flights to the sunny beaches of nearby Florida.

Air Tours on the Bayou ★★ *(every day; 1 Coquille Drive, Belle Chasse, south of New Orleans, ☎ 394-5633)* flies over the city and surrounding swamps. The plane lands in the middle of the swamps or on a bayou.

A number of small and large businesses offer trips on the bayous where you can admire the alligator kingdom and cypress trees. The only problem is figuring out which one to choose. Contact **Captain Terry's Swamp Tour ★** *(☎ 471-4933)* or **Lil Cajun Swamp Tours ★** *(☎ 689-3213 or 1-800-725-3213 from North America)*.

Fun-Day Bayou Tours ★★ *(adults $18, under 12 yrs $12, with transportation to hotel $38 and $18, meal included; leaves the dock at 9:30am and 1:30pm except Sun morning; ☎471-4900)*, offers a guided tour of the Segnette Bayou and the swamps located half an hour away from New Orleans. A traditional meal of rice and beans with sausages is offered on Miss Mary's islet. You are also urged to visit her garden.

Private excursions and photo-safaris (camera included) are available through **Captain Nick's Wildlife Safaris ★★** *(☎ 361-3004 or 1-800-375-3474)*. Their boats are small,

New Orleans and Surroundings

holding from one to four passengers. They will pick you up at your hotel.

Louisiana is a large state and distances are long. The most interesting **plantations** are unfortunately not all located near New Orleans and sometimes you have to drive for a few hours to get there. Nonetheless, three very interesting plantations that are easily accessible by car are listed below. For an exhaustive list of southern Louisiana's large plantations, including the famous Oak Alley, refer to our guide on Louisiana.

Kenner

The **Mardi Gras Museum- Historical Museum of Louisiana ★** *(adults $3, seniors and children $2; Tue to Sat 9am to 5pm; 1922 Third St., Kenner, ☎ 468-7258)* is located in the former home of the ex-sheriff Frank Clancy. Memorabilia from the "green gold" era, the golden era of bounty hunters, is on display.

The **Louisiana Toy Train Museum ★** *(adults $3, seniors and children $2; Tue to Sat 9am to 5pm; 519 Williams Blvd., Kenner, ☎ 468-7223)*. They have toy trains from the beginning of the 19th century, hands-on exhibitions and videos.

The **Jefferson Downs Racetrack** *(opens at 6:30pm, Apr to mid-Nov; 1300 Sunset Blvd., Kenner, ☎ 466-8521)*. Pure-bred racing. Children under 12 are not permitted and 12- to 17-year-olds must be accompanied by an adult. The old train tracks alongside the Hippodrome were converted into a trail bordered by parkland.

Louisiana Wildlife and Fisheries Museum ★★ *(adults $3, seniors and children $2; Tue to Sat 9am to 5pm, Sun 1pm to 5pm; 303 Williams Blvd., Kenner, ☎ 468-7232)*. This is a reserve with 700 species of birds, reptiles and other indigenous animals; the 56,775-litre aquarium houses various species of fish from the region.

Metairie

Lafreniere Park *(free admission, every day 6am to sundown; 3000 Downs Blvd., Metairie, ☎ 838-4389)*. This 62-hectare park is equally suited to both nature lovers and athletes. Botanists will love the landscaped gardens and the rich local flora. For fans of outdoor activities you can rent boats, bikes and pedal-boats, go jogging on the paths, have a picnic or go fishing.

Still along Lake Pontchartrain, continuing on Robert E. Lee Boulevard, you will arrive in the heart of the city of **Bucktown ★★**, in a fishing region. Now integrated into the municipality of Metairie, Bucktown, was for a long time a seaside resort for New Orleanians. It is comprised of an interesting contrast of a country setting and tall skyscrapers. There are seafood restaurants here.

Vacherie

Laura Plantation ★★★ *(adults $7, children and teens $4, discounts for groups; every day 9am to 5pm, guided tours; closed on Thanksgiving, Christmas and New Year's Day; on River Road, Vacherie, LA 70090, ☎ 504-265-7690)*. To get there from New Orleans (35 minutes from Moisant International Airport), take the I-10 in the direction of Baton Rouge, then the I-310 to the LA 3127 (after the bridge), then the LA 20 to the Mississippi where you will turn right onto Route 18. The "Belle Créole" of the Mississippi has unfortunately been unoccupied since 1984; faithful to tradition, its successive occupants made French the language spoken at the plantation until their departure in 1984. Its acquisition by a group of history enthusiasts including the architect and historian Norman Marmillion, himself a descendant of a rich aristocratic Louisiana family, ensured the preservation of this beautiful heritage site, built in 1805, which would have otherwise deteriorated with time and inevitable acts of vandalism. After it was partially restored, the plantation's masters' quarters were opened to the public in 1994. Although other buildings are still under renovation, the site remains, without question, the most inviting and agreeable of all existing plantations. Less famous

---

A Fish and Seafood Restaurant/Market

.If you want to get something to eat before or after your visit to Laura Plantation or Oak Alley, you must drop by the pleasant Breaux family business. Family members fish on the bayous and lakes of the region. At **B & C Seafood - Market of Cajun Delights** *(2155 LA 18, on River Road, Vacherie, LA 70090, ☎ 265-8356)*, you choose your fish or seafood at the counter, which, once it is weighed, is prepared for you either Cajun or Creole style. On the menu: alligator, frogs legs, catfish, shrimp, crawfish, oysters, tortoise, clams, crab, etc.. The establishment also offers a multitude of other choices such as Cajun pudding, smoked chitterling sausages, tasso (dried meat), bread pudding, spices, wild blackberry jelly, red pepper jelly, fig spread and dressings.

---

than other "star plantations", Laura Plantation is nonetheless the most interesting as much for its authentic Creole character, including being painted in bright colours, as for its well-documented and researched history. In fact, the passionate accounts given by the guides during plantation visits are supported by old documents (5000 pages of documents) consulted in the National Archives of Paris and from *Memories of Laura*. This journal of Laura Locoul, relating the daily events of those who lived on the sugar-cane plantation for close to two centuries, was found in St. Louis, Missouri, in 1993. The historical account in no way conceals the slavery practised at the time on the property and the site of the plantation's old slave cabins is poignant evidence of the difficult years that African-Americans endured. It was here in the 1870s that the West African folktales of Compair Lapin, better known as Br'er Rabbit, were first recorded in America. Laura Plantation also offers, to those who ask, five different thematic visits of the property: 1 - Creole architecture; 2 - The feminine presence and the plantation's matriarchy; 3 - Creole slaves: folklore and craft traditions; 4 - The daily lives of children on a Creole plantation; 5 - Wine tasting at Laura Locoul's.

Destrehan

The **Destrehan Plantation** ★★ *(adults $7, students $4, 6-12 yrs old $2, under 6 free, every day 9:30am to 4pm, except holidays; P.O. Box 9999 River Road, Destrehan, LA 70047, ☎ 764-9315)* is located only 16 kilometres from the New Orleans (Moisant) International Airport, on Highway LA 48 (River Road), between St. Rose and Destrehan. The residence, built in 1787 in the French colonial style and remodelled in neoclassical style around 1830, is the oldest residence in the lower Mississippi Valley. There are tall oaks bordering it and it is furnished with beautiful antiques.

Ormond Plantation ★ *(adult $7, seniors and students $4, children $2.50; every day 10am to 4pm; 8407 River Road, Destrehan, LA 70047, ☎ 764-9854)*. This is a colonial-style plantation house built around 1790, with straw and mud walls and old furnishings. There are exhibits of doll, cane and gun collections.

Chalmette

The **Jackson Barracks Military History Museum** ★★ *(free admission; Mon to Fri 7:30am to 4pm, Sat 10am to 4pm; 6400 St. Claude Ave., ☎ 278-8242)*. This museum located in an old powder magazine (1837) has a significant collection of arms, flags and artifacts.

New Orleans Battlefield Park in Chalmette ★★ *(Chalmette, ☎ 589-4428)*.

Fort Pike

Fort Pike State Commemorative Area ★★ *(adults $2, under 12 yrs free; every day 9am to 5pm except legal holidays; Route US 90/Old Spanish Trail, ☎ 662-5703)*. The fort was built in 1827 at Rigolets Channel, between Lake Pontchartrain and Lake Borgne to defend the city. Museum and nature information centre, picnic grounds and washrooms.

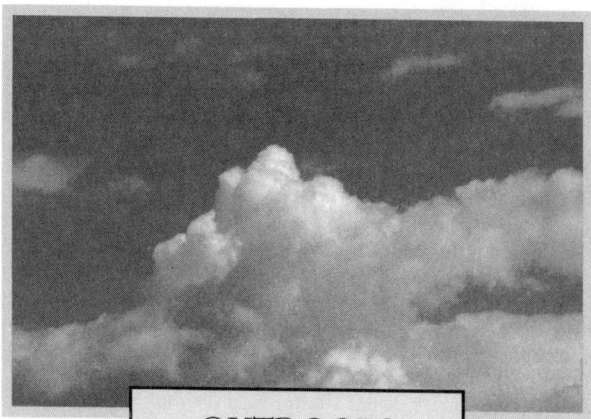

OUTDOORS

A s in all big cities, it is possible to practise your favourite sports and activities, or try out some new ones, in New Orleans.

CYCLING

Since New Orleans' streets are very busy, it's particularly pleasant to cycle in Audubon Park, City Park and along Lake Pontchartrain. Information on cycling activities is available through **Crescent City Cyclists** (☎ 276-2601).

CANOEING

At **City Park** ($5 per hour; ☎ 483-9371), you can rent a canoe and explore the lagoons and subtropical wildlife.

FISHING

You can go fishing for perch or cat-fish in the waters of **City Park** ($2 adults, $1 under 16; ☎ 483-9371). A permit is required and can be purchased on site.

For information on New Orleans fishing permits (including Lake Pontchartrain), contact the **Wildlife and Fisheries Department** *(1600 Canal Street,* ☎ *568-5636).*

SWIMMING

Since the Gulf of Mexico is about 100 kilometres from New Orleans it's not exactly a seaside resort. Also, the thin layer of earth covering the southern Louisiana region doesn't allow for the construction of swimming pools. However, certain hotels have pools: small ones if built in the hotel's courtyard and bigger ones in some of the larger hotels where they are located on the upper floors, if not the top floor or roof itself. To cool off on those scorching hot or extraordinarily humid days, or for swimmers who want to stay in shape, it's better to choose a hotel with a pool because public pools in New Orleans are practically nonexistent.

You will have to go outside New Orleans to find a public swimming pool. The **Bayou Segnette State Park** swimming pool *($8 adults, $4 under 12 yrs; 7777 West Bank Expressway, Westwego,* ☎ *736-7140)* attracts big crowds. There are picnic tables and a playground.

St. Bernard State Park *($2; Highway Saint Bernard, LA 39 South, Poydras,* ☎ *682-2101)* is over 180 hectares in size and offers, as well as a swimming pool, picnic tables, walking trails and campgrounds.

WALKING

Most public parks in New Orleans have walking trails. Walking is by far the best way to see the city and the surrounding area. The **French Quarter**, the **Garden District** and **Algiers Point** are great places to walk while discovering this historic city's many points of interest. Don't forget to take a supply of water or some other refreshment.

One hour from New Orleans, **Jean Lafitte Park** *(*☎ *689-2002 or 589-2330)* has a large number of trails. Some of the paths go through swamps and archaeological sites.

TENNIS

Tennis lovers will find courts at **Audubon Park** *(6400 to 6900 St. Charles Avenue)* and at **City Park**.

GOLF

The following golf courses are open to the public:

Audubon Park
473 Walnut Street
New Orleans
☎ 865-8260
($10; 18 holes)

Brechtel
3700 Berhman Place
Westbank
☎ 362-4761
($8; public 18-hole course)

City Park
1040 Filmore Street
New Orleans
☎ 483-9396
($15; four 18-hole courses, driving range)

SWAMP TOURS

Contact **Captain Terry's Swamp Tour** *(☎ 471-4933)* or **Lil Cajun Swamp Tours** *(adults $16, seniors $14, children $12, with transportation to hotel $15 and $30; departures 10am, noon, 2pm; Highway 301, Crown Point, ☎ 689-3213 or 1-800-725-3213)*, with Cyrus Blanchare, known as "Cyrus the Cajun", captain of the *Moonlight Lady*, a boat that can carry 60 passengers. Tours visit the swamps of Jean Lafitte National Park and last two to four hours.

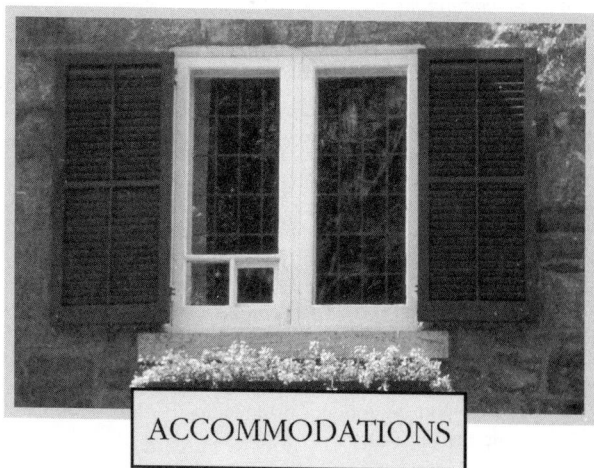

ACCOMMODATIONS

Whether you are looking for a simple *pied-à-terre* or something more luxurious, New Orleans offers a wide choice of hotels, motels and bed and breakfasts to suit all budgets.

Whether you just want to rent a small room or would prefer to stay in a historic manor, **Bed and Breakfast Inc.** *(1021 Moss Rd., New Orleans, LA 70152-2267, ☎ 488-4640 or 1-800-749-4640 from the U.S., ☎ 827-5391)* can provide all of the necessary information and make reservations.

New Orleans Bed & Breakfast and Accommodations *(P.O. Box 8163, New Orleans, ☎ 838-0071)* reserves rooms, apartments, furnished flats and houses.

You can get information on all the different hotels in the Southern Comfort chain in the New Orleans metropolitan area and make reservations through the **Southern Comfort** reservation service *(P.O. Box 13294, New Orleans, ☎ 861-0082 for information or 1-800-749-1928 for reservations)*.

Our Favourites

For warm atmosphere:
> Le Meridien (p 178) and Le Richelieu (p 168)

For New Orleans architecture:
> Hotel Maison de Ville and Audubon Cottages (p 171), Soniat House (p 168), and the Rue Royal Inn (p 166).

For attractive decor:
> Chimes B&B (p 174), Grenoble House (p 170), the Dauphine Orleans Hotel (p 170), Hotel Maison de Ville and Audubon Cottages (p 171) and Soniat House (p 168).

For pleasant courtyards:
> Chimes B&B (p 174), Hotel de la Poste (p 171), Maison Dupuy (p 172), and Soniat House (p 168).

For sophisticated character:
> Claiborne Mansion (p 170), the Bourbon Orleans Hotel (p 172), the Omni Royal Orleans Hotel (p 171), the Pontchartrain Hotel (p 175), Le Meridien (p 178), The Melrose (p 172), and the Monteleone (p 171).

For a warm welcome:
> The Avenue Plaza Hotel and Spa (p 175), Chimes B&B (p 174), Villa Convento Hotel (p 166), Le Meridien (p 178), Le Richelieu (p 168), New Orleans Guest House (p 166).

For period antiques:
> Claiborne Mansion (p 170), Grenoble House (p 170), Cornstalk Hotel (p 168), Girod House (p 170), Duvigneaud House (p 176), and Soniat House (p 168).

For affordable prices:
>   Comfort Inn/Downtown Superdome (p 177), French Quarter Suites (p 166), the Nine-O-Five Royal Hotel (p 165), New Orleans Guest House (p 166), and Prytania Inn I, II and III (p 173).

For the most attractive lobby:
>   The Hyatt Regency Hotel (p 179).

For romantic atmosphere:
>   The Melrose (p 172).

For terraces and balconies:
>   Hotel de la Poste (p 171), the Omni Royal Orleans Hotel (p 171), Girod House (p 170), Soniat House (p 168), Rue Royal Inn (p 166).

For views of the city and the Mississippi:
>   The Westin Canal Place Hotel (p 180).

Most of the major hotel chains are represented in New Orleans, especially in the Central Business District. They obviously do not have the character and ambience that a smaller hotel has, but they offer good quality, service and comfort.

THE FRENCH QUARTER AND FAUBOURG MARIGNY

St. Peter Guest House *($50-$180 bkfst incl.; ≡, pb, tv; 1005 St. Peter St., 70116, ☎ 524-9232 or 1-800-535-7815 in North America, ⇆ 943-6536 or 523-5198).* The wrought-iron balconies of this beautiful 19th century building overlook the French Quarter. There are 17 rooms and 11 suites with period decor.

The **Nine-O-Five Royal Hotel** *($65 and up; ≡, pb, K; 905 Royal St., 70116, ☎ 523-0219),* constructed in 1890, is one of the oldest small hotels in the French Quarter. Its European character, courtyard and balconies looking over Royal Street make it very charming. Credit cards are not accepted.

The **Bourgoyne Guest House** *($75 and up; pb, K; 839 Bourbon St., 70116, ☎ 524-3621 or 525-3983)*, a lovely Creole manor from the 1830s, is located in the heart of the French Quarter. It has three rooms and two suites overlooking a pretty courtyard.

The **New Orleans Guest House** *($79-$99 bkfst incl.; pb; 1118 Ursulines St., 70116, ☎ 566-1177)* is a Creole cottage dating from 1848 with a pleasant courtyard in which breakfast is served. The owners are very friendly. There is private parking.

Rue Royal Inn *($75-$145; ≡, pb, K, ℝ; 1006 Royal St., 70116, ☎ 524-3900 or 1-800-776-3901 in North America, ≈ 558-0566)* is a beautiful Creole house from the 1830s. It offers luxurious suites with balconies and rooms that open onto a courtyard.

The **French Quarter Suites** *($79-$119 bkfst incl.; ≡, pb, tv, ≈; 1119 Rampart North St., 70116, ☎ 524-7725 or 1-800-457-2253 from the U.S., ≈ 522-9716)*, located close to the French Quarter, offers rooms that are modest but comfortable.

The picturesque **Château Motor Hotel** *($79-$129 bkfst incl.; ≡, pb, tv, ≈, ℜ; 1001 Chartres St., 70116, ☎ 524-9636, ≈ 525-2989)* is located in the heart of the historic French Quarter. Free parking.

Villa Convento Hotel *($89-$155 bkfst incl.; ≡, pb, tv; 616 Ursulines St., 70116, ☎ 522-1793, ≈ 524-1902)* is a lovely Creole house built in 1848. This family guest house offers very proficient European-style service.

The **Rathbone Inn** *($90-$145 bkfst incl.; ≡, pb, K, tv; 1227 Esplanade Ave., 70116, ☎ 947-2101 or 1-800-947-2101 in North America, ≈ 947-7454)* is an elegant manor that was constructed in 1850. Well situated in the attractive and historic Faubourg Marigny, the Rathbone has eight cozy rooms and two magnificent suites. Private parking.

Lamothe House Hotel *($90-$195 bkfst incl.; pb, K; 621 Esplanade Ave., 70116-2018, ☎ 947-1161 or 1-800-367-5858 in North America, ≈ 943-6536)*, a hotel tucked away in a grove of oak trees, is well situated one block from the French

Restaurants and Hotels of the French Quarter (Vieux Carré)

◇ Restaurants

1. Acme Oyster House
2. Bacco
3. French Market Restaurant and Bar
4. Bayona
5. Bella Luna
6. Bistro at the Hotel Maison de Ville
7. Café Du Monde
8. Café La Madeleine
9. Alex Patout's
10. Antoine's
11. Arnaud's
12. Brennan's
13. Broussard's
14. Galatoire's
15. Coops
16. Croissant d'Or
17. Di Piazza
18. G&E Courtyard Kitchen
19. K-Paul's Louisiana Kitchen
20. The Court of the Two Sisters
21. Le Richelieu
22. Maison Napoléon
23. Mr. B's Bistro
24. Palace Café
25. Pasta E Vino
26. Pelican Club
27. Peristyle
28. Praline Connection
29. Ristorante di Carmelo

○ Hotels

1. Rathbone Inn
2. Château Motor Hotel
3. Claiborne Mansion
4. French Quarter Suites
5. Grenoble House
6. Holiday Inn Château Le Moyne
7. Bourbon Orleans Hotel
8. Cornstalk Hotel
9. Dauphine Orleans Hotel
10. Hotel de la Poste
11. Eienville House Hotel
12. Hotel Maison de Ville and Audubon Cottages
13. Omni House
14. Omni Royal Orleans Hotel
15. Provincial Hotel
16. Hotel St.Ann Marie-Antoinette and Hotel St.Louis
17. Hotel St.Pierre
18. Hotel St.Helene
19. Villa Convento Hotel
20. Le Richelieu
21. Maison Dupuy Hotel
22. Girod House
23. Lamothe House Hotel
24. St.Peter Guest House
25. Soniat House
26. T.Melrose
27. Montelone
28. Nine-O-Five Royal Hotel
29. Bourgoyne Guest House
30. New-Orleans Guest House
31. Rue Royal Inn

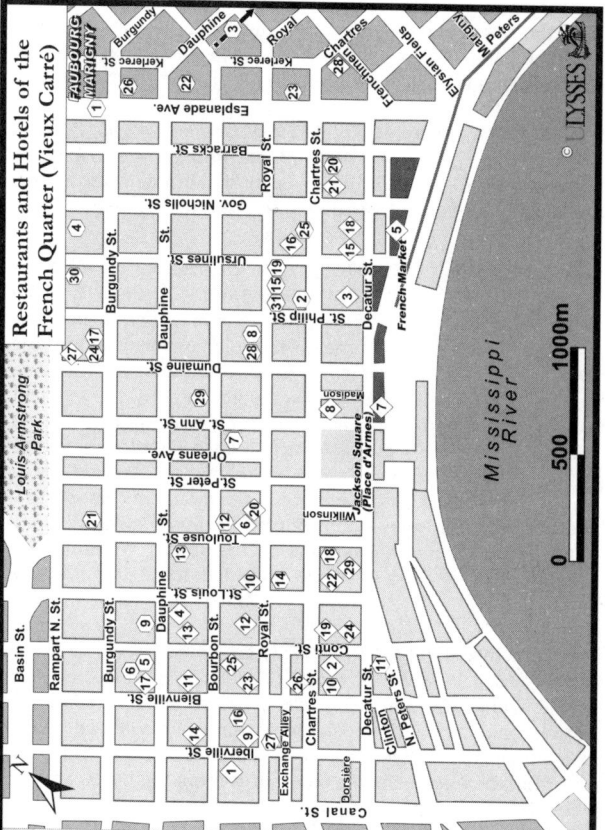

Quarter. Its 11 rooms and 9 suites are furnished in old-fashioned style. Every aspect of the place evokes the charm of the Victorian era – it's pleasant, but a bit stiff.

The **Hotel St. Pierre** *($109-$129 bkfst incl.; ≡, pb, ≈; 911 Burgundy St., 70116, ☎ 524-4401 or 1-800-225-4040 in North America, ⚲ 524-6800)* includes two 18th-century Creole cottages in a peaceful, shady courtyard. Free parking.

Le Richelieu *($95-$150; ≡, ⊗, pb, tv, ℝ, ≈, ℜ; 1234 Chartres St., 70116, ☎ 529-2492 or 1-800-535-9653 in North America, ⚲ 524-8179)* is a highly recommended, wonderful establishment that has earned a four-diamond rating from the AAA auto club. Le Richelieu is located near the Ursuline Convent, the French Market, Faubourg Marigny and elegant Esplanade Avenue. Romantic charm, exceptional service and relatively reasonable prices for the French Quarter merit this hotel particular acclaim. The hotel bar, which also serves as dining room, opens onto a beautiful, flowered courtyard and a pool. At night this marvellous spot is a favourite meeting place in the French Quarter. Everyone on the staff is exceptionally kind. Room service is available on request and there is free parking.

The **Cornstalk Hotel** *($115-$155 bkfst incl.; ≡, pb; 915 Royal St., 70116, ☎ 523-1515, ⚲ 522-5558)* is located in the heart of the French Quarter. This elegant little hotel, declared a historic landmark, offers 14 rooms furnished with antiques, stained-glass windows, fireplaces and canopy beds. Set back a bit from the road, behind a pleasant garden, the hotel is easily recognized by its wrought-iron fence with corn motifs.

The **Hotel St. Ann/Marie-Antoinette** *($119-$139; ≡, pb, tv, ≈, ℜ; 717 Conti St., 70130, ☎ 581-1881 or 1-800-535-9111 in North America)*, a charming hotel with 66 rooms, welcomes everyone in a friendly manner. Pink predominates throughout the hotel: it is the colour of dining-room tablecloths and guest-room bedding, carpets and sofas.

Soniat House *($120 and up bkfst incl.; pb, ≡, tv; 1133 Chartres St., 70116, ☎ 522-0570 or 1-800-544-8808 in North America, ⚲ 522-7208)* is quiet, luxurious and enthusiastically recommended. The historic character of the

Soniat du Fossat House, which was built in 1829 for plantation owner and New Orleans aristocrat Joseph Soniat du Fossat, has been maintained in this unique hotel. Rooms and suites are furnished with antiques from France, Great Britain and Louisiana. Breakfast is served in the charming, rustic courtyard. From the beautiful wrought-iron balcony that overlooks Chartres Street there is a view of the Old Ursuline Convent, a masterpiece of New Orleans' architectural heritage (see p 111). Across the street is another historic house, which originally belonged to Joseph Soniat du Fossat's son and which has also been converted into a hotel by the owners of this establishment. This second house also has a magnificent, abundantly flowered courtyard with a lovely fountain.

Olivier House *($125 and up; ≡, pb, tv, ≈, K; 828 Toulouse St., 70112-3422, ☎ 525-8456, ↵ 529-2006)* is an attractive building that dates from 1836 and is listed in the National Register of Historic Places. It offers large rooms with high ceilings and antique furniture. The hotel opens onto a lush yard.

Hotel Ste. Helene *($130-$225 bkfst incl.; ≡, pb, tv, K; 508 Chartres St., 70116, ☎ 522-5014 or 1-800-348-3888 in North America, ↵ 523-7140)*. Clients will greatly appreciate its 18th-century style as well as the luxuriously furnished rooms.

The **Holiday Inn Château Le Moyne** *($139 and up; ≡, pb, tv, ≈, ℜ; 301 Dauphine St., 70112, ☎ 581-1303 or 1-800-465-4329 in North America, ↵ 523-5709)*, located close to the French Quarter, offers, apart from its rooms, some lovely suites in Creole cottages. The rooms are all tastefully decorated; some have brick walls, canopy beds and fireplaces, and they all feature ceiling-height windows adorned with floral-patterned drapes.

Hotel Saint-Louis *($139 and up; ≡, pb, ⊛; 730 Bienville St., 70130, ☎ 581-7300 or 1-800-535-9111 in North America, ↵ 524-8925)*. Everything here is reminiscent of the New Orleans of bygone days: the Louis XVI decor of the restaurant, the fountains, the subtropical flora, etc. Guests can use the pool at the Hotel Saint-Anne/Marie-Antoinette, a neighbouring establishment (see p 168).

The **Provincial Hotel** *($145 and up; ≡, pb, tv, ≈, ℜ; 1024 Chartres St., 70116, ☎ 581 4995 or 1-800-535-7922 in*

North America, ☎ 581-1018) is a quiet, comfortable hotel in the French Quarter, housing about a hundred rooms. All of the rooms are furnished with antiques and each is decorated differently. Wallpaper with subtle designs adorns the walls, and the large windows are trimmed with attractive printed or solid-colour fabrics. Free parking.

Grenoble House *($145-$195; ≡, pb, tv, ≈, K; 329 Dauphine St., 70112, ☎ 522-1331, ┄ 524-4968)* is a delightful little 17-suite hotel with enchanting decor. The suites are distributed among the three original sections of the estate: the masters' residence, the servants' wing and rooms, and the slave quarters. All of the suites have sofa-beds as well as beds. The kitchenettes are equipped with modern facilities (conventional or microwave oven, stove, refrigerator and dishwasher). Children under the age of 12 are not admitted.

Girod House *($145-$225 bkfst incl.; ≡, pb, K; 835 Esplanade Ave., 70116, ☎ 522-5214 or 1-800-650-3323 in North America, ┄ 522-7288)* is a well-preserved Creole residence that is pleasantly decorated with antiques. This distinctive little hotel offers five rooms and six suites. Every suite includes a bedroom, a living room, a kitchenette and a bathroom. The two largest suites have balconies that overlook either elegant Esplanade Avenue or the rustic courtyard. Rooms and suites combine Creole comfort and luxurious 19th-century furnishings.

Claiborne Mansion *($150-$250; ≡, pb, tv, ≈; 2111 Dauphine St., 70116, ☎ 949-7327 or 1-800-449-7327 in North America, ┄ 949-0388)*, a small hotel located across from Washington Square in Faubourg Marigny, has nine spacious, inviting rooms in a sober yet tasteful decor of neutral tones. Some rooms are furnished with canopy beds.

Dauphine Orléans Hotel *($150 and up; ≡, pb, tv, ≈; 415 Dauphine St., 70112, ☎ 586-1800 or 1-800-521-7111 in North America, ┄ 586-1409)*. Upon arrival, guests are greeted with a complimentary refreshment. Tea is served every afternoon. The hotel has 109 rooms. The "Dauphine" part of the hotel, dating from the beginning of the 19th century, houses 14 magnificent rooms with original exposed ceiling beams and brick walls. The other rooms, with their pale-coloured walls, beige carpeting and flowered bedspreads also have a lot of character. Rooms are equipped with a number of small appliances such as irons and hair dryers.

The adorable **Hotel de la Poste** *($150 and up; ≡, pb, tv, ≈, ℜ; 316 Chartres St., 70130, ☎ 581-1200 or 1-800-448-4927 in North America, ≈ 523-2910)* has about one hundred rooms, each with a balcony overlooking the courtyard or the street. The decor of the rooms is simple but cozy, with dark-wood furniture. The Hotel de la Poste boasts an excellent restaurant, Bacco, renowned for its fine Italian cuisine with strong Creole accents (see p 191).

At the **Monteleone** *($150 and up; ≡, pb, tv, ≈, ℜ; 214 Royal St., 70140, ☎ 523-3341 or 1-800-535-9595 in North America, ≈ 528-1019)*, you will discover the advantages that a high-calibre hotel has to offer. The spacious rooms were renovated in 1996. Light-coloured walls provide a contrast to the finely crafted dark-wood furniture. Some rooms have canopy beds.

The **Omni Royal Orleans Hotel** *($169 and up; ≡, pb, tv, ≈, ℜ; 621 St. Louis St., 70140, ☎ 529-5333 or 1-800-843-6664 in North America, ≈ 529-7089)*. During major events such as Mardi Gras, certain rooms of this hotel offer no respite since it is located in the heart of the action in the French Quarter. The rooms are decorated with wallpaper in a light, striped design with a flowered band, and some of them have canopy beds. There is a pool on a roof-top terrace, from which there is a striking view of the French Quarter.

The **Bienville House Hotel** *($175 and up; ≡, pb, tv, ≈, ☉, ℜ; 320 Decatur St., 70130, ☎ 529-2345 or 1-800-535-7836 in North America, ≈ 525-6079)* is a charming little establishment, and a few of its rooms have balconies. Recently, the building and its 83 rooms were completely renovated. Bedspreads with subtle prints and curtains with flower designs in pink tones complement dark, finely crafted wood furniture. Across from the Aquarium of the Americas and Riverfront, close to Bourbon Street and Jackson Square, the hotel benefits from one of the best locations in the French Quarter. Free parking.

🏨 **Hotel Maison de Ville and Audubon Cottages** *($180 and up, bkfst incl.; ≡, K, pb, ℜ, 727 Toulouse St., 70130, ☎ 561-5858 or 1-800-634-1600 in North America,*

☎ *528-9939).* Located in the heart of the French Quarter, this establishment, of refined architectural beauty, is comprised of 16 rooms and 7 cottages. Originally, John James Audubon and his family lived in the house. He created some of his most beautiful sketches, drawings and paintings here. The principal residence and the outbuildings have all been carefully restored. The varied decor of the rooms – some rustic, some luxurious – reflects different periods in the history of the South. Children under the age of 12 are not admitted. Free parking.

The **Bourbon Orleans Hotel** *($185-$250; ≡, pb, tv, ≈, ℜ; 717 Orleans Ave., 70116, ☎ 523-2222 or 1-800-521-5338 from the U.S., ☛ 525-8166)* is a luxurious hotel in the tradition of 19th-century Europe, with Queen-Anne period antiques and marble bathrooms. Bedspreads and curtains are made of sumptuous floral-patterned fabrics that are set off nicely by bright carpeting.

The **Maison Dupuy Hotel** *($185 and up; ≡, pb, tv, ≈, ℜ; 1001 Toulouse St., 70112, ☎ 586-8000 or 1-800-535-9177 in North America, ☛ 566-7450)*, has 198 rooms and suites, arranged in seven 19th-century cottages which have retained their old-fashioned character despite recent renovations. The spacious rooms have European-style decor. The floral-patterned bedspreads and curtains complement the light-coloured walls. Many rooms have French windows that open onto the pool in the magnificent courtyard. The garden is full of wonderful banana, orange and grapefruit trees. Sunday brunches at the hotel restaurant, Le Bon Créole, are accompanied by jazz.

🏨 **The Melrose** *($250 and up; ≡, pb, tv, ≈; 937 Esplanade Ave., 70116, ☎ 944-2255, ☛ 945-1794)*. The splendid rooms of this elegant historic house are luxuriously decorated. Wealthy romantics can stay in the "Donecio Suite" for the modest price of $425! The hotel provides transportation to and from the airport.

🛏 UPTOWN AND THE GARDEN DISTRICT

Longpre Guest House and Hostel *($12 in the dormitory, $35 for a room; sb, K; 1726 Prytania St., 70130, ☎ 581-4540)* is located between the French Quarter and the Garden District and is close to the St. Charles streetcar. The hundred-year-old house is a bit run down and now houses a youth hostel. This is no-frills accommodation: either a bed in a dormitory or a small private room.

Marquette House New Orleans International Hostel *(2253 Carondelet St., 70130,* ☎ *523-3014)*, a member of the American Youth Hostel Association, has 160 beds, most of them in dormitories *($14-$17; sb)*, and a few in private rooms *($28-$31; ≡, pb)*. There are also two-bedroom suites with living rooms and kitchenettes *($40-$70; ≡, pb, K)*.

Prytania Inn I *($40 and up; pb, 1415 Prytania St., 70130,* ☎ *586-0853)*. Although the decor is somewhat stark, this modest little hotel offers comfortable clean rooms. Under the same administration, **Prytania II** *(2141 Prytania St.)* and **Prytania III** *(2127 Prytania St.)* offer slightly more expensive accommodation.

The **Saint Charles Guest House** *(single $45-65, double $65-$85, continental bkfst incl.; ≡, pb or sb, ≈; 1748 Prytania St., 70130,* ☎ *523-6556)* is small, simple hotel near the Lower Garden District and the streetcar. The house is somewhat old-fashioned and offers no luxuries. Clients tend to be fairly young, sometimes bohemian, low-budget travellers – this is one of the cheapest places to stay in New Orleans. There are 26 rooms overlooking a pretty, sunny courtyard and a pool.

Saint Charles Inn *($50-$90 bkfst incl.; pb; 3636 St. Charles Ave., 70115,* ☎ *899-8888, 1-800-489-9908 in North America, ≈ 899-8892)*. Although the entrance to this hotel is squeezed between a restaurant and a café, you will find the recently renovated rooms inside very inviting.

The **Quality Inn - Maison Saint-Charles** *($65 and up; ≡, pb, ≈; 1319 St. Charles Ave., 70130,* ☎ *522-0187 or 1-800-831-1783 from the U.S., ≈ 525-2218)* is comprised of six historic buildings around a charming courtyard. The modest rooms are impeccable despite the industrial-quality carpeting and nondescript furniture. A good place to stay if you are on a fixed budget.

Fairchild House *($75-$100 bkfst incl.; pb, tv; 1518 Prytania St., 70130,* ☎ *524-0154 or 1-800-256-2043 from the U.S.,*

☏ 568-0063) is a magnificent neoclassical residence built in about 1841 and it is close to the Garden District. It has only 14 Victorian-style rooms. The decor is warm and inviting, and guests are welcome to enjoy the charming courtyard. Private parking.

Quality Inn - Midtown *($75 and up; ≡, pb, tv, ≈, ℜ; 3900 Tulane Ave., 70119, ☏ 486-5541 or 1-800-228-5151 in North America, ☏ 488-7440)*. The rooms are comfortable and the prices are among the most affordable. Clients can take advantage of free service shuttle to various points in the French Quarter. Free parking.

The **Columns Hotel** *($75-$175 and up, bkfst incl., pb or sb, ≡; 3811 St. Charles Ave., 70115-4638, ☏ 899-9308 or 1-800-445-9308 in North America, ☏ 899-8170)* is listed in the National Register of Historic Places. The very same grand staircase that leads to the rooms can be seen in the film *Pretty Baby*. Although the furnishings are somewhat sparse, the rooms shine like a new penny! Nineteen rooms are available, nine of which have private bathrooms. Every Thursday night, the hotel bar hosts a jazz-rock band. On Sundays there is a brunch with mellow jazz.

🌴 **Chimes Bed & Breakfast** *($90-$125 bkfst incl.; ≡, pb; 1146 Constantinople St., ☏ 899-2621 or 1-800-749-4640 from the U.S.)* are attractive suites with bathrooms that can house up to six people. Smoking is permitted outside only. Charles, the Lebanese owner, also works as the head waiter at Arnaud's, in the French Quarter (see p 194). He is very friendly and loves to chat. A charming place to stay, Chime Cottages are highly recommended by the authors of this guide and easily accessible via the St. Charles streetcar, which can also take you to the heart of the French Quarter in a matter of minutes.

Terrell House *($100-$125 bkfst incl.; ≡, pb, tv; 1441 Magazine St., 70130, ☏ 524-9859)*, erected in 1858, has been converted into a nine-room guest house. The house maintains its old-fashioned character and its furnishings appear to be authentic. It is located in the residential Lower-Garden District, also the site of many galleries and antique shops. Two dogs keep watch over a lush English garden where. Your hosts will make restaurant and guided-tour reservations for you upon request.

The **Park View Guest House** *($90 - $120 and up; ≡, pb, tv, ℜ; 7004 St. Charles Ave., 70118, ☎ 861-7564, ↔ 861-1225)*, located on the edge of Audubon Park, was constructed for visitors to the World's Industrial and Cotton Centennial Exhibition in 1884. The rooms on the St. Charles Avenue side of this charming Victorian house have period furniture. The other rooms have less character but offer a magnificent view of the park. All 23 rooms are clean and comfortable. Breakfast is served in the dining room, which offers a splendid view of the park.

Avenue Plaza Hotel and Spa *($125 and up; ≡, pb, tv, ≈, ℜ; 2111 St. Charles Ave., 70130, ☎ 566-1212 or 1-800-535-9575 in North America, ↔ 525-6899)*. The hotel's spacious and inviting rooms have recently been renovated. Some of them are decorated with attractive Art Deco furniture.

The **Pontchartrain Hotel** *($150 and up; ≡, pb, tv, ℜ; 2031 St. Charles Ave., 70140, ☎ 524-0581 or 1-800-777-6193 in North America, ↔ 529-1165)*, a luxurious European-style hotel, is located in the heart of the Garden District. As well as offering standard rooms, there are a few romantic suites. Prince Aly Khan and Rita Hayworth stayed in one of this illustrious hotel's suites during their honeymoon in New Orleans.

MID-CITY

The **Degas House** *($100-$200 bkfst incl.; pb; 2306 Esplanade Ave., ☎ 821-5009)*, built in 1854, exhibits Italian-inspired style. The painter Edgar Degas stayed here in 1873, while visiting his mother's family. It was during his time in New Orleans that Degas painted *Le Portrait d'Estelle* (owned by the New Orleans Museum of Art, see p 124) as well as *Le Bureau de coton de La Nouvelle-Orléans*. The house has been renovated in keeping with its original character. Rooms on the second floor are spacious and furnished with antiques; one has a large private balcony. Although the rooms on the third floor have a bit of an attic feel, they have the advantage of being less expensive.

The **New Orleans First B & B** *($100-$125; by; 3660 Gentilly Boulevard, ☎ 947-3401)* is a splendid Art-Deco-style house flanked by magnificent oaks. The three rooms are rented to non-smokers only.

The **Mentone Bed And Breakfast** *($125 and up, bkfst incl.; ≡, pb, K; 1437 De Pauger St., 70116, ☎ 943-3019)* is five blocks from the French Quarter and offers one suite with a private entrance and a separate living room. The kitchen is small but complete. Decor consists of Oriental rugs and antique furniture (some pieces are reproductions), that overall make this a pleasant place to stay. Children under the age of twelve are not admitted. Smoking is permitted outside only.

Mechling's Guest House *($125 and up, bkfst incl.; ≡, pb, 2023 Esplanade Ave., 70116, ☎ 943-4131 or 1-800-725-4131 from the U.S.)*, a Victorian-style historic manor from the 1860s, is close to the French Quarter.

Duvigneaud House *($135 bkfst incl.; pb, tv, K; 2857½ Grand Route St. John, close to St. John Bayou, 70116, ☎ 821-5009, ↝ 948-3313)* is a plantation residence built in 1834 that has been completely restored. The spacious, homey, four-person suites have high ceilings and wood floors. Rooms are furnished with antiques and guests have access to a pretty courtyard. Almost all services and facilities for an extended stay are available (laundry, housekeeping, grocery store a few blocks away). The house is located near Esplanade Avenue and City Park. Free parking.

🛏 CENTRAL BUSINESS DISTRICT

The **YMCA International Hotel** *($50 and less; ≡, tv, pb, ℜ, ☺, ≈; 920 St. Charles Ave., 70130, ☎ and ↝ 568-9622)* is a favourite among budget travellers, fans of Jack London and Jack Kerouac, and the young at heart in general.

Comfort Studios *($55-$105; pb, ≡, tv, ≈, ⊛, ℝ, 346 Baronne St., 70112-1627, ☎ 524-1140 or 1-800-228-5150 in North America, ↝ 523-4444)*, located four blocks from the French Quarter, is ideal for people looking for comfortable rooms at reasonable prices. Free parking.

The **Roadway Hotel** *($65 and up, bkfst incl.; ≡, pb, tv, ≈; 1725 Tulane Ave., ☎ 529-5411 or 1-800-635-1976 from the U.S.,*

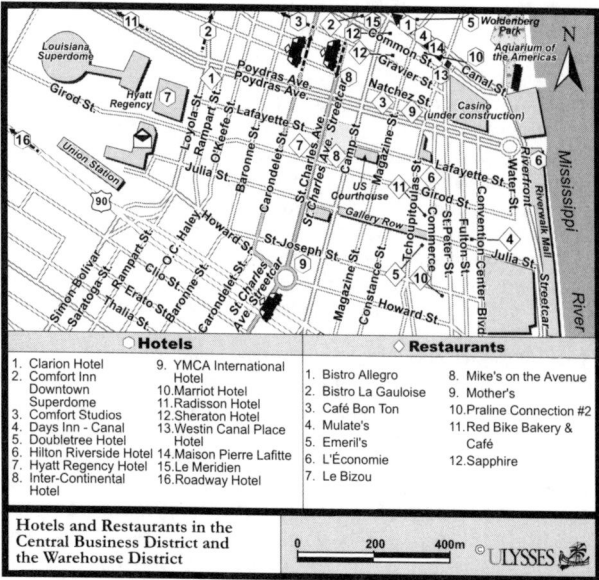

Hotels

1. Clarion Hotel
2. Comfort Inn Downtown Superdome
3. Comfort Studios
4. Days Inn - Canal
5. Doubletree Hotel
6. Hilton Riverside Hotel
7. Hyatt Regency Hotel
8. Inter-Continental Hotel
9. YMCA International Hotel
10. Marriot Hotel
11. Radisson Hotel
12. Sheraton Hotel
13. Westin Canal Place Hotel
14. Maison Pierre Lafitte
15. Le Meridien
16. Roadway Hotel

Restaurants

1. Bistro Allegro
2. Bistro La Gauloise
3. Café Bon Ton
4. Mulate's
5. Emeril's
6. L'Économie
7. Le Bizou
8. Mike's on the Avenue
9. Mother's
10. Praline Connection #2
11. Red Bike Bakery & Café
12. Sapphire

Hotels and Restaurants in the Central Business District and the Warehouse District

0   200   400m   © ULYSSES

≈ 524-1059) is located at the highway off-ramp, just north of the French Quarter. Although the rooms of this hotel, a member of an American chain, have no particular character, they are clean and comfortable. Free parking.

The **Comfort Inn Downtown Superdome** (*$65-$90; ≡, pb, tv, ℝ, ℜ; 1315 Gravier St., 70112-2003, ☎ 586-0100 or 1-800-535-9141 in North America, ≈ 588-9230 or 527-5263)* benefits from an ideal location, mid-way between the Superdome and the French Quarter. Rooms are simple and inviting, all equipped with contemporary furnishings. Every room has useful small appliances such as irons, hair dryers and microwave ovens.

The **Clarion Hotel** (*$89-$109; ≡, pb, tv, ≈, ☉, ℜ; 1500 Canal St., 70112, ☎ 522-4500 or 1-800-824-3359 from the U.S., ≈ 525-2644)*, a highly rated hotel located close to the Superdome, offers free shuttle service to the French Quarter. Rooms are tastefully decorated, mostly in pastel tones and have attractive, finely crafted dark-wood furniture. The hotel offers families a list of reliable people who provide child-care services.

The **Days Inn - Canal** *($95-$135; ≡, pb, tv, ≈, ℜ; 1630 Canal St., 70112, ☎ 586-0110 or 1-800-232-3297 in North America, ⇝ 581-2253)* is only a few minutes away from the French Market, close to the I-10 (exit 235B). This 211-room, eight-floor hotel has classic decor. Each standard room is furnished with either one king-size bed or two large beds. All the rooms are comfortable, adorned with wall-to-wall carpeting, and equipped with a chest of drawers and small appliances (hair dryers, coffee machines, voice message service). Free parking.

The **Maison Pierre Lafitte** *($105 and up; pb, tv, K; 108 University Place, 70112, ☎ 527-5800 or 1-800-726-5800 from the U.S.)* is two steps from the French Quarter, at the corner of Canal Street.

The **Doubletree Hotel** *($129 and up; ≡, pb, tv, ≈, ℜ; 300 Canal St., ☎ 581-1300 or 1-800-222-8733 in North America, ⇝ 522-4100)*, less expensive than other hotels in the same category, has the advantage of being situated just a few minutes from the French Quarter. The lobby of this 363-room hotel is unassuming, but the rooms are cozy. Their pale wood furniture is well matched with the pastel-coloured curtains and bedspreads.

Le Meridien *($185 and up; ≡, pb, tv, ≈, ℝ, ☉, ℜ; 614 Canal St., ☎ 525-6500 or 1-800-543-4300 in North America, ⇝ 586-1543)*. This luxurious, up-market hotel has 494 spacious, elegant, comfortable rooms. A work table completes the furnishings that are composed, most notably, of an easy chair and a sofa whose colours harmonize with the drapes and the bedspread. Modern luxury is combined with all the traditional charm of the South. The rooms on the upper floors of this 30-floor building offer a superb view of the city. Staff members see to every detail of guests' needs, right down to the complimentary toiletries in the washrooms. An outdoor pool and an exercise room are on the eighth floor. The hotel has a bistro, **La Gauloise** (see p 197), and numerous conference rooms with all necessary services for business people. Jazz performances are presented every evening and during the hotel's famous Sunday brunches.

The **Hilton Riverside Hotel** *($185 and up; ≡, pb, tv, ≈, ℝ, ☺, ℜ; 2 Poydras St.,* ☎ *561-0500 or 1-800-445-8667 in North America, ✉ 568-1721)* is definitely one of the biggest hotels in the city with more than 1,500 rooms. Furnishings are contemporary, and the decor in the standard rooms is comfortable, if not especially creative. The "concierge rooms", designed for business people, are equipped with fax machines. Suites are also available, some with pool tables and private terraces. Other services and facilities include bars, tennis courts, a health club and two pools.

Hyatt Regency Hotel *($185 and up; ≡, pb, tv, ≈, ℝ, ☺, ℜ; 500 Poydras St.,* ☎ *561-1234 or 1-800-233-1234 in North America, ✉ 587-4141)*. The lobby and lounge areas are spacious and bright, creating a luxurious and comfortable environment. Rooms are large and tastefully decorated. Some rooms are specially designed for women and, apparently out of chivalry, are located near the elevators. Other amenities include bars, a health club and a beauty salon.

Hotel Inter-Continental *($185 and up; ≡, pb, tv, ≈, ℝ, ☺, ℜ; 444 St. Charles Ave.,* ☎ *525-5566 or 1-800-332-4246 from the U.S., ✉ 585-4387)*. A few blocks from the French Quarter, the comfort and elegance found here are the reasons for this international chain's distinguished reputation. Approximately 450 vast rooms with simple, inviting decor are available. Some of the rooms are designed for people with physical disabilities. Everyone on the hotel's staff shows great concern for the well-being of guests. Other services and facilities offered are bars, a health club and a beauty salon.

The **Marriott** *($185 and up; ≡, pb, tv, ≈, ℝ, ☺, ℜ; 555 Canal St.,* ☎ *581-1000 or 1-800-228-9290 in North America, ✉ 523-6755)*, a modern hotel with 1,300 rooms and 54 suites, is located a few steps away from the French Quarter. The Marriott often hosts important conferences. The rooms are comfortable and very well equipped. Those on the upper floors have a spectacular view of the city, the French Quarter and the Mississippi. The staff is very courteous.

The **Radisson Hotel** *($185 and up; ≡, pb, tv, ≈, ℝ, ☺, ℜ; 1500 Canal St.,* ☎ *522-4500 or 1-800-333-3333 in North America)*, part of another large hotel chain, is listed in the National Register of Historic Places. The warmth and ambience of the

South are present in every one of the 759 spacious, elegantly decorated rooms. The dark tones of the wood furniture blend well with attractive floral fabrics. The Radisson offers a number of luxurious suites, as well as rooms for people with physical disabilities. Staff members speak many languages. Reception and service are among the most courteous. The hotel offers guests free shuttle service to the French Quarter.

The **Sheraton Hotel** *($185 and up; ≡, pb, tv, ≈, ℝ, ⊙, ℜ; 500 Canal St., ☎ 525-2500 or 1-800-325-3535 in North America, ⇆ 592-5615)* is another hotel in demand for mega-conferences. The enormous lobby was designed to accommodate the comings and goings of thousands of people. The 1,100 comfortable rooms are functionally furnished. Staff members make every effort to pay particular attention to each visitor.

The **Westin Canal Place Hotel** *($185 and up; ≡, pb, tv, ≈, ℝ, ⊙, ℜ; 100 Iberville St., ☎ 566-7006 or 1-800-228-3000 in North America, ⇆ 553-5133)*. This hotel's expansive rooms are attractively decorated in pastel colours; each has a marble fireplace and a large marble bathroom. From the outdoor pool, on the 30th floor, there is a fantastic panoramic view of the city. The restaurant Le Jardin offers room service 24 hours a day and weekly Sunday jazz brunches. Among the other facilities offered are a fully equipped exercise room and two bars.

CAMPING

Metairie

KOA New Orleans West *($21 for tents, $27 for recreational vehicles; ≈; 11129 Jefferson Hwy.: from the I-10, take exit 223A-Williams, travel south on Williams to Jefferson Hwy. and take it east, ☎ 467-1792)*, located on the Mississippi riverbank, is open all year. There are 96 sites, showers, washrooms, laundry facilities, a playground and a grocery store. Many of the sites are paved, shaded from the sun and bordered by grass.

Close to Downtown

Quite close to downtown, the **Mardi Gras Campground** *($15-$25; ≈; 6050 Chef Menteur Hwy., exit 240B from the I-10, ☎ 243-0085)* is a AAA-rated campground with 200 tent sites. There are also a guaranteed security service, showers, laundry facilities and public transportation to downtown.

Jude Travel Park *($19 and up; ≈, ⊛; 7400 Chef Menteur, exit 240B from the I-10, ☎ 241-0632 or 1-800-523-2196 in North America, ⤶ 245-8070)* This "Good Sam" campground has 43 shady sites for recreational vehicles, showers, washrooms, and laundry facilities. It is located close to bus routes and there is a car-rental agency on site, a shuttle to the French Quarter and a security service.

The **Parc d'Orléans Travel Park 1** *($50 and less; ≈; 7676 Chef Menteur Hwy., 70126, exit 240B from the I-10, ☎ 241-3167 or 1-800-535-2598 from the U.S.)* is a 74-site campground with showers, washrooms and laundry facilities. Transportation to the French Quarter and guided tours are offered.

The **Parc d'Orléans Travel Park 2** *($50 and less; ≈; 10910 Chef Menteur Hwy., exit 240B from the I-10, ☎ 242-6176 or 1-800-535-2598 from the U.S.)*, open all year, has 125 sites, showers, washrooms and laundry facilities. Shuttle service to the French Quarter and guided tours are also available.

RESTAURANTS

R estaurants abound both in and around the French Quarter, serving Creole, French, African-American (soul food) or Cajun cuisines. New Orleans is a city to indulge (oneself) in where gourmets are sure to make all sorts of delectable discoveries. Unless otherwise indicated, all major credit cards are accepted in the following establishments.

The prices in this guide are for a meal for one person, including taxes, but not drinks and tip.

$	$10 or less
$$	$10 to $20
$$$	$20 to $30
$$$$	$30 or more

RESTAURANTS BY TYPE OF CUISINE

Our Favourites

For their trendy side:
> Emeril's (p 199), Palace Café (p 192), Peristyle (p 195), Mike's on the Avenue (p 198), and Straya (p 200).

For their warm ambiance:
> Bacco (p 191), Bayona (p 189), Café Degas (p 204), Économie (p 198), Martinique Bistro (p 202), and Upperline (p 203).

For its balcony:
> K-Paul's (p 193)

For their lovely interior courtyards:
> Bayona (p 189), Bistro at the Hotel Maison De Ville (p 193), Café Volage (p 200), Broussard's (p 194), Brennan's (p 195), G & E Courtyard (p 193).

For their inviting decor:
> Upperline (p 203) and Sapphire (p 198).

For their preppy side:
> Brennan's (p 195), Antoine's (p 194), Commander's Palace (p 204), Galatoire's (p 192), The Court of Two Sisters (p 192).

For their dinner concerts:
> Bistro La Gauloise - Le Meridien (jazz) (p 197), Mulate's (Cajun music) (p 197) and Praline Connection #2 (gospel) (p 196).

For their romantic ambiance:
> Bayona (p 189), Bella Luna (p 189), Arnaud's (p 194), Bistro de Ville (p 206) and Upperline (p 203).

For the best French cuisine:
> Bistro de Ville (p 206).

For their service:

> Christian's (p 205), Emeril's (p 199), G & E Courtyard (p 193), K-Paul's (p 193), Praline Connection (p 189) and Upperline (p 203).

For their healthy menu:

> Bella Luna (p 189), Croissant d'Or (p 188), Kim Son (p 207), Mr. B's Bistro (p 190) and Mike's on the Avenue (p 198).

For its view of the Mississippi:

> Bella Luna (p 189).

For their quintessential New Orleans surroundings:

> Acme Oyster House (p 188), Café du Monde (p 187), Coops (p 187), Galatoire's (p 192), Mother's (p 196), Napoleon House (p 188) and Uglesich's (p 199).

For its desserts:

> Windsor Court (p 201)

For their breakfasts:

> Le Richelieu (p 189) and Mother's (p 196).

✕ THE FRENCH QUARTER AND FAUBOURG MARIGNY

For the locations of these establishments, see map on p 167.

The world-famous **Café du Monde** *($; 24 hours a day; 800 Decatur St., French Market, ☎ 581-2914)*, located right in front of the French Market, near the riverfront promenade, has been around since 1860. Its chicory-flavoured *café au lait* (coffee with steamed milk) is served with tasty *beignets*. It is relatively inexpensive; you can eat here for as little as $5 at noon or in the evening. Good value for your money.

A small, rather plain restaurant, **Coops** *($; 1109 Decatur St., French Quarter, ☎ 525-9053)* serves good gumbo and delicious po'boys.

The **Croissant d'Or** pastry shop *($; every day 7am to 5pm; 615-617 Ursulines, French Quarter, ☎ 524-4663)* offers a lunch special that might include delicious green-pea soup with a ham and cheese sandwich, served with salad. It is best to avoid the microwave-oven-heated sandwiches. The coffee is mediocre, but the croissants and brioches prepared by Maurice Delechelle are exceptional for New Orleans. Classic French pastries are also available here. The lovely interior courtyard with its fountain is the ideal place in which to eat when the temperature allows, but should be avoided on very humid days. Good value.

Acme Oyster House *($-$$; lunch $5 to $10/person; 724 Iberville St., French Quarter, ☎ 522-5973)*. Generations of New Orleanians have passed through this restaurant over the years. The establishment specializes in fresh fish and seafood; it is particularly renowned for oysters, shrimp and catfish. Accepted credit cards: Visa, American Express.

The **French Market Restaurant and Bar** *($-$$; Mon to Thu 11am to midnight, Fri to Sun 11am to 1am; 1001 Decatur St., French Quarter, ☎ 581-9855)* is popular with locals and tourists alike. Depending on the season, crab or crayfish in a spicy court-bouillon, a fabulous po'boy or a muffaletta, pasta dishes and Creole food are prepared here. This is another good place for savouring oysters.

Café de la Madeleine *($-$$; every day, morning to night; 547 St. Ann St., French Quarter, ☎ 568-9950)* is close to what used to be Place d'Armes but is now Jackson Square. Both its ambiance and breakfast are French. This bistro and café, which is also a bakery, boasts wonderful bread, baked right on the premises, in a wood-burning oven. Expect to pay about $5 for breakfast.

Napoleon House *($-$$; Mon to Thu 11am to midnight, Fri and Sat 11am to 2am, Sun 11am to 7pm; 500 Chartres St., French Quarter, ☎ 524-9752)*. It is said that this residence, dating from 1791, had been reserved for the Emperor Napoleon, should he come to seek refuge in Louisiana. Having a cocktail in the charming back courtyard is a must. With classical music playing in the background, patrons can enjoy good sandwiches; a small, inexpensive menu *($5)* is also offered.

🦞 The café of the **Le Richelieu** hotel *($-$$; every day 7am to 9pm; 1234 Chartres St., French Quarter,* ☎ *529-2492)* serves good breakfasts, even at night. The mood on the terrace, which faces a lovely interior courtyard and its pool, is pleasant and fancy-free. The bar crowd consists of local regulars. Sandwiches and steaks are featured on the menu. Everyone here is very friendly, from the big boss Frank S. Rochefort to the manager Joanne Kirkpatrick, the barman Armand and the waiter Michael (an ace at breakfast), as well as Lester, the waiter who takes over in the evening.

Praline Connection *($$; Sun to Thu 11am to 10:30pm, Fri and Sat 4pm to midnight; 542 Frenchmen St. at Chartres St., in the Faubourg Marigny,* ☎ *943-3934)* features Creole specialties and family fare typical of Southern Louisiana. The Creole and African-American (soul food) cuisines are excellent, the ambiance is relaxed and the bill is never high. Featured dishes include gumbo, Creole-style stuffed crab, stuffed peppers, crayfish étoufée, grilled chicken, jambalaya, rice with lima beans, bread pudding with praline sauce and sweet-potato pie. The restaurant also has a sweetshop where clients can purchase cookies and the most famous pecan pralines in all of Louisiana (an old recipe whose origins date back to the French Colonial era).

🦞 A very talented chef presides at **Bayona** *($$-$$$; Mon to Fri 11:30am to 1:30pm, Mon to Sat 6pm to 10:30pm; reservations required; 430 Dauphine St., French Quarter,* ☎ *525-4455)*. Susan Spicer prepares exquisite meat and fish dishes, inspired by early fruits and vegetables, which prove to be both successful and flavourful. Patrons have the choice of eating in the charming dining room or the magnificently flowering interior courtyard, all the while being lulled by the gentle murmur of the fountain. On the fixed-price dinner menu: rabbit aiguillette in a pecan crust with a mustard glaze; braised sea kale with mustard; young rabbit and Portobello mushroom cream soup; lemon sole with spicy red beans and fresh coriander pesto with avocado "salsa"; ginger-rhubarb cake with custard, fresh blackberries and crème fraîche. Excellent California wines are offered by the glass. Good value.

🦞 **Bella Luna** *($$-$$$; every day 6pm to 10:30pm, until 9:30pm on Sun; reservations recommended; 914 North Peters*

St., French Quarter, ☎ *529-1583)* is located behind the French Market. This fashionable restaurant, with lovely table settings and a well-trained staff, offers an unobstructed view of the Mississippi. Chef Horst Pleifer's cuisine reveals Creole and European flavours. Savoured dishes included shrimp soup garnished with carrots julienne, mussels, roasted garlic, fresh basil and dill; fresh peach, strawberry and blackberry sorbet; redfish in a cashew crust with *beurre blanc* and blood orange; Tahitian vanilla *crème brulée* with a banana biscuit and chocolate ice cream. Good value.

Di Piazza *($$-$$$; lunch $10 to $15, dinner $15 to $20; Tue to Thu 11:30am to 10:30pm, Fri 11:30am to 11pm, Sat 5pm to 11pm, closed Sun; reservations required; 337 Dauphine St., French Quarter,* ☎ *525-3335)*. This Italian trattoria has been established in the French Quarter for a few years now and has maintained a clientele of regulars. Others have gone in search of novelty. Its specialties include fried conch, veal cutlet stuffed with prosciutto and mozzarella, oysters poached in olive oil, and more. The menu has lovely and delicious culinary finds in store for diners.

Mr. B's Bistro *($$-$$$; every day, lunch and dinner; 11:30am to 3pm and 5:30pm to 10:30pm, brunch on Sun 10:30am to 3pm; 201 Royal St., French Quarter,* ☎ *523-2078)*. With its marble tables scattered throughout a large dining room and lunchtime clientele of bureaucrats and business people, this establishment is warmly reminiscent of a Parisian bistro. Waiters don the customary service uniform: black vest, white shirt, bow tie and long white apron. The concoctions of Michelle McRaney, the talented chef whose menu changes with the season, are flavourful and aromatic and inspired by New Orleans' Creole and French culinary heritages. Savoured dishes included cream of crayfish and cauliflower soup; "jambalaya pasta" with fettucini and spinach, fresh tomatoes, Gulf shrimp, chitterlings (smoked sausage), duck, beef and chicken; bread pudding with whiskey sauce. The restaurant offers a few good Louisiana wines. Service is prompt and amiable. Live jazz is featured during brunch on Sundays.

Pasta E Vino *($$-$$$; Tue to Sun 5pm to 12:30am; reservations recommended; 240 Bourbon St., French Quarter,* ☎ *523-3181)*. Legend has it that this magnificent house, built in 1807 and better known as the Old Absinthe House, was once frequented by the famous pirate/patriot Jean Lafitte. The fresh pasta is made on the premises, and all the great Italian culinary classics are featured here. Its wine list enjoys an excellent reputation.

Ristorante di Carmelo *($$-$$$; lunch $5 to $10, dinner $15 to $20; reservations recommended; 541 Decatur St., French Quarter, ☎ 522-0074).* Ceilings with cypress beams hand-squared by artisans, superb Italian ceramic tiles and luxurious mahogany appliqués make up this restaurant's exceptional decor. The restaurant also boasts a balcony on which guests can dine. Among the specialties to be sampled are the grilled or sautéed salmon and *antipasto fredo* as well as exquisitely prepared veal in all its guises. The following languages are all spoken here: English, Italian, French, Spanish, German and Swedish.

Bacco *($$-$$$$; breakfast $5 to $10, lunch $10 to $15, dinner $15 to $20; Mon to Sat 7am to 10am, 11:30am to 3pm and 5:30pm to 10:30pm, brunch on Sun 10:30am to 3pm; reservations recommended; 310 Chartres St., French Quarter, ☎ 522-CIAO or 522-2426)* is located right next to the Post Office. Gothic arches, Venetian chandeliers and Baroque-style murals are part of the eccentric and extravagant decor. The place is pleasant nonetheless; service is courteous and attentive toward a relaxed clientele of all ages. Here, Italian-inspired Creole cuisine is prepared, or is that Creole-inspired Italian cuisine? No matter what the definition, the presentation of the dishes is exquisite and you are sure to be pleased with the food. A few of their specialties include oyster and eggplant ravioli; crayfish pizza; pasta with wild mushrooms and herbs; "jambalaya" risotto; barbecued duck or lamb. The restaurant also offers valet parking. Languages spoken: Italian, Spanish and English. Good value.

The **Pelican Club** *($$-$$$$; every day from 5:30pm on; 312 Exchange Alley, ☎ 523-1504)* offers a fixed-price menu at $19.50 (a 17% tip is added for groups of eight or more) between 5:30pm and 6pm. The large bar and its round tables make it reminiscent of a private club in the Edwardian era. The menu features little crayfish and shrimp cakes; escargots and crayfish *à la duxelle* of mushrooms, with a tequila, garlic and butter sauce; smoked and roasted duck supreme with mushroom ravioli; fillet of fish in a pecan and coconut crust;

vanilla and brandy *crème brulée*; orange and sour cream cheesecake.

Alex Patout's *($$$; every night 5:30pm to 10pm; 221 Royal St., French Quarter, ☎ 525-7788)* serves cuisine typical of Southern Louisiana, prepared with local ingredients. The menu features Louisiana-style won tons; shrimp in a remoulade sauce; seafood and smoked tasso (dried-meat) pasta; Cajun-style roasted duck étoufée; suckling pig; sautéed crayfish; bread pudding and brownies. The soberly decorated 125-seat dining room is most welcoming. One unfortunate drawback is that groups making their way to the other dining rooms (which are spread out over three levels) have to pass behind your table. Service, however, is very amiable. Reservations are recommended. Parking is available. Good value.

Unless you want to wait in line, it's best to make reservations at the **Palace Café** *($$$; Mon to Sat 11:30am to 2:30pm, every day 5:30pm to 10pm, brunch on Sun 10:30am to 2:30pm; 605 Canal St., French Quarter, ☎ 523-1661)*. The service and decor are reminiscent of great Parisian cafés, and the cuisine is both Creole and French. On the menu: shrimp and pasta Provençale; shrimp barbecued in Abita beer (a good local beer); Maine lobster or grilled fish; bread pudding with white chocolate.

The Court of Two Sisters *($$$-$$$$; lunch buffet $21, dinner $25-$30; every day 9am to 3pm and 5:30pm to 11pm; 613 Royal St., French Quarter, ☎ 522-7273)*. This magnificent oasis in the heart of the French Quarter boasts an enchanting terrace. In the evening, it is illuminated by antique gas torches and jazz bands play there. Unfortunately, the staff can be brusque and the establishment has lost its good reputation with the locals. Its cuisine is nothing more than a mass of clichés. Every day, a buffet is set out, offering about fifty different dishes. The staff speaks English and Spanish.

Galatoire's *($$$-$$$$; Tue to Sat 11:30am to 9pm; Sun noon to 9pm; 209 Bourbon St., ☎ 525-2021)*. The *ne plus ultra* of New Orleans cuisine, this restaurant is prized for its lunchtime fare. The establishment does not take reservations – first come, first served! To avoid the queue, show up after 1pm. Men are required to wear a tie at dinner.

G & E Courtyard *($$$-$$$$; Fri to Sun 11am to 2:30pm, Tue to Thu and Sun 6pm to 10pm, until 11pm Fri and Sat; 1113 Decatur St., French Quarter, ☎ 528-9376)* serves Italian food that is good though inconsistent from lunch to dinner; dishes here are invariably seasoned with vinegar – sometimes a bit too much? In any case, this does not seem to deter clients. Indeed, its interior courtyard is very popular, though only the lucky ones manage to snare a table there. Nevertheless, the air conditioned interior is charming and its two carriage gateways open out on the street, allowing patrons to observe the constant stream of motley tourists walking past. Lovely fresh artichokes are charmingly arranged on a shelf, but these merely serve as decoration and are nowhere to be found on the menu. The dishes are artfully presented and beautifully cooked. The menu features such dishes as Caesar salad with fried oysters; shrimp tempura with deep-fried straw potatoes; roasted pullet with rosemary; lamb sausages with tomato and basil pasta.

K-Paul's Louisiana Kitchen *($$$-$$$$; Mon to Fri 11:30am to 2:30pm and 5:30pm to 10pm, closed Sat and Sun; 416 Chartres St., French Quarter, ☎ 524-7394, reservations ☎ 596-2530).* This establishment owes its good reputation to the famous Cajun chef Paul Prudhomme. The restaurant is on two levels: the upstairs and balcony are for those with reservations; the ground floor looks more like a bistro. The kitchen is open and a double of Paul, only thinner but still well-padded, presides there. The menu is peppered with Cajun and Creole classics as well as original dishes, composed of early produce and fresh products from the market. Among dishes not to be missed are the traditional chicken and sausage gumbo, the famous blackened fish (the celebrated chef Prudhomme's creation) and the gorgeous sweet potato and pecan pie with Chantilly cream, laced with cognac and Grand Marnier.

The **Bistro at the Hotel Maison de Ville** *($$$$; Mon to Sat 11:30am to 2:30pm, Sun to Thu 6pm to 10pm, Fri and Sat 11am to 11pm; reservations required; Hotel Maison de Ville, 727 Toulouse St., French Quarter, ☎ 528-9206)*, recreates a Parisian bistro atmosphere (very popular in New Orleans) and can accommodate 40 people in its dining room and 20 more on its pleasant flowered courtyard. Excellent wine list and tastings by the glass.

Broussard's *($$$$; every night 5:30pm to 10pm, brunch and jazz on Sun 10:30am to 2pm; 819 Conti St., French Quarter, ☎ 581-3866)* is a must with its very European cachet and lovely flowering courtyard set with tables. New owners have taken over. Among the treats are crab and shrimp cheesecake; Napoleon sea perch and Broussard veal. Reservations are required. Diners can be served in English, French, Spanish, German or Italian.

Antoine's *($$$$; approx. $50; Mon to Sat 11:30am to 2pm and 5:30pm to 9:30pm, closed Sun and public holidays; 713 St. Louis St., French Quarter, ☎ 581-4422)*. This restaurant, well-known on both a national and international level, has been around since 1840. Since Antoine Alciatore of Marseilles first opened it, the establishment has been run by five generations of his descendants. The famous Rockefeller oysters were first created in this very restaurant. The establishment has several reception rooms, and some can accommodate up to 700 people. The rather rustic decor features countless photographs of celebrities who have set foot here. The menu is made up of French and Creole classics (the menu is in French) and its dishes are well-prepared and particularly delicious. Service is very professional. The staff speaks French, Spanish and English.

Arnaud's *($$$$; approx. $50, not including wine, service and taxes; reservations recommended; parking at 912 Iberville St.; lunch Mon to Fri 11:30am to 2:30pm, dinner Sun to Thu 6pm to 10pm, Fri and Sat 6pm to 10:30pm, brunch on Sun 10am to 2:30pm, closed for lunch Sat; 813 Bienville St., French Quarter, ☎ 523-5433)* was founded by Arnaud Cazenave in 1918 and now belongs to the Casbarians. The Cazenaves enjoyed celebrating Mardi Gras, and from 1937 to 1968, Irma Cazenave never missed the festivities; she made her own dazzling costumes as well as those of her husband's. She was queen of the Carnival on several occasions. Upstairs, a museum exhibits Dame Cazenave's fabulous collection. The Gulf of Mexico is teeming with fish, crustaceans and seafood and these fresh products are prepared in a variety of ways: Arnaud shrimp, potted turtle, oysters Suzette, Bourgeois crayfish mousse, seafood court-bouillon, shrimp and eggplant casserole, *pompano* in a crust, alligator with hot sauce, Provençale frogs legs. Meat dishes include quail in red wine sauce, Rochambeau braised chicken, rack of lamb diablo, Caën-style tripe, and more. Cheeses, salads, classic desserts and Arnaud's *café brûlot* round off this dazzling menu. Service is impeccable.

Brennan's *($$$$; approx. $40, including wine, service and taxes; reservations required; every day brunch 8am to 2:30pm, Tue to Fri lunch 11:30am to 2:30pm and dinner 6pm to 10pm; 417 Royal St., French Quarter, ☎ 525-9711)* is renowned for its breakfasts and brunches. All the same, it is hardly a gourmet's paradise; their eggs Benedict are smothered by a mass of béchamel sauce, and their other preparations are as heavy as they are uninspired. It is very expensive and quite disappointing. The dining rooms do, however, give out on a magnificent and serene subtropical garden, with a fountain, banana trees, flowers and plants, that is best enjoyed with good friends. This place is a must when visiting New Orleans. Among the overpriced items offered for breakfast, brunch or dinner: oyster soup, Creole-style onion soup, eggs *sardou*, eggs *hussarde*, Rockefeller oysters, Chantecler fillet steak, grill-smoked red mullet, Cajun pepper chicken, Gulf shrimp chitterlings, chef Roussel's sautéed veal, lemon tartlets and bananas Foster.

The talented chef Anne Kearny officiates at **Peristyle** *($$$$; lunch Fri 11:30am to 2pm, dinner Tue to Thu 6pm to 10pm, until 11pm Fri and Sat; 1041 Dumaine St, French Quarter, ☎ 593-9535)*. Her French-inspired cuisine has retained a distinctive New Orleans flavour, as demonstrated by the earthiness of the cream of mushroom soup, well-seasoned with pepper and chillies. The crab and horseradish salad is served on a bed of roasted beets with marinated red onions. The grilled puppy drum fillet, a Gulf of Mexico fish, is well-prepared and served on a bed of sticky rice with tomatoes and spinach, enhanced by a spoonful of pesto; a shrimp and saffron sauce surrounds this delightfully prepared dish. Among the fabulous desserts is the lemon pudding, spread over sponge cake and garnished with crystallized lemon rinds and blackcurrant jam. Good French and American wines. Service is rather aloof, however. An affluent and stylish clientele of all ages frequents this dining room, which makes itself out to be a bistro despite the austerity of the place; many come out of curiosity and some are confined to small spaces here and there.

CENTRAL BUSINESS DISTRICT AND WAREHOUSE DISTRICT

The following establishments are located on the map on p 177.

Red Bike Bakery & Café *($; Mon to Fri 11am to 3pm, Tue to Thu 6pm to 9:30pm, until 11pm Fri and Sat; 746 Tchoupitoulas St., ☎ 529-2553)* serves home-made bread as well as turkey or sausage gumbo soups, sandwiches and a few cooked meals such as fettucini with mushrooms, sesame chicken, and more.

Café Bon Ton *($-$$; 11am to 2pm and 5pm to 9:30pm; 401 Magazine St., at Natchez, ☎ 524-3386)*. Since 1953, the Pierces have been preparing dishes here derived from family recipes: "Bon Ton" red snapper, crayfish étouffée, shrimp and oysters in every shape and form as well as wonderful bread pudding.

Mother's restaurant *($-$$; Mon to Sat 5am to 10pm, Sun 7am to 10pm; 401 Poydras St., ☎ 523-9656)* is close to Riverwalk. Traditional New Orleans cuisine is prepared here. Mother's is the best restaurant in the world for smoked ham. The establishment offers a wide choice of po'boys, with ham, of course, but also with roast beef, crayfish, oysters or chicken. The standard American breakfast is served at all times. Cafeteria-style setting.

Bolstered by the success of their enterprise in the Faubourg Marigny, Curtis Moore and Cecil Kaigler, have opened **Praline Connection #2** *($-$$; every day 11am to 10pm; 901 and 907 South Peters St., between St. Joseph and North Diamond, ☎ 523-3973)* in a huge space, in a soulless neighbourhood where renovation efforts are being carried out. In addition to the restaurant, a stage is set up for jazz, R&B or gospel groups (see "Entertainment", p 217). The trademark black and white room is surrounded by a backdrop of façades of Creole houses. The food is the same as on Frenchmen Street, but not as tasty, that is heavy and mostly deep-fried family fare. On the menu: head cheese, battered with deep-fried soft-shell crab; peppers stuffed with sausage and shrimp; meat loaf; barbecued pork chop (huge and overcooked on this occasion) with hot sauce; fried chicken in brown sauce. Everything is well-seasoned with chillies. The restaurant also serves deep-fried alligator... The bread pudding with praline sauce is not to be missed.

Bizou *($-$$$; lunch and dinner, except Mon; 701 St. Charles Ave., ☎ 524-4114)* was opened by Daniel Bonnot, former chef-owner of the Chez Daniel restaurant, now the Bistro de Ville, in Metairie. In this bistro, the cooks transform the classics in their own way, but not always with success. The vichyssoise was nothing more than a purée of cream and green onions, the spring roll (sushi) bland and the garnishes usually found in the Niçoise salad conspicuously missing. For lunch, it is perhaps best to have one of their delicious sandwiches, as the regulars do. On the afternoon of our visit, the waiter was neither eager nor friendly.

The decor at **Bistro Allegro** *($$; every day 11:30am to 2:30pm; 1100 Poydras St., room 101, ☎ 582-2350)* is Art Deco. As it is right downtown, business people crowd in at lunch time. Here, Creole cooking is influenced by Italian cuisine and the fusion of the two, it is said, is utterly harmonious. Free parking. The staff speaks French, Spanish, Italian and English.

Mulate's *($$; every day 11am to 11pm, Mon to Fri lunch Cajun buffet; 201 Julia St., ☎ 522-1492)* is situated in the Warehouse District, across from the convention centre. This restaurant is very popular with tourists. Unfortunately, the cuisine is not what it used to be, but the music is authentic and the performers are genuine Cajun musicians and singers from Lafayette, Abbéville, St. Martinville, Eunice or New Iberia. The ambiance is terrific. Reservations are recommended.

Bistro La Gauloise *($$-$$$; breakfast $5 to $15, lunch $10 to $20 and dinner $15 to $30; every day 6:30am to 10pm; Le Meridien, 614 Canal St., ☎ 527-6712)*, the famous bistro in the Meridien hotel, faces bustling Canal Street, across from the French Quarter. The ambiance is warm and relaxed. À la carte dishes, a daily menu and a buffet are offered, providing something for everyone. On the menu: crayfish gumbo; shrimp Provençale; "vetiver" lamb (in a cabbage leaf); seafood pennine with olive oil and basil; grilled veal chop seasoned with tarragon, served with spinach gnocchi; bread pudding; Creole-style cheesecake. The place is renowned for its Sunday brunch, livened by a jazz band *(10:30am to 2:30pm, valet parking at 609 Common Street)*.

Those who do not know their way around the neighbourhood may have trouble locating the entrance to the **Économie** restaurant *($$-$$$; Tue to Fri 11:30am to 2pm and 5pm to 10pm, until 11pm Fri and Sat; 325 Girod St., at Commerce St., ☎ 524-7405)*. The restaurant is set in buildings that once flourished as warehouses and factories. Despite the neighbourhood's monotony, the inside reveals an amazing ambiance and Mexican colours adorn the walls on which lovely paintings by contemporary artists hang; in short, it is attractive, vital and fresh. The chef-proprietor Keith Mallini – whose father and mother are Italian and Japanese, respectively – demonstrates perfect skill in the kitchen. What a treat to find a genuine and delicious vegetable soup, a Caesar salad made with spinach and enhanced with a perfect dressing. The menu offers several choices: salmon, crayfish, chicken, guinea fowl and pork. They also serve an excellent New York strip steak, nice and rare if you so desire, with a true cream, pepper and cognac sauce; this tasty cut of meat comes with fried scalloped potatoes and sautéed snowpeas. The *crème brulée* and the gargantuan chocolate truffle cake with custard are equally divine. All this and more can be enjoyed at marble-topped tables. Good value.

Sapphire *($$-$$$$; lunch $7 to $12, dinner $14 to $30; 228 Camp St., ☎ 571-7500)*. Good things are being said about this newcomer; though it has yet to prove itself. Poached oysters in hollandaise sauce, Peking duck and rack of lamb are a few selections from its menu. The restaurant was designed by Mario Villa, a New Orleans artist.

Mike's on the Avenue *($$$$, $$-$$$ lunch; Mon to Fri 11:30am to 2pm, every day 6pm to 10pm; 628 St. Charles Ave., Lafayette Hotel, ☎ 523-1709)* is run by the very esteemed and very popular chef Mike Fennelly along with Vicky Bayley. The dining room is decorated with watercolour paintings done by the chef himself, who also holds a degree in architecture. The restaurant is on the hotel's ground floor and its dining room opens out on Lafayette Square and Gallier Hall. Their clientele mainly consists of business people. The food here is a blend of Californian, Mexican, Japanese and Louisianian cuisines. This fusion is rather successful, as demonstrated by the delicious rice rectangles (sushi) stacked like sandwiches with nori seaweed, blackened tuna, a remoulade of crayfish and smoked salmon; the grilled tomato tortilla soup appears as a delectable creamed, peppered and spiced purée with a faintly smoky flavour; strips of trout tempura are served with pecan rice and a purée of green onions that is somewhat bland but impressively presented; for dessert, there is the traditional New Orleans bread pudding served in a pie crust, covered in raisins and chocolate sauce (a real treat!) and *crème brulée* made with real cream. The bread is home-made. It is less expensive at lunch. Apparently, Mike Fennelly is about to open a restaurant in California: let us just hope this won't affect the St. Charles Avenue establishment.

Emeril's *($$$-$$$$; lunch $10 to $15, dinner $15 to $20; Mon to Fri 11:30am to 2pm, Mon to Sat 6pm to 10pm; reservations required; 800 Tchoupitoulas St., ☎ 528-9393).* Housed in an old warehouse, the restaurant is currently enjoying great popularity and people come here from all across the United States. Groups of stylish patrons gather round large tables; jeans, casual jackets and other unconventional attire are prohibited. Creole or American *nouvelle cuisine* is featured here. Service is warm and friendly and most of the waiters are Latino. Real gourmets, however, will find their flashy cuisine disappointing. The staff speaks Spanish, French, German and English.

✕ UPTOWN

Piccadilly Cafeteria *($-$$; every day 11am to 8:30pm; 3800 South Carrollton Ave., ☎ 482-0776).* There are several Piccadilly's in Louisiana. Many daily specials are offered here, with something for everyone. No credit cards accepted.

Uglesich's *($-$$; Mon to Fri 9:30am to 4pm; 1238 Barron St., ☎ 523-8571).* Small places that are little known to tourists – the neighbourhoods being somewhat disreputable – often have pleasant surprises in store for visitors. Large onion and potato sacks are piled up between the tables in this café, with its concrete floors and look of an old neighbourhood grocer's shop. For lunch, patrons come and eat shrimp or oyster po'boys at the counter. A mixed clientele of business people, blue-collar workers and students crowd the dining room to savour gumbo enhanced by brown roux, spicy crayfish bisque, fresh oysters in their half shells from the Gulf of Mexico or a soft-shell crab sandwich. Between orders, the amiable Karin peels and cuts up the potatoes, the major ingredient of some of the best fries in town. No credit cards accepted. Good value.

After having travelled around the world, Felix Gallerani finally settled in New Orleans. For the last few years, the affable host has been the heart and soul of **Café Volage** *($-$$$; Sun brunch $12,95; every day 11am to 3pm and 4pm to 10pm; 720 Dublin St., Riverbend district, one street west of Carrollton,* ☎ *861-4227)*. He has built a lovely terrace behind the little "shotgun" house, classified as a historic monument. The place, however, is a bit run down and could certainly use a thorough cleaning. A small menu offers Italian, French and Creole specialties. Among these are onion or gumbo soup; seafood fettucini in wine and cream sauce; veal scallopini Marsala; steak and fries (the fries are home-made); chocolate mousse or *crème brulée*. The host, holding court at a table like a prince upon his throne, welcomes patrons with a huge Havana cigar in the corner of his mouth!

Pizzas, pasta, and a terrace beneath the trees, that is what you'll find at **Figaro's Pizzeria** *($$; Mon and Tue 11:30am to 10:30pm, until 11:30pm Fri and Sat, noon to 10pm Sun; 7900 Maple St., two streets north of St. Charles Ave., just after Audubon Park,* ☎ *866-0100)*. The restaurant makes Neapolitan-style pizza with garlic butter and Mozzarella cheese, and a choice of toppings such as shrimp, smoked salmon, spinach, feta cheese, etc. Standard American pizza garnished with tomato sauce, pepperoni, green peppers, onions and mushrooms is also served as are a few pasta dishes. For dessert: New York cheesecake, fudge pie, brownies and peanut-butter pie.

Eating at **Straya** *($$; Sun to Thu 11am to midnight, until 2am Fri and Sat; 2001 St. Charles Ave.,* ☎ *593-9955; 4517 Veterans Boulevard, Metairie,* ☎ *887-8873)* is somewhat like dining in a discotheque. Star-studded black tables and gaudily-coloured couches are dispersed throughout a vast space, dotted with Hollywood-esque gilded banana trees. In this galactic universe, the star theme dominates all accessories. The current trend for fusion cuisine is apparent here, with a selection of Creole, Eurasian, Cajun and Californian cuisines to which are added Italian and Japanese touches. Servings are

JoAnn Clevenger - Epicure and Gourmet

The generous and epicurean JoAnn Clevenger, proprietor of the superlative Upperline restaurant (see p 203), bestows a list of her favourite restaurants and dishes to her clients: **Uglesich's** for its shrimp gumbo and barbecued oysters (see p 199); **Mandich** for its oysters *à la bordelaise (\$-\$\$; 3200 St. Claude Ave., in the east, near Louisia St., ☎ 947-9553)*; the home-made ice cream at **Gabrielle's** (see p 205); **Windsor Court** for its desserts *(\$\$\$\$; 300 Gravier St., in the Central Business District, ☎ 522-1992)*; **Bayona**'s vegetarian dishes (see p 189); **Praline Connection** for its Creole cuisine and soul food (see p 189); the "specials" and "extras" at **Peristyle** (see p 195); the gumbo at the fast food counter at **Krauss** *(store, 1201 Canal St.)*, at **Gumbo Shop** *(\$-\$\$; 630 St. Peter St., French Quarter, ☎ 525-1486)*, at **Alex Patout's** (see p 192) and at **Dooky Chase** (see p 205); **Galatoire's** crab (see p 192); calf's sweetbreads at **Clancy** *(\$\$-\$\$\$; 6100 Annunciation St., Uptown, south of Magazine St., ☎ 895-1111)*; the crab cakes at **Gautreau's** *(\$\$\$\$; 1728 Soniat St., Uptown, ☎ 899-7397)*; **Brigtsen** for its fish (see p 203); **K-Paul's** for its pasta with tasso cream (see p 193); the bread pudding soufflé at **Commander's Palace** (see p 204); the lamb at **La Provence** *(25020 Hwy. 190, Lacombe, on the north shore of Lake Pontchartrain, ☎ 626-7662)*; and **Emeril's** for its crayfish cakes (see p 199). JoAnn takes part in all culinary events and adds to this list the garlic festival and theme dinners (Jane Austen, Monet, Thomas Jefferson, *le Festin de Babette* [Babette's Feast], etc.) that she organizes during her sumptuous brunches at the **Upperline** restaurant.

huge. A few specialties include nori seaweed California rolls; sushi made of rice, crab and avocado with horseradish and ginger; crispy pizza topped with cheese; fillet of trout in an almond crust; barbecued shrimp fettucine; roasted chicken; tiramisu crepe; bread pudding laced with white chocolate and apple pizza with Amaretto cream. Patrons are warmly greeted and service is as sparkling as the decor. Good Californian wines served by the glass.

At the very popular bistro-creperie **La Crepe Nanou** *($$-$$$; every day 6pm to 10pm, until 11pm Fri and Sat; 1410 Robert St., between Magazine and St. Charles, ☎ 899-2670)*, the menu is in French (it features the classic *escargots de Bourgogne*). Specialties include whole grilled fish; *moules marinière* (mussels cooked in white wine); onion soup; Greek chicken and rice soup; leg of lamb and veal scallopini. There are also crepes, of course: with crab and spinach; ratatouille; cheese and onion; crayfish; beef bourguignon and about fifteen different dessert crepes.

Kelsey's *($$-$$$; Tue to Fri 11:30am to 2pm, Fri and Sat 5:30pm to 10pm; 3923 Magazine St., ☎ 897-6722)* with its warm French-café ambiance is set in a very quaint neighbourhood full of charming boutiques. Randy Barlow's fusion cuisine draws its inspiration as much from Cajun and Creole schools as it does from other cuisines world-wide. Perusing his menu is tantamount to a culinary tour of the world, as the following savoured dishes attest to: cream of artichoke hearts and mushroom soup; chicken and chitterlings gumbo; tomatoes and *provolone* cheese on a bed of lettuce and red onions, with a mustard vinaigrette; oyster, Brie and herb tartlet; crayfish fritters with honey and Meaux mustard sauce; stuffed breast of smoked duck; soft-shell crab stuffed with seafood and green mayonnaise; chocolate nut cake and lemon pie.

Kyoto *($$-$$$; lunch Mon to Fri 11:30am to 2:30pm, Sat noon to 3:30pm, dinner Mon to Thu 5pm to 10pm, until 10:30pm Fri and Sat; 4920 Prytania St., ☎ 891-3644)* is currently the most popular sushi place in town; what matters here is the freshness of the ingredients. Besides the rolls, there are shrimp tempura; *miso*, noodle, shrimp and vegetable soups; as well as chicken or beef teriyaki and sashimi.

The affable Hubert Sandot of the **Martinique Bistro** *($$-$$$; fixed-price menu $23,50; every day 5:30pm to 9:30pm; 5908 Magazine St., ☎ 891-8495)* is quite loquacious, and a real charmer who enjoys chatting with the customers. He prepares a few classic French dishes and improvises with a range of Italian, Caribbean or Indian dishes, depending on deliveries. The menu features such items as leek and carrot soup; eggplant with goat cheese; endives with nuts, apples and blue cheese;

steamed mussels cooked in white wine and herbs; sautéed shrimp with dried mangoes and curry as well as Provençale braised leg of lamb. This warm and friendly little restaurant remains a place worth visiting in New Orleans. Good value.

Pascal Manale *($$-$$$; lunch approx. $10, dinner $15 to $20; Mon to Fri 11:30am to 10pm, Sat 4pm to 10pm, Sun 4pm to 9pm; 1838 Napoleon Ave., ☎ 895-4877)* is a classic, renowned for its grilled shrimp, its seafood, as well as its shellfish and oyster bar.

One of New Orleanians' great favourites remains **Brigtsen's** *($$$$; Tue to Sat 5:30pm to 10pm; 723 Dante St., at Leake Ave., Riverbend District, ☎ 861-7610)*, comfortably nestled in a lovely cottage in the residential district of Riverbend. Its chef, Frank Brigtsen, prepares innovative food inspired by Cajun and Creole cooking that is the delight of gourmets; it is best to make reservations. The menu features tomato, crouton and blue cheese salad with avocado vinaigrette; rabbit and sausage gumbo; "Bienville" oyster gratin; zucchini flowers stuffed with ricotta, crayfish and mushrooms, flavoured with basil oil; grilled fish, crispy crab with Parmesan and lemon purée; blackened tuna with smoked corn sauce; sautéed veal and crayfish with mushrooms, topped with Parmesan sauce; bread and banana pudding with rum sauce; pecan pie with caramel sauce; champagne zabaglione with fruit and a hint of crème fraîche.

At the **Upperline** restaurant *($$$-$$$$; Wed to Sun 5:30pm to 9:30pm, brunch on Sun 11:30am to 2pm from $13.50 to $22.50; 1413 Upperline St., near Magazine St., ☎ 891-9822)*, JoAnn Clevenger, the owner, is only too happy to take the time to chat with customers; she likes to share and it is with this enthusiastic spirit of generosity that diners are invited to her table. The place is positively dazzling and adorned with paintings by Martin LaBorde (see p 231). The beautiful bouquets on each of the tables come from the small flower garden surrounding the house. Chef Richard Benz's cuisine is particularly flavourful; there are two gumbos: seafood and okra gumbo or the more intense duck and chitterlings gumbo, enhanced by a spicy roux. Among the restaurant's fine hors d'oeuvres, the fried green tomatoes with shrimp remoulade and the fried veal sweetbreads on crisp corn polenta, on a bed of mushrooms, with *demi-glace* sauce. Dishes include grilled Gulf fish with warm Niçoise salad, tapenade and basil lemon-butter;

braised lamb in wine, with saffron risotto and *gremolata*; port and garlic crispy duck. A couple of tasty desserts: *tarte Tatin* with apple sorbet and chocolate truffle cake.

Commander's Palace *($$$$; $40 to $50; Tue to Fri 11:30am to 2pm, Sat 11am to 2pm, Sun 10am to 2pm, every night 6pm to 10pm; 1403 Washington Ave., ☎ 899-8221),* situated in the historic Garden District, enjoys an excellent reputation with New Orleanians. Without being jingoistic, some even classify it as the best restaurant in the country – and they truly believe it. The establishment offers classic Creole cuisine, and its chef occasionally tries his hand at unexpected concoctions. The restaurant's Victorian style is very appealing. The dining rooms can accommodate up to 100 guests; other lovely little private rooms are ideal for smaller, more intimate gatherings.

MID-CITY

Café Degas *($-$$; lunch and dinner $5 to $10; every day 10:30am to 2:30pm and 5:30pm to 10:30pm, brunch Sat and Sun; 3127 Esplanade Ave., ☎ 945-5635).* This friendly little place, on elegant Esplanade Avenue, bears the name of the celebrated French painter, engraver and sculptor Edgar Degas, whose brothers, who still signed their name de Gas, endeavoured to make their fortune here. This restaurant's honest prices make it ideal for those on limited budgets. Specialties include shrimp and couscous salad with mustard vinaigrette; smoked trout with garlic mayonnaise; veal sweetbreads *à la grenobloise*; a variety of omelettes; rack of lamb; sirloin steak with shallots; key-lime pie and chocolate and peanut butter pie. Good value.

Some restaurants don't look like much and **Lola's** *($-$$; every day 6pm to 10pm; 3312 Esplanade Ave., facing Gabrielle's, ☎ 488-6946)* certainly falls into this category. Though it's run down and its few rows of tables lack decor, it does offer a wide range of specialties such as garlic soup; grilled squid; beef, vegetarian or Valencia-style paella; grilled tuna; spinach linguine; *caldereta* (lamb stew with tomatoes, wine and peppers) and caramel cream with nougat icing.

Mandina's *($-$$; Mon to Thu 11am to 10:30pm, until 11pm Fri and Sat, Sun noon to 9pm; 3800 Canal St., ☎ 482-9179)* restaurant, which is really more of a snack bar, attracts a local crowd with its popular turtle soup, red beans and rice, fried oyster platter or soft-shell crab, oyster po'boy, fried shrimp and catfish, all served with fries. The menu also offers daily specials, Creole-American-Italian family fare (trout Amandine, cabbage and corned beef, turkey breast in oyster sauce and sweet potatoes, Creole shrimp on a bed of rice and green peas). The establishment is located in a middle-class residential neighbourhood, close to City Park. Dining there is a gustative experience. No credit cards accepted.

The **Dooky Chase** restaurant *($-$$$; buffet $19.95, daily menu $8,25, dinner $25; 2301 Orleans Ave., ☎ 821-0535)* enjoys a legendary reputation in Mid-City, a disadvantaged neighbourhood. Leah Chase, the chef, is a local celebrity. The restaurant exhibits very beautiful works by African-American artists. The traditional New Orleans cuisine served during the lunch buffet is the specialty of the house. Among the choices are gumbo, court-bouillon fish, *"Clémenceau"* shrimp, stuffed crab, Creole or fried chicken and bread pudding topped with praline sauce.

Gabrielle's *($$-$$$; fixed-price lunch menu $16.95; Fri 11:30am to 2pm, Tue to Sat 5:30pm to 10pm; 3201 Esplanade Ave., ☎ 948-6233)* stands apart from other establishments and, with its modern cuisine, attracts numerous devoted patrons. Taking the magnificent Esplanade Avenue to get there is a truly enchanting experience. The menu features fillet of rabbit wrapped in prosciutto, in a mustard sweet and sour sauce; crayfish *enchilada* with cheese; blackened ribeye steak with crispy bacon and *shitake* étouffée with grilled red pepper and horseradish sauce; grilled red snapper with roasted garlic and crab meunière; pork chop with a Root beer, pear and caramelized onions glaze; upside down apple pudding with vanilla sauce; and home-made ice cream.

Christian's *($$-$$$$; Tue to Fri 11:30am to 2pm, Tue to Sat 5:30pm to 10pm; reservations recommended; 3835 Iberville St., ☎ 482-4924)*. Christian Ansel and Henry Bergeron could not have found a more noble location than the old Lutheran church, built in 1914, in which to relocate their restaurant, previously in Metairie. The welcoming building retains its stained-glass windows as well as the original woodwork, and offers delicious Creole and French cuisine. Savoured dishes included "Roland" oysters with garlic and mushrooms; okra gumbo; onion soup with Parmesan and croutons; swordfish with artichokes and mushrooms sautéed in black butter; angel hair pasta with shrimp, crayfish and artichoke hearts, in a tomato-flavoured cream and butter sauce; as well as chocolate profiteroles. Service is very warm and attentive. Take care, the man at the table next to you could be the owner's son, listening in on your comments! Good value.

✖ THE SUBURBS

Chalmette

If those hunger pangs hit while in Chalmette, the friendly and inexpensive **Rocky and Carlo's** cafeteria *($-$$; open late every day; St. Bernard Highway West, ☎ 279-8323)* is sure to satisfy your appetite. The restaurant features family fare, with a menu consisting of macaroni & cheese, hamburger steak with onion sauce, and white beans and pork. The place is hardly luxurious, but very popular at lunch time. No credit cards accepted.

Metairie

Bistro de Ville *($$-$$$; Tue to Sat 5pm to 9pm, French guitar player Fri and Sat; 2037 Metairie Rd, Exit 229-Bonnabel off Highway 1-10 heading south, ☎ 837-6900)* is a small restaurant that seats 70 and looks like a Parisian bistro. This used to be the restaurant Chez Daniel. The new owner is Daniel's former sous-chef and she offers Creole cuisine imbued with French and Mediterranean flavours. One dining room wall depicts a country dinner scene inspired by French impressionists. The restaurant is situated in Metairie, 15 minutes from downtown New Orleans.

Gretna

Gretna is less than a half hour from downtown New Orleans. Visitors can get there by taking the Greater New Orleans Bridge, which links the two. **Kim Son** *($-$$; Mon to Sat 11am to 3pm and 5pm to 10pm; 349 Whitney Ave., first exit off West Bank Expressway after the bridge, keeping to the right, second light on the left, behind the Oakwood Shopping Center,* ☎ *366-2489)*, a delicious Vietnamese and Chinese restaurant, is worth the trip. For those who love this type of cuisine, this is unquestionably one of the best Asian restaurants in and around New Orleans. Savoury spring rolls, complemented with coriander when there is no fresh mint, are prepared here. The seafood soup as well as the vegetable and soya soup are tasty, the chicken strips sautéed with citronella and broccoli are delectable, and the Singapore noodles are judiciously seasoned with curry. The staff here speaks Vietnamese, Chinese and English. Good value.

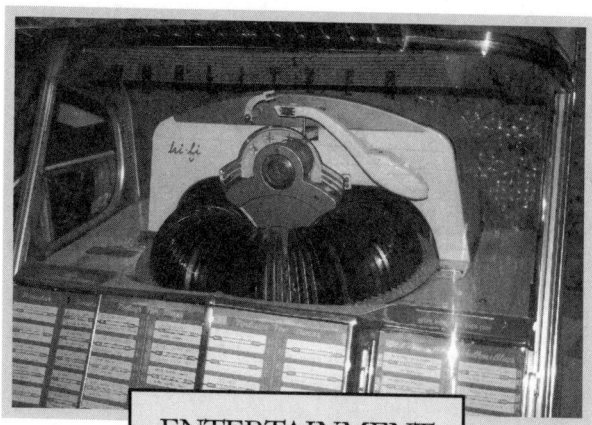

ENTERTAINMENT

Just before the first world war, jazz was born in New Orleans, and whether it's blues, ragtime, old Creole songs or haunting spirituals, it always gets your blood flowing. Fans should hit Bourbon Street, in the French Quarter: a long-established spot for all-night revelry to explosive and nostalgic music.

BARS AND NIGHTCLUBS

The French Quarter and Faubourg Marigny

The **Café Brazil** *(2100 Chartres St., Faubourg Marigny,* ☎ *947-9386)* is considered one of the best places in the city for dancing to reggae and Afro-Caribbean music. Julia Roberts has been spotted there.

At the Royal Sonesta Hotel's **Can Can Café** *(300 Bourbon St., French Quarter,* ☎ *553-2372)*, the Silver Leaf Jazz Band plays traditional Dixieland from Thursday to Sunday.

The **Café Istanbul** nightclub *(cover charge; 534 Frenchmen St., Faubourg Marigny,* ☎ *944-4180)* is open every night, with dancing on Fridays and Saturdays. As well as English, they speak Italian and Turkish here. Parking is available after 8pm. The only Turkish restaurant in Louisiana is on the main floor. They are open for lunch and dinner and offer traditional Turkish hors-d'oeuvres, lamb, grilled chicken and salads. There is live music at lunch.

At **Checkpoint Charlie** *(501 Esplanade Ave., Faubourg marigny,* ☎ *947-0979)*, you can munch on a Charlie Burger while listening to live music.

The **Club 544** *(544 Bourbon St., French Quarter,* ☎ *566-0529)* presents different traditional-jazz celebrities every night.

The **Club Second Line** *(216 Bourbon St., French Quarter,* ☎ *523-2020)*, open every night, is one of the rare spots in New Orleans where they present Dixieland as well as contemporary jazz.

The **Famour's Door** *(339 Esplanade Ave., Faubourg Marigny,* ☎ *522-7626)*, in existence since 1934, is one of the oldest bars on Esplanade Avenue. There is jazz in the afternoon and evening, and dancing to jazz and blues.

The **Hard Rock Café** *(418 Peters St. North, French Quarter,* ☎ *529-5617)*. All the big cities of the world have Hard Rock Cafés. In New Orleans, Fats Domino's piano hangs over the guitar-shaped bar and you can even see Elton John's shoes.

The **Hotel Fairmount** *(123 Baronne St., French Quarter,* ☎ *529-7111)* has three different bars, each with its own music: The **Fairmount Court**, The **Sazerac Bar** which is a bit more stylish, and **Bailey's** for the end of the evening.

The **House of Blues** *(225 Decatur St., French Quarter,* ☎ *529-2624)* is the latest trend for its music as much as its food. Different artists perform each week.

Howlin' Wolf *(828 South Peters St., French Quarter,* ☎ *523-2551)*. This bar was converted from an old cotton-seed warehouse. They offer shows by contemporary rock bands.

Jimmy Buffet's in the **Margaritaville Café at Story Ville** *(1104 Decatur St., French Quarter,* ☎ *592-2560)* features different solo artists or groups each week. They also serve some traditional dishes.

Maxwell's Toulouse Cabaret *(615 Toulouse St., French Quarter, ☎ 523-4207)* is renown for the quality of its artists. You will find the New Orleans style at its best here. Harry Connick, the father of the famous singer of the same name, takes time off from his job as New Orleans' district attorney to sing here two nights a week.

The **Palm Court Jazz Café** *(1204 Decatur St., French Quarter)* presents high-calibre jazz seven nights a week. Danny Barker, considered one of the best banjo players in the world, plays here regularly. You can also listen to their exceptional collection of rare and out-of-print records. Prices for both the drinks and their local cuisine are among the most reasonable.

Preservation Hall *(726 St. Peter St., French Quarter)* remains the definitive choice for traditional jazz. A different group plays here every night, bringing together the grand masters for unforgettable jam sessions. There's neither food nor drinks, only jazz.

Rhythms *(227 Bourbon St., French Quarter, ☎ 523-3800)* offers intoxicating blues in an old courtyard enhanced with a babbling fountain and beautiful wrought-iron balconies.

The **Snug Harbor** *(626 Frenchmen St., Faubourg Marigny, ☎ 949-0696)* presents two shows a night, at 9pm and 11pm, of contemporary jazz and rhythm and blues.

Favourites of the Gay Community

In New Orleans, most of the establishments visited by members of the gay community are located in the French Quarter and are easy to spot. The most popular small café, the **Bourbon Pub** *(801 Bourbon St., French Quarter, ☎ 529-2107)*, is open 24 hours a day.

Café Lafitte in Exile *(901 Bourbon St., French Quarter, ☎ 522-8397)*, one of the oldest and most popular meeting places, is open all the time. A disc jockey plays the music.

Charlene's *(940 Elysian Field, Faubourg Marigny,* ☎ *945-9328),* although outside the French Quarter, offers an atmosphere that is worth going out of your way for. Friendly advice: take a cab!

The **Golden Lantern** *(1239 Royale St., French Quarter,* ☎ *523-6200)* is an old corner pub.

The **Good Friends Bar** *(740 Dauphine St., French Quarter,* ☎ *566-7191)* has all the charm of the French Quarter and offers a quiet ambience, perfect for conversation.

Rawhide *(740 Burgundy St., French Quarter,* ☎ *525-8106)* plays the best music in town and squeezes in a crowd with a fondness for dressing in leather.

Uptown

The Pontchartrain Hotel's **Bayou Bar** *(2031 St. Charles Ave.,* ☎ *524-0581)* is an enjoyable meeting place for business people and local residents.

The **Carrollton Station** *(8140 Willow St.,* ☎ *865-9190)* is a small quiet bar that nonetheless attracts talented singers and musicians.

Jimmy's Music Club *(8200 Willow St.,* ☎ *866-9549)* presents all different styles of music indiscriminately (rock, reggae, rap, etc.).

The **Maple Leaf Bar** *(8316 Oak St., past South Carrollton St.,* ☎ *866-5323)* is open seven days a week. Their program includes blues on Wednesdays, cajun music on Thursdays and poetry readings on Sunday afternoons.

At **Michaul's Live Cajun Music Restaurant** *(701 Magazine St.,* ☎ *529 3121)* you can take free cajun dancing lessons, and then move up to the huge dance floor.

Muddy Water's *(8301 Oak St., past South Carrollton St.,* ☎ *866-7174)* welcomes young aspiring musicians as well as larger bands on tour. Relaxed atmosphere and original decor.

Tipitina's *(501 Napoleon Ave.,* ☎ *895-8477)*, which witnessed the growth of the Neville Brothers and Professor Longhair, has shows every night. You will find the best local and regional rock bands, New Orleans funk, gospel, zydeco, rhythm and blues, jazz, cajun and reggae music.

The **Victoria Lounge** in the Columns Hotel *(3811 St. Charles Ave.,* ☎ *899-9308)* offers a plush setting that accommodates professionals of all ages.

The Warehouse District

Mulate's *(201 Julia St., by South Peters St.,* ☎ *522-1492)*. At this establishment, which also doubles as a cajun restaurant (see p 197), all kinds of Louisiana Cajun singers and groups perform every night.

On the third floor of the **Hilton** *(2 Poydras St., close to the French Quarter,* ☎ *523-4374)* you'll find famous jazz-man **Pete Fountain's** nightclub.

At the **Jazz Meridien** *(Hotel Meridien, 614 Canal St.,* ☎ *525-6500)*, a jazz pianist performs during the week and a Dixieland band on weekends.

Other Styles...

Karaoke fans can get themselves recorded on video performing their favourite songs at both the **Cat's Meow** *(701 Bourbon St., French Quarter,* ☎ *523-1157)* and at **White Horse Bar & Grill** *(526 St. Louis St., French Quarter,* ☎ *566-1507)*.

The **Mid-City Lanes Rock'n'Bowl** *(4133 South Carrollton St.,* ☎ *482-3133)*, where you can dance to a live band or sample steamed shrimp or crayfish between games, has been a local attraction since it opened in 1941.

Pat O'Brien's *(718 St. Peter St., French Quarter,* ☎ *525-4823)* serves its famous "hurricane" cocktail in blown-glass tumblers, while artists provide entertainment from 8pm to 4am.

The Captain's Tour

In the social atmosphere of New Orleans' cafés it's easy to meet interesting characters. This is how, one night at the Hotel Richelieu's bar in the French Quarter, we were approached by Captain Roger C. Johnson, who, having learned that we were from Quebec (he has a pied-à-terre in the port of Quebec City), invited us for a tour of his favourite spots. The Captain, who has been frequenting the French Quarter for 30 years, knows a lot of out-of-the-way spots that the average tourist might not otherwise find. Here's the route he suggests, preferably not all at once.

In the bars...

We start with **The Blacksmith Shop** *(914 Bourbon St., French Quarter, ☎ 523-0066)*, practically the oldest bar in the United States and the only one to escape the numerous fires that have ravaged the city. Regular customers; sometimes a pianist in the evening.

At **Molly's on the Market** *(1107 Decatur St., French Quarter)*, beside Coops, you will be greeted by Jim Monaghan. Thursday is media night. From 10pm to midnight, newspaper and television people get together with a guest bartender each time. This guest could be the city mayor, the state governor, a member of Congress or someone else making headlines at the time.

The Captain likes the **Chart Room** *(at the corner of Chartres St. and Bienville, French Quarter)* for its fine cocktails at reasonable prices.

For a little "buffet" break, he recommends **Lord V.J.'s Bar** *(at the corner of Bienville and Decatur, French Quarter)*. On Monday nights, the regulars indulge in delicious corn bread and red beans

Johnny Whites *(733 St. Peter St., French Quarter)* and **Johnny Whites Sports Bar** *(at the corner of Toulouse St. and Bourbon St., French Quarter)* are both open all the time. They have a regular clientele; at the Sports Bar, you can see rebroadcasts of big sporting events.

At **Bar 711** *(711 Bourbon St., French Quarter)*, the late-night bartender "Freak", has great sideburns and a sense of humour, and knows about everything that goes on in the city.

Maison Napoléon *(500 Chartres St. at St. Louis, French Quarter, ☎ 524-9752)*. "One of the best bars in the world." Good background music, good food, good service. No juke-box. The house was built to welcome Napoleon who died before being able to visit. Say "hello" to the manager, Ray Fox (an aspiring writer), on behalf of the Captain.

At **Giovanni's - The Sequel** *(625 St. Phillip St., French Quarter)*, you can expect the unexpected. Here, say "hello" to Johnny (Giovanni) on the Captain's behalf. On Wednesdays and Sundays, between 9pm and 3am, you can replenish your proteins during an evening of liberal liquor consumption with a juicy steak.

The **Richelieu** bar, at Arnaud's restaurant *(813 Bienville St., French Quarter)*, is a favourite for a quiet afternoon drink.

Other food and drink establishments...

The Abbey *(1123 Decatur St., French Quarter)*. On Saturday afternoons after 3pm, for $5 you can enjoy fried chicken and a game on the tube. All types of New Orleanians mix at The Abbey. It's open all the time. If Laura is working at the bar, be sure to order one of her remarkable Bloody Marys and also say "hi" from the Captain. Nights, starting at 2am, it's "Big Dave's" shift. He's a veritable fountain of information about life in the area.

The charming little bar in the **Provincial Hotel** *(1024 Chartres St., French Quarter)* has only five bar-stools and six tables; it's calm and the regulars appreciate the cocktails. The Captain wouldn't ordinarily recommend hotel restaurants but he makes an exception for this one, called **Le Honfleur**, where, in his opinion, from 5pm every day, they serve perfect food.

Where the Captain grabs a bite to eat...

At **Andrew Jaeger's** *(622 Conti St., French Quarter, ☎ 522-4964)*, the crabs are cooked to order and all the seafood is remarkably fresh.

At **Bayona** *(430 Dauphine St., French Quarter, ☎ 525-4455)* Susan Spicer is the owner and prepares the food. It is excellent, expensive, charming and elegant, although less expensive for lunch. See "Restaurants", p 189.

The **Bella Luna** *(914 Peters St. North, French Quarter, ☎ 529-1583)* isn't within everyone's price range but there's a marvellous view of the river. See "Restaurants", p 189.

At **Coops** *(1100 Decatur St., French Quarter)*, they serve the best gumbo in town and shrimp po-boys on French bread. Don't let the decor bother you, the important thing is what's on your plate.

Greco's *(1000 Peters St. North, French Quarter, ☎ 523-7418)* is, in the Captain's opinion, as good as it is relaxed.

Tony Moran welcomes patrons in the evenings at the **Maison de la Vieille Absinthe** *(240 Bourbon St., French Quarter)*. Mr. Moran prepares excellent pasta at very reasonable prices. The house is open from 9am to 4am every day.

CULTURAL ACTIVITIES AND FESTIVALS

Gospel

For the best gospel in town, go to the **St. Stephen** Baptist Church during Sunday services *(Sun 8am and noon; 7pm on the 2nd, 4th and 5th Sundays of the month; 2308 South Liberty St., in the Mid-City area, seven streets north of St. Charles St., access from Philip St., ☎ 822-6800)*. Their singing is sometimes broadcast on local radio stations *(Mon-Fri 9:15am on WYLD 940 AM and 10:45am on KKNO 1750 AM)*. The church has a devout following among local blacks.

The **Praline Connection #2 Gospel and Blues Hall** restaurant *($19.95; Sun 11am and 2pm; 901-907 South Peters St., Warehouse District, ☎ 523-3973)* offers gospel performances during their Sunday brunches.

Films

There are a number of movie theatres in New Orleans. Among them are the theatres of **Canal Place** *(333 Canal St., ☎ 581-5400)*, located close to the French Quarter. The **Prytania** *(5339 Prytania St., ☎ 895-4513)* presents mostly repertory films. There is an **IMAX** theatre *(☎ 581-4629)* a few steps away from the Aquarium of the Americas. Finally, **Movie Pitchers** *(3941 Bienville Ave., ☎ 488-8881)* shows mostly foreign films.

Films set in New Orleans available on video

Pretty Baby, directed by Louis Malle in 1978 and starring Susan Sarandon and Brooke Shields, takes place at the Columns Hotel. Many of the outdoor scenes were filmed in the Garden District.

Panic in the Streets, 1950. An atmospheric film shot partly at the New Orleans port.

JFK (Oliver Stone), 1991. In this film, the New Orleans District Attorney is unsatisfied with official explanations surrounding the assassination of President John F. Kennedy.

Interview with the Vampire, 1994. In this film, based on a book by Anne Rice, Tom Cruise is seen in the French Quarter, Lafayette Cemetery and Oak Alley Plantation.

Big Easy, 1986. A fine little thriller which takes place near Lake Pontchartrain and the Piazza d'Italia with zydeco background music.

The Pelican Brief, 1993. Julia Roberts tries to solve the dark mystery at the Faculty of Law at Tulane University.

Dance and Opera

The **New Orleans Ballet Association** *(☎ 522-0996)* is the only professional dance ensemble in New Orleans. They perform at the Theater of the Performing Arts. At the same theatre, the **New Orleans Opera Association** *(☎ 529-2278)* presents operas.

Theatre

The **Saenger Performing Arts Centre** *(143 North Rampart St., French Quarter, ☎ 524-2490)*, a superb renovated theatre, puts on Broadway shows.

The **Petit Théâtre du Vieux-Carré Français** *(616 St. Peter St., French Quarter, ☎ 522-2081)* is the oldest surviving theatre troupe in the United States. Every year in March, the famous Tennessee Williams Festival takes place here.

The **Marigny Theatre** *(616 Frenchmen St., Faubourg Marigny, near Chartres St., ☎ 944-2653)* has a reputation for choosing the most avant-garde plays.

The **Contemporary Arts Center** *(900 Camp St., near Julia St., ☎ 523-1216)* presents experimental theatre.

The **Southern Repertory Theater** *(Canal Place, 333 Canal St., 3rd floor, ☎ 861-8163)* offers regional works as well as classics.

Casinos

Although casinos were legalized in 1993, their presence continues to be controversial among residents. There are currently four casinos that are open 24 hours a day, seven days a week in the New Orleans metropolitan area; must have been set up in boats. Theoretically they must leave the dock for gambling to be permitted, though in practice things don't always work that way!

For fans of games of chance, the **Flamingo Casino New Orleans** boat *($5 entrance fee; cruises 11:45am to 1:15pm, 2:45pm to 4:15pm, 5:45pm to 7:15pm; Poydras St. Pier, adjacent to the New Orleans Hilton Riverside and to the Riverwalk Market,* ☎ *587-7777)* offers 1000 square metres of floor space on its four decks and is able to accommodate up to 2,400 passengers. There are more than 100 slot machines, video lottery terminals, blackjack tables, roulette wheels, etc.. They also offer a restaurant, jazz and a free shuttle to downtown hotels. There is free parking with validation from the ticket office at the Hilton, the World Trade Center or at Riverwalk.

On Lake Pontchartrain, close to Lakefront airport, **Bally's Casino Lakeshore Resort** *(1 Stars and Stripes Boulevard, South Shore Harbor,* ☎ *248-3200)* also has a large selection of slot machines and gaming tables for dice games, mini-baccarat, roulette, blackjack, etc..

Located in Kenner, on Lake Pontchartrain, the **Treasure Chest** *(5050 Williams Boulevard,* ☎ *443-8171)* is a replica of a nineteenth-century paddleboat. They recently invested five million dollars to renovate the interior.

On the right bank of the Mississippi, anchored at the Harvey Canal Pier, the **Boomtown Belle Casino** *(4132 Peters Route, Harvey,* ☎ *366-7711)*, a 75-metre, three-deck ship, has 850 video lottery terminals, 50 gaming tables, as well as a dance floor, a bar and a café.

Calendar of Annual Events

January

Sugar Bowl Football Classic *(Jan 1; Superdome, 1500 Sugar Bowl Drive, LA 70112,* ☎ *525-8573)*. The Sugar Bowl is the final match between the two best American college football teams. In celebration of it there is a colourful parade in the city's streets.

Beginning of the Mardi Gras season *(starting Jan 6).*

Mardi Gras in New Orleans

Mardi Gras became part of Louisiana history as of March 3rd, 1699. In that year, the French explorer Pierre Le Moyne, Sieur d'Iberville, named an area near the future New Orleans "Bayou Mardi-Gras". As of 1740, under the French regime, masquerade balls took place in New Orleans, then were banned by the Spanish governors. Prohibition continued with the Americans as of 1803. Nevertheless, the Creole population ignored this ban and revived the tradition of the masquerade ball in 1823.

Four years later, the first Mardi Gras parade made its way through the streets and the tradition has repeated itself every year since. One of the most spectacular and surprising elements of the parade is the "Indian Mardi Gras". Blacks strut about in clans with hand-made, glittering feathered and beaded costumes. Next come the Tchopitoulas, the Pocahontas and other colourfully-clad traditional native characters, and of course there are the popular zulus.

There are also a few rules to follow during the Mardi Gras parade: use plastic glasses only, no glass or metal allowed; no streamers to be thrown from balconies; don't park your car along the parade route, in fact parking regulations change during the parade so to avoid a $100 ticket or, worse, getting your car impounded *(400 Claiborne Ave., ☎ 826-1900)*, double-check that you are legally parked; wear comfortable clothes and shoes; and don't carry your valuables with you. Finally portable toilets can be found throughout town.

Mardi Gras is the festive period preceding the fast or Lent. It falls 46 days before Easter.

In Louisiana, parish rulings declare the season officially open 12 days before Mardi Gras itself. There are about 70 parades in the four parishes Orleans, Jefferson, St. Bernard and St. Tammany - during this period.

Since 1872, the colours of Mardi Gras are purple which represents justice, gold symbolizing power and green for faith.

Every year, each krewe chooses a different theme for their floats and masks. "Krewe" comes from the word "crew", probably "hispanicized". They are non-profit organizations, often associated with charity groups whose main goal is to contribute to the preparation and financing of floats before presenting them at Mardi Gras. The originator of this venerable tradition, the krewe of Comus was born in 1857. In honour of this, the krewe of Comus concludes the Mardi Gras procession.

Krewes parade with a captain at the head, on horseback or in a convertible. The captain is followed by officers, then the king and queen, accompanied sometimes by a few dukes and always by young girls, and behind them, the float with costumed krewe members on it. All this is followed by bands, dance troupes, clowns and public entertainers, etc.. In all, there are over 3000 participants.

Kings and queens get chosen in a different manner from one krewe to another. For some it's done by a draw, but regardless of the method, most require a monarch. The King of Carnival is chosen by a committee from the School of Design, the parade's sponsor.

Arrive early because space is limited and good spots are precious, and be careful when the doubloons and necklaces start getting thrown from the floats, because there's a lot of jostling to catch them. Also think about stocking up on sandwiches and water because it's as hard to break through the crowd as it is to find a free table at a restaurant. St. Charles Avenue, between Napoleon Avenue and Lee Circle gets transformed into a huge picnic area for the whole family. The crowd is more restless toward Canal Street and in the French Quarter.

New Orleanians prefer attending the Metairie Mardi Gras, whose parades rival those from their own city.

Lundi Gras, a recent addition, takes place the day before at Spanish Plaza, adjacent to Riverwalk *(Poydras St.)*. This is where, at around 5pm, Rex, the King of Mardi Gras, arrives. The program for this first evening includes a masquerade ball, fireworks and a concert.

Mardi Gras is always more fun in disguise. There is even a competition reserved for visitors for the best costume. To participate, contact Mardi Gras **Maskathon** *(☎ 527-0123)*. There is a good selection of masks at the French Market.

On the day of Mardi Gras, watch for bands going by, they call them marching clubs. The traditional Jefferson City Buzzards and Pete Fountain's Half-Fast Walking Club are the most famous. The parade starts at 8:30am with the arrival of the Zulus and then at 10am, the most spectacular event of the day occurs, the arrival of Rex, the King of Carnival, followed by 200 thematic floats.

During Mardi Gras, the public transportation service, the **RTA** *(☎ 560-2700)*, offers day-passes *($3)*.

Mardi Gras in the Gay Community

The costume competition near the bar Rawhide, at Burgundy and St. Ann, is one of Mardi Gras' most popular shows. It starts at noon. Two pieces of advice: come early and leave the kids at home!

Black Arts and Martin Luther King Jr. Festival *(mid-Jan; Tulane University, office of multicultural affairs, ☎ 596-2697)*. Peace Week.

February

Festival of the Zulu Family *(day before Mardi Gras 10am to 5pm; Woldenberg Park, ☎ 822-1559)*. More Mardi Gras festivities.

Lundi Gras (Fat Monday) on Spanish Plaza *(Riverwalk, ☎ 522-1555)* celebrates the eve of Mardi Gras with fireworks and a masquerade ball (a mask is required).

Mardi Gras *(☎ 566-5068 or 525-6427)*. Festivities and parades throughout the city streets and the French Quarter.

Mardi Gras dates for coming years:

1998: February 24   **2001**: February 26
1999: February 16   **2002**: February 12
2000: March 7   **2003**: March 4

March

St. Patrick's Day Parade *(mid-Mar; French Quarter,* ☎ *525-5169)*. As in a lot of major American cities, this Irish holiday is celebrated in fine splendour in the French Quarter.

St. Patrick's Day Parade in the Irish Channel area *(mid-Mar;* ☎ *565-7080)*. Another neighbourhood, another Irish gathering, another party!

Black Heritage Festival *(mid-Mar; Audubon Zoo,* ☎ *861-2537)*. For two days, this event highlights the cultural, musical, artistic and gastronomical contributions of the black community.

St. Joseph Day Festivities *(mid-Mar; St. Joseph Tabernacle, Piazza d'Italia, at Poydras and Tchoupitoulas,* ☎ *891-1904)*. This day celebrating the patron saint of workers is also celebrated in grand style.

The **Crescent City Classic** *(3rd weekend in March;* ☎ *861-8686)* is a 10,000-metre marathon starting at Jackson Square and finishing at Audubon Park.

The **Tennessee Williams Literary Festival** *(last weekend in March; Conference Services of New Orleans University,* ☎ *286-6680 or 581-1144)* focuses on the works of the famous writer, born Thomas Lanier, author of, among others, *A Streetcar Named Desire* and *Suddenly Last Summer*. For three days there are various theatre productions, poetry recitals and other cultural activities taking place in the city that the writer loved so much and where he wrote his early plays including *The Glass Menagerie*.

The **Earth Festival** *(last weekend in March, 9:30am to 6pm; Audubon Zoo,* ☎ *861-2537)*. Even spring's reawakening is a reason to celebrate in New Orleans!

April

At the **French Quarter Festival** (☎ *522-5730)*, there are a dozen or so bands on as many stages. Refreshments, fireworks, etc..

Spring Festival (☎ *581-1367)*. For five days the public is invited to visit historic sites and houses, plantations, etc.. The festival opens with a parade of horse-drawn carriages.

The **Jazz and Heritage Festival** *(last weekend in April; New Orleans Hippodrome Fairgrounds,* ☎ *522-4786)* is one of the most popular celebrations in the world. For ten days, more than 4,000 artists, musicians, chefs and artisans share their talent with more than 250,000 visitors.

Louisiana Crayfish Festival *(Breaux Bridge,* ☎ *318-332-6655)*. During this two-day festival you can sample all kinds of food, attend concerts and craft exhibitions.

Uptown Free Street Festival *(1st weekend in April; New Orleans Jazz and Heritage Foundation,* ☎ *522-4786)*. There is a lot of frenzied crowd participation at this huge celebration devoted to music.

May

Greek Festival *(last weekend in May; Greek Cultural Centre, 1200 Robert E. Lee Boulevard,* ☎ *282-0259)*. This event presents folk dancing, music and art exhibitions.

June

Reggae Riddums Festival *(2nd weekend in June; City Park,* ☎ *367-1313)*. This festival brings together reggae and calypso performers from around the world.

Carnival Latino *(last weekend in June; and Mississippi River Front and Canal,* ☎ *522-9927)*. Throughout the four days of this festival you can hear bands from Latin America, Spain and Portugal.

Great French Quarter Tomato Festival *(1st weekend in June; French Market,* ☎ *522-2621).* A number of popular events are presented with the tomato as central theme; June is tomato season here.

Zydeco Bay-Ou *(3rd weekend in June; Crown Point,* ☎ *689-2663).* A number of shows are presented with zydeco singers and musicians.

July

Independence Day *(Riverfront,* ☎ *528-9994).* The fourth of July is celebrated with various activities and performances that always attract a diverse and joyous crowd.

Wine and Food Experience *(end of July; Ernest N. Morial Convention Center, 900 Convention Boulevard,* ☎ *529-9463).* Wine-tastings and a variety of foods are both offered in the French Quarter. Approximately 40 restaurants participate in this event.

August

International Festival of African Heritage *(end of Aug and beginning of Sep;* ☎ *949-5600 or 949-5610).* Festivities are devoted to African-American art of all forms and disciplines.

October

Swamp Festival *(Audubon Zoo and Wodenberg Park,* ☎ *861-2537).* For two weekends, the zoo offers free admission. You can also enjoy some cajun food and examine distinctive swamp wildlife.

Festival of Film and Video *($3-$6; 365 Canal St.,* ☎ *523-3818).* For one week, various film and video productions from all over the world are shown. The festival takes place at the Canal Place theatres.

Festa D'Italia *(*☎ *891-1904).* Celebrating, it's something that Italians do so well!

Gumbo Festival *(beginning of Oct; Bridge City, Westwego,* ☎ *436-4712).* There's gumbo, music and...more gumbo!

Gay Pride Weekend *(Oct 11 and 12;* ☎ *1-800-345-1187).* A very lively weekend for the gay community. A parade, dancing and shows are held at Washington Square.

Hallowe'en *(Oct 31;* ☎ *566-5055).* Throughout the city costume parties are organized but the most popular is the one in the French Quarter. There is also a parade.

Boo at the Zoo *($10; Oct 29 to 31; Audubon Zoo, 6500 Magazine St.,* ☎ *871-2537).* Special Hallowe'en activities are organized at the Zoo. Profits go to the city's children's hospital.

Octoberfest *(all month).* Approximately 20 establishments in the city serve beer and German food. You can also polka at the Deutches Haus *(*☎ *522-8014).*

November

Luling Suckling Pig Festival *(1st weekend in Nov; on the west bank of the river, route US90, Luling).* This festival celebrates the suckling pig. The highlight is of course tasting it either roasted or prepared in a variety of other ways.

Celebration in the Oaks *(evenings, end of Nov to beginning of Jan; City Park).* The park's trees are decorated with hundreds of thousands of lights. This brilliant spectacle is accompanied by music.

December

Creole Christmas *(*☎ *522-5730).* The public is invited to take part in carolling at Jackson Square, candlelight walks, bonfires and Christmas celebrations.

New Year's Eve at Jackson Square *(Jackson Square,* ☎ *566-5046).* New Orleanians and visitors get together to say goodbye to the year and ring in a new one.

Orange Festival and Parish Persimmon Fair *(1st weekend in Dec; Port Sulphur,* ☎ *656-7752)* proposes food, music, a catfish cooking contest, a duck-calling competition and "fais do-do", a traditional cajun dance.

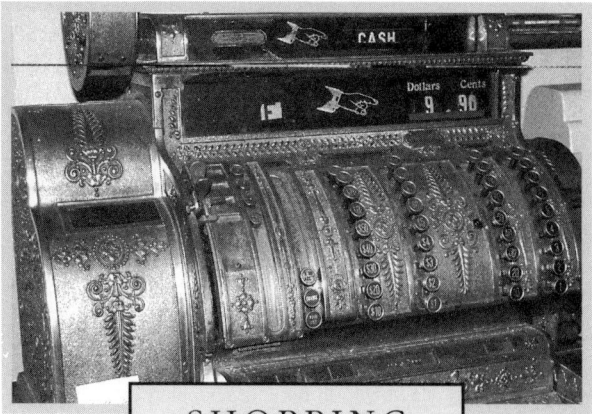

SHOPPING

More than one thousand New Orleans businesses participate in the state's sales-tax-reimbursement program. Simply present your passport and airplane ticket at the time of purchase to receive the tax-refund voucher that is filled out and submitted to **Louisiana Tax Free Shopping (LTFS)** at the New Orleans International Airport (Moisant). Amounts of less than $500 are reimbursed in cash; larger amounts are paid by cheque sent to the visitor by mail.

NEIGHBOURHOODS

Each New Orleans neighbourhood has its own specialty. The French Quarter, essentially a tourist area, brings together many different businesses from the most elegant gallery to the simplest souvenir stand. Uptown, a residential district, is known for the row of antique shops on Magazine Street; there are also a number of restaurants, food markets and a few cafés here. In the Riverbend neighbourhood, around Carrollton Street and St. Charles Avenue, there are a few good restaurants, jazz clubs and clothing stores.

SHOPPING CENTRES

A main point of interest for window-shoppers is **Canal Place Fashion Mall**, with more than 60 stores and cafés. Of course **Jax**, or **Jackson Brewery**, is also a choice spot for shoppers.

The recently opened **New Orleans Centre**, near the Superdome and the Hyatt Hotel, offers three floors of elegant boutiques under a glass dome.

On the site of the 1984 Universal Exposition along the Mississippi, **Riverwalk** is a market of 140 stores, boutiques and restaurants that allows you to do your shopping while enjoying a unique view of the river.

GALLERIES AND ANTIQUE SHOPS

Royal Street is the address of about 40 of the over 60 boutiques and galleries in the French Quarter that specialize in antiques of all kinds. Paintings, jewellery, furniture, glass, porcelain, bronze, etc., whether for decoration or collection, authentic or reproduction, there is something for all tastes if not for all budgets. There's no point in naming them all: the best thing to do is stroll along and enjoy the ambience.

Like Royal Street, **Julia Street**, in the Warehouse District, is renowned for its many galleries. They are located near the Contemporary Arts Center.

A Gallery for Fine Photography *(322 Royal St., ☎ 568-1313)* sells posters by American and international photographers.

The **French Antique Shop** *(225 Royal St., ☎ 524-9861)* specializes in pieces from the 18th and 19th centuries: light fixtures, marble, porcelain, bronze.

At **Dixon & Dixon** *(237 Royal St., ☎ 524-0282 or 1-800-848-5148)* you can find exceptional collections of paintings, Oriental rugs, European and Oriental porcelain and antique jewellery.

Endangered Species *(619 Royal St.,* ☎ *568-9855)* sells sculpted ivory figures, ritual objects, icons and masks.

The **Morton M. Goldberg Auction Galleries** *(547 Baron St.,* ☎ *882-7422)*, one of the most important auction houses in North America, offers imported furniture, paintings and various other objects. They regularly hold estate auctions.

La Belle Gallery *(309 Chartres St.,* ☎ *529-3080)* houses one of the most important collections of African-American art in the United States.

Martin LaBorde Gallery *(631 Royal St.,* ☎ *587-7111)* exhibits paintings by the artist. His richly coloured works display a Mexican influence, for example, in those that represent a figure floating freely through the air. Some of LaBorde's paintings can be seen at the cozy **Upperline** restaurant (see p 203).

The portrait artist **Johnny Donnels** *(634 St. Peter St.,* ☎ *525-8550)* presents work from throughout his career, spanning over fifty years, as well as an attractive collection of photographs of New Orleans.

Macon Riddle *(*☎ *899-3027)*, an expert consultant, conducts visits to antique shops and galleries on Royal and Magazine Streets.

Magazine Street is a paradise for antique enthusiasts. Stretching over almost 10 kilometres, boutiques, arcades and galleries offer ceramics, pewter pieces, glassware, and other old objects.

The boutique **Antiques-Magazine** *(2043 Magazine St.,* ☎ *522-2043)* offers a whole range of items from the Victorian era to 1920s Art Deco: glassware, lamps, furniture, silverware and various oddities.

On the same street, **Aurat Antiques** *(3005 Magazine St.,* ☎ *897-3210)* has the biggest collection of English and Portuguese colonial furniture in all of the southern states.

Accent Antiques *(2855 Magazine St.)* and **Collection Antiques** *(3123 Magazine St.)* have fine fabrics, quilts, inkwells and old frames.

BOOKSTORES

Book Star *(414 North Peters St., French Quarter, ☎ 523-6411)* has a wide selection of books including a complete section on the history, culture and food of Louisiana and New Orleans.

The ideal place to hunt down a book of recipes from rural Louisiana and New Orleans is **Aunt Sally's Praline Shop** *(810 Decatur St., French Quarter, ☎ 524-3373 or 524-5107)*.

At the **Arcadian Books & Art Prints - Librairie d'Arcadie** *(714 Orleans St., French Quarter, ☎ 523-4138)* the pleasant and erudite owner Russel Desmond, a history and literature enthusiast, proposes the best authors "for the study of French and Francophone Louisiana": Barry Ancelet *(Contes Bilingues 'cadiens et créole)*, Jeanne Castille *(Moi, Jeanne Castille de la Louisiane)*, Maurice Denuzière *(Je te nomme Louisiane)*, and the Reverend Mother Saint Augustin de Tranchepain *(Relation du voyage des premières Ursulines à La Nouvelle-Orléans et leur établissement en cette ville - published in 1859)*.

Louisiana Cookbooks

Local cuisine in Louisiana is an important preoccupation and you will probably want to take home a few books dedicated to Cajun, creole, southern or African-American cooking. Here is a list of some of the most popular books in New Orleans.

Creole Gumbo and All That Jazz: New Orleans cuisine.

River Road Recipes I: Two million copies sold since 1959.

La Bonne Cuisine: Creole cuisine of New Orleans.

The Little New Orleans Cookbook: New Orleans' cuisine.

La Bouche Créole I: Authentic creole recipes.

Commander's Palace Cookbook: Recipes from the gastronomic mecca of New Orleans.

Recipes & Reminiscences of New Orleans I: Written by the Ursuline nuns of New Orleans.

The Best of New Orleans: A marvellous little book, fully illustrated with beautiful colour photos, bringing together the best creole and Cajun recipes from New Orleans and Louisiana, including a few from Paul Prudhomme and from prominent restaurants such as Antoine's.

MUSIC

Tower Records - Video *(every day 9am to midnight; Jackson Brewery, 408-410 North Peters St., at Decatur, ☎ 529-4411)*. Excellent selection of local music.

Record Ron's *(every day 11am to 7pm; 239 Chartres St., ☎ 522-2239; 1129 Decatur St., ☎ 524-9444)*. One of the largest selections of vinyl: pop, R & B, jazz, soul, Dixieland, rock, blues, gospel, Cajun, etc.. Credit cards accepted.

Rock & Roll Records *(10am to 10pm; 1214 Decatur St., ☎ 561-5683)*. Records (33, 45 or 78 rpm), cassettes, compact discs and videos.

Louisiana Music Factory *(every day 10am to 7pm; 225 North Peters St., French Quarter, ☎ 523-1094)*. Regional music, books, photos, videos and posters.

FOOD, COFFEE AND WINE

At **Aunt Sally's Praline Shop** *(810 Decatur St., French Quarter)*, you can buy cookbooks, jars of pepper sauce, other pickles and preserves, and typical local foods. Just look for the glassed-in counter facing the street where staff prepare mountains of sugary pralines.

You'll find good coffee just about everywhere in New Orleans; **Community** coffee is roasted according to tradition.

At **Croissant d'Or** *(7am to 5pm; 615-617 Ursulines St., French Quarter, ☎ 534-4663)*, Maurice Delechelle, a French-pastry chef, prepares delicious (and huge) butter croissants, chocolate croissants, Danish pastries and other treats. The café also serves quiche and a small menu of daily lunch specials (soup, sandwich and salad). The building has a lovely courtyard, but it can be very hot on humid days. Thankfully, the café has air conditioning.

Visits to Agricultural or Industrial Sites

The Louisiana Seafood Exchange *(by appointment, Mon to Sat 7am to 3pm; 428 Jefferson Highway, Kenner, ☎ 834-9393)*. Wholesaler of a wide variety of fresh seafood. New Orleans-style restaurant, with po'boys, hot meals, boiled or poached seafood (take out).

The **Vietnamese Farmer's Market** *(Sat mornings; 13344 Chef Menteur Hwy, Route US 90, at the east exit of the city, ☎ 254-9646)* is the most interesting vegetable market in New Orleans. You have to get there early.

You can't visit New Orleans without stopping in at the historic **French Market** *(Decatur St., French Quarter)*. In addition to local produce there is produce from other states: Texas oranges, Georgia peaches and California grapes, to name a few. Garlic braids and small jars of pepper sauce are popular items.

It's not easy to find good cheese in New Orleans. **Martin Wine Cellar** *(3827 Baron St., two streets north of St. Charles Ave., Uptown, ☎ 899-7411)* imports stilton, goat cheese, brie and parmesan. They also have one of the largest selections of wine in New Orleans and a sandwich counter.

The **Praline Connection** restaurant *(542 Frenchmen St., Faubourg Marigny)* has a gift shop where they sell products from New Orleans including traditional, chocolate and coconut pralines.

Progress Grocery *(912 Decatur St., French Quarter, ☎ 525-6627)*, best known for its muffalettas (sandwiches of Italian meats, cheeses and olive salad), also carries some groceries, cigarettes, magazines and newspapers.

At the **Saint Roch Seafood Market** *(2381 St. Claude Ave., east of the French Quarter at St. Roch St., ☎ 943-5778 or 943-6666)*, you can get locally caught fish and seafood including soft crab (in season), shrimp, crawfish, oysters, etc..

Vieux Carré Wine and Spirits *(422 Chartres St., French Quarter, ☎ 568-9463)* is run by an Italian who started out in the catering business in New Orleans. It stocks a wide variety of good wines from many different countries and a large selection of beers.

There are many stores in the residential area of **Uptown**, including **Zara's** *(4838 Prytania St.)* for food, **McKenzie's** *(4926 Prytania St.)* for baked goods, **The Wine Seller** *(5000 Prytania St.)* for wine, and coffee roasters on Magazine Street and Maple Street such as **P.J.'s Coffee and Tea** *(7624 Maple St., ☎ 866-7031)*. There is also **Don Jefes Uptown Cigar Shop** *(5700 Magazine St. and 5535 Tchoupitoulas)*.

PHOTOGRAPHY

Photography stores throughout the city offer developing, a number of them in the area of Canal Street near Decatur, Chartes and Royal and on the other side of Canal. Professionals will find a good selection of film at the **Liberty Camera Center** *(337 Carondelet St., one street north of St. Charles, between Gravier and Union, ☎ 523-6252)*.

MARDI GRAS

You can relive the atmosphere of Mardi Gras throughout the year by visiting the **Louisiana State Museum** (see p 100) *(751 Chartres St., ☎ 568-6972 or 568-6978)*, with its permanent collection of costumes, old floats, documents and accessories (invitation cards, decorations) dating back to the last century.

You can get a closer look at and a better feel for costumes, masks and other finery at the following specialty shops.

The **Accent Annex** *(1120 Jeff Davis Parkway South,
☎ 821-8999 or 838-8818)* wholesales all kinds of decorations
and objects.

Barth Brothers *(4346 Poche Court West, ☎ 254-1794)* is a
business that has made Mardi Gras celebration an art in itself.
They specialize in the design and construction of elaborate
floats. Their work is exhibited at the Museum of American
History in Washington.

Blaine Kern's Mardi Gras World *(233 Newton St., Algiers Point,
☎ 361-7821)* makes floats and sells all the requisite Mardi Gras
accessories.

Jefferson Variety Store *(239 Iris Ave., Metairie, ☎ 834-5222)*.
Costumes and doubloons, which are tokens used in Mardi Gras
festivities.

Costume Headquarters *(3635 Banks St., ☎ 488-9523 or
488-6959)*. All sorts of costumes, wigs and masks for rent.

Garage Antiques and Clothing *(1234 Decatur St., French
Quarter, ☎ 522-6639)* specializes in selling Mardi Gras
accessories; you'll find a wonderful selection of old costumes
and masks. The owner, Marcus Fraser, is up on all the latest
trends.

Neighborhood Art Gallery *(2131 Soniat St., ask for Sandra
Berry, ☎ 891-5537)*. This African-American artists co-op
exhibits members' work.

Bergen Galleries *(Sun to Thu 9am to 9pm, Fri and Sat 9am to
10pm; 730 Royal St., ☎ 523-7882 or 1-800-621-6179)*. The
largest selection of Mardi Gras posters, new and old. They can
be shipped anywhere in the world.

Little Shop of Fantasies *(523 Dumaine St., French Quarter,
☎ 529-4243)* has one of the most dazzling selections of Mardi
Gras masks.

French Market Flea Market *(every day; at the corner of St.
Peter and Decatur, ☎ 522-2621)*. At this 200-year-old market
you will find a bit of everything, including Mardi Gras masks.

Rumors *(513 and 319 Royal St., French Quarter, ☎ 525-0292 or 523-0011)* is a favourite spot for buying Mardi Gras masks. There's a large selection of earrings, from the most classic to the most eccentric.

FLORIST

The staff at **Scheinuk The Florist** *(2600 St. Charles Ave., at Washington Ave., ☎ 895-3944 or 1-800-535-2020)* takes care of customers without delay. An attractive selection of cut flowers and tastefully arranged bouquets are offered at reasonable prices.

RECOMMENDED READING

Non-fiction

Ancelet, Barry Jean. *Cajun Country*. Jackson: University Press of Mississippi, 1991.

Arthur, Stanley Clisby.*Walking Tours of the French Quarter*. Gretna, Louisiana: Pelican Publishing Company, 1995.

Bizier, Richard and Roch Nadeau. *Louisiana*. Montréal: Ulysses Travel Publications, 1998.

Brasseaux, Carl. *Acadian to Cajun - Transformation of a People, 1803-1877*. Jackson: University Press of Mississippi, 1992.

Calhoun, Milburn and Jeanne Frois, eds. *Louisiana Almanach 1997-1998 Edition*. Gretna, Louisiana: Pelican Publishing Company, 1997.

Cowen, Walter G., Charles L. Dufour and John Wilds, eds. *Louisiana Yesterday and Today - A Historical Guide of the State*. Baton Rouge: Louisiana State University Press, 1996.

Hall, Gwendolyn Midlo. *Africans in Colonial Louisiana - The Development of Afro-Creole Culture in the Eighteenth Century*. Baton Rouge: Louisiana State University Press, 1995.

Stacey, Truman. *Louisiana's French Heritage*. Lafayette, Louisiana: Acadian House Publishing, 1990.

Novels, Short Stories and Poetry

Anderson, Geneviève and John Miller, eds. *New Orleans Stories: Great Writers on the City*. San Francisco: Chronicle Books, 1992. Biographies and works by well-known authors, with a preface by Andrei Codrescu.

Arceneaux, Jean. *Je suis 'Cadien*, Cajun Writers (chapbook 2), A Cross-Cultural Communications (Merrick, New York), 1994. (Bilingual book.)

Gaines, Ernest J. *Bloodline.* New York: Dial Press, 1968. Most recent published version New York: Vintage Contemporary, 1997.

Coffee-table Books

Ancelet, Barry Jean. *Musiciens 'cadiens et créoles - The Makers of Cajun Music*. Montréal: Les Presses de l'Université du Québec.(Bilingual book.)

Delehanty, Randolph and Richard Sexton. *New Orleans - Elegance and Decadence*. San Francisco: Chronicle Books, 1993.

Guirard, Greg. *Cajun families of the Atchafalaya - Their Ways & Words*. Lafayette, Louisiane: self-published, 1991.

Savoy, Ann Allen. *Cajun Music - A Reflection of a People, Vol 1*. 3rd ed. Eunice, Louisiane: Bluebird Press, 1988.

Books in French

Non-fiction

Bizier, Hélène-Andrée and Jacques Lacoursière. *Nos Racines - L'histoire vivante des Québécois*. Montréal: Éditions Transmo et Robert Laffont, 1979.

Bizier, Richard.*Le tour du monde en 300 recettes*. Montréal: La Presse, 1986. Cajun and Louisianian recipes by the author.

Chenu, Bruno. *Dieu est noir - Histoire, religion et théologie des Noirs américains*. Paris: Éditions Le Centurion, 1977.

Clark, John P. and Ronald Creagh. *Naissance et renaissance de la societé acadienne louisianaise - Les Francais des États-Unis: D'Hier à aujourd'hui*. Montpellier, France: Éditions de l'Université de Montpellier III, 1995. (The English version of this book is out of print.)

Denuzière, Jacqueline and Maurice. *Les années Louisiane*. Paris: Éditions Denoël, 1987.

Lugan, Bernard. *La Louisiane française 1682-1804*. Paris: Éditions Perrin, 1994.

Montbarbut, Johnny. *Si l'Amérique française m'était contée - Essor et chute*. Montréal: Éditions de L'Hexagone - Coll. Itinéraires, 1990.

Smith-Thibodeaux, John. *Les francophones de la Louisiane*. Paris: Éditions Entente, 1977.

Novels, Short Stories and Poetry

Denuzière, Maurice. *Louisiane*. Paris: Éditions Jean-Claude Lattès, 1977.

Denuzière, Maurice. *Rivière*. Paris: Éditions Jean-Claude Lattès, 1979.

Feux Follets, Revue Littéraire des Écrivains et Poètes Louisianais. Lafayette, Louisiana: Éditions de la Nouvelle-Acadie, Les Études Francophones de l'Université du Sud-Ouest de la Louisiane, 1995.

Coffee-table Books

Denuzière, Maurice. *La Louisiane du coton au pétrole*. Paris: Éditions Denoël, 1990.

INDEX

■ ULYSSES TRAVEL GUIDES

- ☐ Affordable Bed & Breakfasts in Québec .... $12.95 CAN / $9.95 US
- ☐ Atlantic Canada .... $24.95 CAN / $17.95 US
- ☐ Beaches of Maine ...... $12.95 CAN / $9.95 US
- ☐ Bahamas .... $24.95 CAN / $17.95 US
- ☐ Calgary .... $17.95 CAN / $12.95 US
- ☐ Canada .... $29.95 CAN / $21.95 US
- ☐ Chicago .... $19.95 CAN / $14.95 US
- ☐ Chile .... $27.95 CAN / $17.95 US
- ☐ Costa Rica .... $27.95 CAN / $19.95 US
- ☐ Cuba .... $24.95 CAN / $17.95 US
- ☐ Dominican Republic .... $24.95 CAN / $17.95 US
- ☐ Ecuador Galapagos Islands .... $24.95 CAN / $17.95 US
- ☐ El Salvador .... $22.95 CAN / $14.95 US
- ☐ Guadeloupe .... $24.95 CAN / $17.95 US
- ☐ Guatemala Belize ...... $24.95 CAN / $17.95 US
- ☐ Honduras .... $24.95 CAN / $17.95 US
- ☐ Jamaica .... $24.95 CAN / $17.95 US
- ☐ Lisbon .... $18.95 CAN / $13.95 US
- ☐ Louisiana .... $29.95 CAN / $21.95 US
- ☐ Martinique .... $24.95 CAN / $17.95 US
- ☐ Montréal .... $19.95 CAN / $14.95 US
- ☐ New Orleans .... $17.95 CAN / $12.95 US
- ☐ New York City .... $19.95 CAN / $14.95 US
- ☐ Nicaragua .... $24.95 CAN / $16.95 US
- ☐ Ontario .... $24.95 CAN / $14.95US
- ☐ Ottawa .... $17.95 CAN / $12.95 US
- ☐ Panamá .... $24.95 CAN / $16.95 US
- ☐ Portugal .... $24.95 CAN / $16.95 US
- ☐ Provence - Côte d'Azur .... $29.95 CAN / $21.95US
- ☐ Québec .... $29.95 CAN / $21.95 US
- ☐ Québec and Ontario with Via .... $9.95 CAN / $7.95 US
- ☐ Toronto .... $18.95 CAN / $13.95 US
- ☐ Vancouver .... $17.95 CAN / $12.95 US
- ☐ Washington D.C. ...... $18.95 CAN / $13.95 US
- ☐ Western Canada .... $29.95 CAN / $21.95 US

■ ULYSSES GREEN ESCAPES

- ☐ Cycling in France ...... $22.95 CAN / $16.95 US
- ☐ Hiking in the Northeastern United States .... $19.95 CAN / $13.95 US
- ☐ Hiking in Québec ...... $19.95 CAN / $13.95 US

■ ULYSSES DUE SOUTH

- ☐ Acapulco .... $14.95 CAN / $9.95 US
- ☐ Cartagena (Colombia) ... $12.95 CAN / $9.95 US
- ☐ Cancun Cozumel ...... $17.95 CAN / $12.95 US
- ☐ Puerto Vallarta .... $14.95 CAN / $9.95 US
- ☐ St. Martin and St. Barts . $16.95 CAN / $12.95 US

■ ULYSSES TRAVEL JOURNAL

- ☐ Ulysses Travel Journal (Blue, Red, Green, Yellow, Sextant) .... $9.95 CAN / $7.95 US

QUANTITY	TITLES	PRICE	TOTAL

NAME:_____

ADDRESS:_____

_____

Payment: ☐ Money Order ☐ Visa ☐ MasterCard

Card Number:_____Exp.:_____

Signature:_____

Sub-total	
Postage & Handling	$8.00*
Sub-total	
G.S.T.in Canada 7%	
TOTAL	

ULYSSES TRAVEL PUBLICATIONS
4176 St-Denis, Montréal, QC, H2W 2M5
(514) 843-9447 fax (514) 843-9448
www.ulysse.ca
*$15 for overseas orders

U.S. ORDERS: **GLOBE PEQUOT PRESS**
P.O. Box 833, 6 Business Park Road,
Old Saybrook, CT 06475-0833
1-800-243-0495 fax 1-800-820-2329
www.globe-pequot.com